Scaffolds of the Church

Scaffolds of the Church

Towards Poststructural Ecclesiology

CYRIL HOVORUN

CASCADE *Books* • Eugene, Oregon

SCAFFOLDS OF THE CHURCH
Towards Poststructural Ecclesiology

Copyright © 2017 Cyril Hovorun. All rights reserved. Except for brief quotations in critical publications or reviews, no part of this book may be reproduced in any manner without prior written permission from the publisher. Write: Permissions, Wipf and Stock Publishers, 199 W. 8th Ave., Suite 3, Eugene, OR 97401.

Cascade Books
An Imprint of Wipf and Stock Publishers
199 W. 8th Ave., Suite 3
Eugene, OR 97401

www.wipfandstock.com

PAPERBACK ISBN: 978-1-4982-8420-2
HARDCOVER ISBN: 978-1-5326-0754-7
EBOOK ISBN: 978-1-5326-0753-0

Cataloguing-in-Publication data:

Names: Hovorun, Cyril.

Title: Scaffolds of the church : towards poststructural ecclesiology / Cyril Hovorun.

Description: Eugene, OR: Cascade Books, 2017 | Includes bibliographical references and index.

Identifiers: ISBN 978-1-4982-8420-2 (paperback) | ISBN 978-1-5326-0754-7 (hardcover) | ISBN 978-1-5326-0753-0 (ebook)

Subjects: LCSH: Church | Christian union | Eastern churches | Orthodox Eastern Church

Classification: BV600.3 H68 2017 (print) | BV600.3 (ebook)

Manufactured in the U.S.A.   MARCH 28, 2017

To my teacher Andrew Louth

Table of contents

List of Pictures, Maps, and Figures ix
Acknowledgments xi
List of Abbreviations xiii

Introduction 1
1. Fine Pencil Lines: Distinctions 11
    The Church as an historical phenomenon and as an object of
        faith 11
    The Church for Everyone and the Church for Some 16
    The Dualism of the Sacred and Profane 25
    The Church Universal and Particular 40
2. Partition Walls: Territory and Administration 50
3. Ditches: Sovereignty 73
4. Strongholds: Autocephaly 88
    The Case of Bulgaria 94
    The Case of Serbia 99
    The Case of Greece 110
    The Case of Bulgaria II 116
    The Case of Ukraine 121
    The Case of the Orthodox Church in America 125
5. Pyramids: Primacy 128
6. Strata: Ministry 145
7. Frontiers: The Boundaries of the Church 163
Conclusions: From Structuralism to Poststructuralism and Beyond 181

Appendix 1: The Structure of the Roman Empire in the Fourth
    Century 199
Appendix 2: Rulers 203
Appendix 3: Bishops of Constantinople 215
Appendix 4: Bishops of Rome 225

Bibliography 235
Index 249

List of Pictures, Maps, and Figures

Picture 1: Sacred zones in the Temple of Herod. 27
Picture 2: Cosmas Indicopleustes's pattern of the universe. 40
Map 1: Plan of Dura–Europos. 55
Picture 3: Plan of the Christian household in Dura–Europos. 56
Map 2: Administrative divisions of the Roman empire in the fourth century AD. 65
Figure 1: Hierarchy and interconnectedness of beings according to Proclus. 138
Figure 2: Hierarchy of primacies. 142
Map 3: Roman frontiers in North Africa in time of Cyprian of Carthage. 180
Figure 3: Causality of the "ecclesiological sins." 193

Acknowledgments

I BEGAN WRITING THIS book during my fellowship at Yale University, continued at Columbia University in the City of New York, and finished at Loyola Marymount University in Los Angeles. Therefore I want to primarily express gratitude to my colleagues at these Universities. I would particularly like to acknowledge support from Christopher Beeley and Nicholas Denysenko. I am also thankful to my Italian colleagues and friends who shared with me resources and hospitality at the John XXIII Foundation of Religious Sciences in Bologna and the monastic community in Bose. Alberto Melloni, Davide Dainese, and Adalberto Mainardi are among dear friends there. My special thanks to Vitaly Demianiuk, who was always ready to support my studies. Since English is not my first language, I heavily relied on the help of my friends who endured a heavy editorial burden: Sarah Hinlicky Wilson, Peter Eaton, and Joseph Clarke. I acknowledge their help with a lot of appreciation.

List of Abbreviations

ACO	*Acta Conciliorum Oecumenicorum*, (De Gruyter):
	ACO1: series prima, ed. Eduard Schwarz;
	ACO2: series secunda, ed. Rudolf Riedinger.
CPG	Maurice Geerard and Jacques Noret, *Clavis Patrum Graecorum*, 5 vols, (Turnhout: Brepols, 1974–2003).
CPL	Eligius Dekkers and Emil Gaar, *Clavis Patrum Latinorum*, (editio tertia aucta et emendata; Steenbrugis: In Abbatia Sancti Petri, 1995).
Mansi	Giovanni Domenico Mansi, *Sacrorum conciliorum nova et amplissima collectio*.
PG	J.-P. Migne, *Patrologiae Cursus Completus. Series Graeca*.
PL	J.-P. Migne, *Patrologiae Cursus Completus. Series Latina*.
WCC	World Council of Churches.

Introduction

IN THE CONCLUSION TO his study *Structures of the Church*, Hans Küng set as a task for modern theology the reexamination of the original meaning of the ecclesial structures:

> There have been times in the history of the Church when it was theology's task to establish the structures of the Church. The task was a necessary one. Today the task of theology should be to lay bare the original structures that have been covered over in the changes wrought by time. This too is a necessary task.[1]

The main task of this book is to lay bare the structures that define the life of the eastern churches nowadays. In pursuing this goal, I apply techniques of the critical theory, particularly as they have been employed in structuralism and poststructuralism. I believe these techniques are applicable to the church insofar as it is not only transcendental but is also a social phenomenon, with administrative and ministerial structures. I distinguish the *nature* of the church and its *structures*. My critical assessment targets primarily the latter. This does not mean that the nature of the church cannot be critiqued, provided it comprises the human and social elements in it. Nevertheless, distinguishing between the nature and the structures of the church allows me to make criticism more pointed.

The goal of the book is not so much to critically assess the most recent scholarship on particular church structures, as to explain the mechanisms behind the evolution and interaction of these structures. In some sense, I follow Avery Dulles in constructing ecclesiological models.[2] In contrast to Cardinal Dulles, however, I propose models not of the church

---

1. Küng, *Structures of the Church*, 352.
2. Dulles, *Models of the Church*.

as such, but of ecclesial structures. My hope is to present through these models a dynamic picture of how the structures of the church emerged for good reasons, often became abused and failed, and eventually were either abandoned or reinvented. At every stage of their evolution, they have had the potential to turn toxic for the body of the church. At the same time, they should not be stigmatized because of this potential, but should be viewed as capable of being restored to their original meaning and purpose.

I present the ecclesial structures through the semiotics of different kinds of borderlines and edifices: partition walls, ditches, strongholds, pyramids, and strata. These images reveal the characteristic features, the strong and weak points of the ecclesial institutions—supra-communal administrative structures (dioceses, metropolises, patriarchates), canonical territory, autocephaly, primacy, and ministry—which are central to the Orthodox churches' relations with one another and with other churches. I narrow the scope of study to the eastern Christianity, because critical analysis of its structures is practically missing in the modern scholarship.

The book begins with the propaedeutic image of fine lines drawn by a pencil on a piece of paper. This image illustrates the distinctions between the church as it appears and as it is in effect, between the church as it is perceived to be for everyone and as it is for the elect only. These contrasts are imagined, not real. They are often caused by a bipolar worldview that tends to see the world and the church in the terms of profane and sacred, black and white. Such a worldview, despite its speculative character, often contributes to real divisions in the body of Christ. Also a schematic distinction between the church universal and particular, when abused, can be divisive. Thus, exaggerations of universalism in the western church provoked the great schism in the eleventh century. Particularisms of the eastern churches draw them to nationalism and recently led to the difficulties that the much-awaited Panorthodox council experienced. These are illustrations of how the ecclesial structures can act against the nature of the church, causing tensions and disagreements in it.

Initially, however, the structures of the church were designed to contain tensions and disagreements. In accordance with the classical definition of social structures, they were supposed to correct the behavior of those who subscribed to them.[3] In reality, however, the patterns

---

3. "The social factors that are held to influence our behaviour are known as social structure." Elder-Vass, *The Causal Power of Social Structures*, 1.

of behavior often changed the rationale and functionality of the church structures.

The fine pencil lines made up blueprints for building real things capable of both uniting and dividing the church. Let us take, for example, the evolution of the administrative structures of the church, which are presented here by the image of partition walls. Partition walls organize the space within a house to facilitate its inhabitants' communication and peaceful coexistence. At the same time, they can alienate the inhabitants from each other and encapsulate hostility. So also in the church: its administrative and territorial borders have both served and damaged the communal life of the Christians. Their gradual evolution has demonstrated an innate ambivalence.

Initially, the Christian communities were largely independent from each other. They did not have to give account to one another, unless they chose to do so. However, very soon the communities faced problems that they were unable to solve on their own. This was particularly the case when they had to pass judgment on their leaders or to install new ones. These two problems constituted the main driving force for the development of supra-communal structures. Such structures were intended to serve the communities and to help them develop with as few hindrances as possible. In contrast to the communities themselves, these structures were "virtual": they emerged as an additional function bestowed on chosen communities by other communities. Supra-communal structures evolved in several stages, which are presented in this book as the models of neighborhood, metropolis, diocese, patriarchate, pentarchy, monarchy, *millet*, and nation.

Neighborhood was the earliest and the most egalitarian model of arranging the relations between different communities. According to it, the problems of a community were solved with assistance of nearby communities. Any community could ask its neighbors for help and any community could be asked for help in return. This principle secured the ethos of equality which the church had inherited from the apostolic times. I argue that equality or even kenotic anti-hierarchism are foundational for the church and constitute the properties of its very nature.

The principle of hierarchy, in contrast, can be *useful*, but is *not essential* for the church. It was implemented for the first time in the metropolitan system, which succeeded the neighborhood model. This happened when the network of the Christian communities became more widely distributed and more complex. Some communities were entrusted with the permanent privilege of arranging matters for other communities. The main criterion by which communities were chosen for this role was their location in the important urban centers of the Roman Empire: metropolises.

The metropolitan system underwent further modifications in the diocesan (based on the grid of the Roman civil *dioecesae*) and patriarchal models. The latter became the most viable. Many elements of it, including the name, have survived until our days. By the end of Late Antiquity, the patriarchates composed a network, which later would be called "pentarchy" ("the rule of five"). This network allowed them to take *ad hoc* decisions related to the entire church. As the Middle Ages advanced, the two most prominent patriarchates, Rome and Constantinople, turned into a kind of monarchies, and the whole of Christendom became focused and dependent on one or the other. The rise of the monarchical model in the church led to the schism between the East and the West. It also imposed uniformity and intensified stratification in the church.

Ottoman rule created a new model of administrative structure in the eastern church based on social groupings with diverse cultural backgrounds but the same religious identity. They were called in the beginning *tâ'ifse* and later *millet*. The Orthodox population of the Ottoman Empire was organized to a single *millet-i Rum*, with one head, *millet başı*, who was the patriarch of Constantinople. The sultans endowed the patriarchs of Constantinople with unprecedented ecclesial and political control over the Orthodox in the empire, which led to a further decline in the authority of the other eastern patriarchates and a strengthening of the monarchy of the *millet başı*. Simultaneously, the circumstances of Ottoman rule forced the eastern churches to realign more closely with their communities. Communities became important in the church again. As a result, the Ottoman period turned out to be no less effective—if not indeed more effective—than the Byzantine period in the formation of modern eastern church structures.

The process of the emancipation of the hierarchical structures continued when the new national states emerged from the collapsing Ottoman Empire. Enlightenment ideas of national statehood were adopted by the majority of the eastern churches, and led them to redesign the partition walls between them. National identity has played a key role in this model, which remains dominant even now under the guise of the model of patriarchate. In most cases, modern patriarchates are ethnic churches that promote nationalistic ideology and give it sacred forms.

Their primates play the role of ethnarchs and take care that the people remain faithful to the modern identity of nation.

All administrative models were supposed to safeguard the integrity of the church. Each of them was only partially successful in achieving this goal and had its shortcomings. Thus, the metropolitan model facilitated the spread of Arianism. The patriarchal model led to the schism between the Chalcedonian and non-Chalcedonian churches. The monarchical model caused another great schism—between the Orthodox and Roman Catholic. The *millet* model infected the church with unprecedented corruption. Finally, the national model has brought nationalism to the church.

This story of the supra-communal structures separated by partition walls clearly demonstrates the ambivalence of these structures. What originated as a means of unity often became a means of separation and had to be redesigned. These structures also caused changes in theoretical ideas about the church and its properties. Thus, the partition walls led the church to refocus from community to territory. The principle of territorial sovereignty became important in the church and was embodied in the notion of "canonical territory." As a term, "canonical territory" is a recent invention, but as a principle of the church's organization it extends back before the age of Constantine. Borderlines demarcating canonical territories are illustrated in the book by the metaphor of ditches, features that once protected the Roman frontiers. They served, however, not to lock up already possessed lands, but as platforms for further limitless expansion of the *Pax Romana*. So it was with the early church, whose earliest territorial structures did not impede its worldwide mission. Both the Roman state and the Christian church changed their attitude to territory when they refocused from furthering their influence beyond their temporal borders to protecting what they already held. Territory became a thing of value in itself, over which medieval states and churches fought. Church battles over territory contributed to the schism between Rome and Constantinople.

The Peace of Westphalia in the seventeenth century created a new philosophy of territory with state sovereignty at its cornerstone. The Orthodox churches embraced this philosophy. It is difficult to say whether they were aware about its western roots. Joseph de Maistre (1753–1821), a conservative Catholic and ambassador of the kingdom of Piedmont-Sardinia to Russia, who was a proponent of the sovereignty of the Catholic church, might have planted the seed of this philosophy to the Orthodox soil.[4] Whatever is the story of the transmission of the western ideas of sovereignty to the eastern churches, in their relations with each other, they began behaving like sovereign political entities. The principles of the Peace of Westphalia, although they are outdated in international relations now, still define the Orthodox churches' attitudes to the "diaspora" and the "canonical territory." In line with these principles, the idea of "diaspora" remains a rudiment of the colonial mentality in the post-colonial era.[5]

It is as ditches surrounding strongholds that we can best illustrate the institution of autocephaly. This is an ancient structure which goes back to the time of the council of Ephesus (431) and even earlier, when congregations were not yet organized into established supra-communal structures and were, in effect, autocephalous. With the passage of time, however, supra-communal structures borrowed the understanding of autocephaly from communities. Autocephaly in its early supra-communal form, supported by the council of Ephesus (431), served as an instrument to secure church independence from the state. It was, in some sense, counter-cultural. During the Middle Ages, it reversed, becoming an attribute of statelike political status and an instrument of *transitio imperii* from Constantinople to the new Slavic empires. In the nineteenth century, it became a token of the cultural and ethnic maturity of a people. In the twentieth century, it was a symbol of struggles for decolonization, an instrument of the deconstruction of the imperial projects. These transformations of the institution of autocephaly are illustrated in this book with the cases of the Orthodox churches of Bulgaria, Serbia, Moscow, Greece, Ukraine, and in the United States. Autocephaly is an example of a church structure that was reinvented several times during its evolution. In different periods it meant different—sometimes opposite—things, but always under the same name. Instead of abandoning it altogether, the church chose to recast it. This is because autocephaly appeared to be helpful in protecting the rights and privileges of the local churches, turning them into strongholds.

The rise of patriarchates, in combination with the structures of canonical territory and autocephaly, made primacy a pivotal issue of inter-church relations. Primacy is the most-discussed topic in the

---

4. See Miltchyna, "Joseph de Maistre's Works in Russia," 241–70; DeVille, "Sovereignty, Politics, and the Church," 366–89.

5. See Demacopoulos and Papanikolaou, "Orthodox Naming of the Other," 1–22.

Orthodox-Catholic dialogue,[6] and one of the most troublesome issues in the relations between the Orthodox churches. Unlike other issues that are discussed between and within the churches, it is the one that goes far beyond the formal rhetoric and hits a raw nerve in the church. It is the issue which must be solved if we want to make real steps towards Christian unity and to sustain the unity within the families of the churches that participate in the dialogue. At the same time, it is the hardest one to reach an agreement upon.

Everyone in the dialogue agrees that primacy is important in the life of the church. Everyone also agrees that it should be balanced by conciliarity.[7] Only a balanced primacy can be healthy. The difference between healthy and unhealthy primacies can be illustrated through the theory of social hierarchical pyramids. According to this idea, there are on the one hand productive hierarchies,[8] which facilitate complex organizations, such as universities or governments, in organizing their work. These hierarchies function in a constructive way. On the other hand, there are so-called dominance hierarchies,[9] which emerge from the struggle for access to limited resources. These primacies are oppressive. The same distinction is applicable to the church, where only productive hierarchies can facilitate the restoration and sustainability of unity. There are, however, also dominance hierarchies in the church, which are often confused with productive hierarchies and perceived as divinely established structures.

Although hierarchy is commonly understood as a super-structure that encompasses other ecclesial structures, this book argues that it cannot be associated with the nature of the church any more than any other structure. Otherwise, the hierarchical principle would come to clash existentially with the dictum of Christ, who, in response to the dispute among his disciples about who would be regarded greater in his kingdom, said: "The kings of the Gentiles lord it over them, and those in authority over them are called 'benefactors.' Not so with you; instead the one who is greatest among you must become like the youngest, and the leader like the one who serves" (Luke 22:25–26). The early Christian ethos stemmed from the equality of the Father, the Son, and the Holy Spirit. The Incarnation provided an even more radical premise for Christian egalitarianism:

---

6. See Küng, *Structures of the Church*, ix.
7. See Weisgerber, "Primacy and Collegiality," 696–99.
8. See Rubin, "Hierarchy," 259–79.
9. See Sidanius and Pratto, *Social Dominance*.

the fact that the supreme God became a humble human in a God-forgotten corner of the world and preferred to associate himself with the lowest social class was received as a powerful message that Christianity was different from the social and religious hierarchies of the world around. Therefore, the ranks of prophets, teachers, miracle workers, healers, givers of support, interpreters of tongues (1 Cor 12), admonishers, benefactors, and those who show mercy (Rom 12:6–8) reflected the multiple gifts of the Spirit and not positions in the church "hierarchy."

Nevertheless, as soon as the initial Jesus movement expanded and embraced more pieces of the Greco-Roman world, Christian ministry increasingly adopted its features. This world was structured hierarchically,[10] which also affected the Christian communities coming in contact with it. Hierarchization of the church, however, was not like an infection contracted from a diseased organism, that is, a lose-lose situation. It was a lose-win situation. On the one hand, the church compromised its initial egalitarian ethos. On the other hand, it realized the potential of hierarchical models to address problems it faced, such as defining procedures for admission to and expulsion from the community, regulating the balance between the integrity of communities and the variety of charismatic gifts, and maintaining coherence in relations between the expanding communities. Ignatius of Antioch implied these problems when suggesting that the ministry of *episkopos* play a key role in resolving them:

> You should act in accord with bishop's mind, as you surely do. Your presbytery, indeed which deserves its name and is a credit to God, is as closely tied to the bishop as the strings to a harp. Wherefore your accord and harmonious love is a hymn to Jesus Christ. Yes, one and all, you should form yourselves into a choir, so that, in perfect harmony and taking your pitch from God, you may sing in unison and with one voice to the Father through Jesus Christ.[11]

Ignatius became an advocate for mono-episcopacy as a new instrument for securing the integrity of ecclesial communities and harmony in relations between them. This instrument was not the only possible one, and it was certainly not the most perfect, but it turned out to be the most effective in addressing the problems of the church at the time. As a

---

10. See Eckstein, *Rome Enters the Greek East*, 342; Haldon, "The Byzantine Successor State," 8.

11. *Ephesians* (CPG 1025) 4, in Richardson, *Early Christian Fathers*, 89.

result, the church gradually embraced mono-episcopacy, which eventually became central to its life and the basis for subsequent hierarchical structures.

The downside of the convenience of hierarchy was a transformation in the ethos of ministry from a servant duty to a privilege. Hierarchy came to replace the early Christian egalitarianism and ministers became "hierarchs." They turned into an *ordo clericorum*, a distinct ecclesial *stratum* or class departing from the "laity." As a result, the laity emerged as a separate category, and this category was regarded as inferior to the clergy. The church became stratified. The image of geological strata is employed in the book to illustrate the hierarchical structure of ministry. They are layers of rocks and soil, consistent within the same stratum, but different from those above and below. What is important about this image is how the elements of different strata come from the same source: volcanic or other geological activity. Only with the passage of time did elements of the church form into hierarchical structures and become separated from each other. They look as if they were always like that, but they were not: there was time in the history of the church when there were no hierarchical strata.

A hypothesis of this book is that the formation of administrative structures in the church increased the distance between ordained clergy and laity. Indeed, the growth of administrative institutions helped to intensify divisions between ecclesial strata. The church, with its stratified clergy and laity, turned into a pyramid. The top of this pyramid claimed exclusive rights to be associated with the church proper, thereby contributing to the secularization of the bottom part: laypeople, told for centuries that they were not quite the church, one day decided to accept this idea and dissociated themselves from the church. The church, in result, was left to those at the top who had appropriated the ecclesial identity for themselves.

Another hypothesis of the book is that the development of the internal borderlines in the church strengthened its imagined external boundaries. The boundaries of the church are projections of its administrative structures. As a result, the church passed from the idea of local strongholds to perceiving itself as a universal stronghold surrounded by non-church. To correct this mistake and differentiate the internal and external borderlines of the church, the book employs the metaphor of frontiers, which is applicable to the boundaries of the church more than any other metaphor explored here. The argument of this book is that it is impossible to draw a clear line between the church and the non-church. The rationale of a frontier is not to protect the territory inside, but to expand and to cover as much uncultivated land as possible. This metaphor relates to the dynamism of mission, which constitutes an intrinsic feature of the nature of the church.

The conclusion of the book is that all of the church's borderlines are ambivalent. On the one hand, they are helpful in organizing church life, making it more manageable, and protecting the integrity of the church. On the other hand, they can cause tensions within the church and even lead to schisms. This happens when they turn to different sorts of *-isms*: hierarchism, institutionalism, ecclesiocentrism, *etc.* These and other *-isms* falsify the church and function in the capacity of ideology, to use a term from critical theory.[12] In poststructuralist parlance, they turn the structures of the church into simulacra. The book concludes with an experiment, attempting to speak about the structures of the church in the language of structuralism and poststructuralism. This language is helpful in the critical assessment of these structures. At the same time, it protects the church itself from accusations that are properly addressed to the ecclesial structures. It is therefore a liberating language, capable of correcting the ecclesiological *-isms* and of making the structures coherent with the mission and nature of the church.

---

12. See Bailey, *Critical Theory and the Sociology of Knowledge*.

1

Fine Pencil Lines: Distinctions

THERE ARE BORDERLINES WITHIN the church, which are purely imagined, not real. They are drawn by theologians with a pencil on the pages of ecclesiological treatises. This kind of distinction is similar to the distinction between Christ's divinity and humanity in Christology. Cyril of Alexandria distinguished the humanity and divinity of Christ only "in thought" (τῇ θεωρίᾳ μόνῃ).[1] This distinction stressed the idea of the inseparable oneness of Christ as a single being. The same distinction, when applied to the church, stresses that the church is *one single reality*. There are aspects of the church that can be distinguished only theoretically.

THE CHURCH AS AN HISTORICAL PHENOMENON AND AS AN OBJECT OF FAITH

The distinction that is the most difficult to explore is the one between the church as an historical phenomenon and the church as it is believed to be. There are big gaps between the church in theory and in reality. Theologians have applied various languages to describe this distinction. Hans Küng, for instance, distinguishes between "an ideal Church situated in the abstract celestial spheres of theological theory" and the "real Church," which "is first and foremost a happening, a fact, an historical

---

1. *Quod unus sit Christus* (CPG 5228) 736.27.

event."[2] For Edward Schillebeeckx, the single reality of the church can be described in two irreducible languages. The one is theological language, which conceptualizes the church as it is related to God. The other language consists of historical and sociological morphemes.[3] Daniel Ott in his unpublished doctoral dissertation explores the difference between the real and the conceptualized church by engaging the "process theology" of Alfred North Whitehead and the critical ecclesiology of Hans Küng. He has borrowed from Whitehead the idea that God is dynamic and always at work in the world.[4] The way that God works in the world as it is described in "process theology" also applies to the church. Ott dwells on Küng's concept of "real church" and the distinction between "what the church IS [capitalized by Ott] and what the church can be."[5] This combination of Whitehead's process ecclesiology and Küng's ecclesiological realism creates a picture of the church that is called to change in order to correspond more truly in its human and historical dimension to what God wants it to be:

> God can and does work through both continuity and change. God works to preserve and deepen the good in the church's tradition while at the same time creatively transforming the church toward ever-deeper forms of inclusive love and justice. This model avoids both a fear of change that leads to stagnation and a blind affirmation of change that disregards the value of tradition and continuity.[6]

Neil Ormerod, following the nineteenth century's schemata, describes the difference between theoretical and realistic approaches to the church by employing an analogy between Platonic and Aristotelian philosophical methods:

> One might characterise the difference between these two possibilities as one between an Aristotelian and a Platonic (idealist) approach to ecclesiology. The Aristotelian (realist) approach takes as its starting point the historical data of the Church, a Church of historically constituted communities which develop and change over time. It will then seek to draw historical lessons

---

2. Küng, *The Church*, 5.
3. Schillebeeckx, *Church: the Human Story of God*, 210–13.
4. Ott, "The Church in Process: A Process Ecclesiology," 20.
5. Ibid., 66.
6. Ibid., 3.

for the current life of the Church, often by reflecting on some golden age, perhaps the communities of the New Testament, the patristic era, or the high middle ages. The Platonic approach will usually take as its starting point a highly charged theological symbol of the Church, such as the Church as a body of Christ, the people of God or a divine communion. It will then seek to draw conclusions from these religious symbols for the concrete operation of the Church we all live in.[7]

Roger Haight thinks that "the historical church will not yield to theory"[8] and therefore "there will always be a tension between the ideal and the real in ecclesiology."[9] Haight articulates the distinction between theory and the reality of the church in the terms of the ecclesiologies "from above" and "from below" correspondingly. The essential difference between them is that the former is "abstract, idealist, and a-historical," while the latter is "concrete, realist, and historically conscious."[10] Haight lists features of both ecclesiologies and compares them. Ecclesiology "from above," for him, tends

- to transcend any given historical context;
- to remain confined within the limits of one given tradition;
- to build its self-understanding on authority;
- to increase the distance between the church and the world;
- to keep the doctrine about the church separated from the church's history;
- to be Christocentric;
- to ground its ministry on hierarchical principles.[11]

The last feature is fundamental for the ecclesiology "from above." It implies that

> the levels of power and authority have their foundation in God, and they descend. . . . This structure in some measure reflects or corresponds to the monarchical structure of the universe, or reality itself . . . .
>
> A hierarchical structure such as this is concomitant with a hierarchical imagination. . . . The church as institution is willed

---

7. Ormerod, "Recent Ecclesiology: A Survey," 58.
8. Haight, "Systematic Ecclesiology," 273.
9. Ibid., 270.
10. Haight, *Christian Community in History*, vol. 1, 4–5; see Mannion, *Comparative Ecclesiology*, 19–20.
11. Haight, *Christian Community in History*, vol. 1, 19–25.

by God, informed by God in Christ and as Spirit, so that the church is holy in its institutional forms. The institutions of the church enjoy a certain sacrality: scripture is holy, sacraments are holy, but so too are the bishops and priests who administer them. The word of God is holy, but so too is the sacred authority with which the leaders of the church speak. One objective state or way of life may be considered holier than another.[12]

An approach to the church from above, in Haight's description, corresponds to a theoretical and idealistic outlook, which is often confronted by empirical and historical data about the church. Haight suggests an approach that embraces the full historical reality of the church as "from below." He has identified four aspects of ecclesiology "from below":

1. Such ecclesiology has to be "concrete, existential, and historical";
2. it goes "back to Jesus to find the origins of the church";
3. it should take seriously sociological and historical realities, without which one cannot properly understand church's "full reality";
4. at the same time, ecclesiology should not be reduced to sociology or history—it remains a theological discipline.[13]

Haight prefers ecclesiology "from below" to ecclesiology "from above" and explains why. In his judgment,

1. It is more suitable for the contemporary mentality. Unlike ecclesiology "from above," it does not cause cognitive dissonance with postmodernity. It helps people with a postmodern way of thinking to comprehend what the church is.
2. Whereas ecclesiology "from above" focuses on particular confessions, ecclesiology "from below" tends to deal with the "whole Christian movement." It is therefore ecumenical and welcoming of pluralism. It encourages "an effort to imagine ecclesial forms that are open to and accommodate other perspectives on the church."
3. While ecclesiology "from above" relies on intellectual conceptualization, ecclesiology "from below" bases itself on experience. This experience is not individual, but communal.

---

12. Ibid., 23–24.
13. Ibid., 4–5.

4. Unlike ecclesiology "from above," which authoritatively imposes itself, ecclesiology "from below" "does not take its suppositions and premises for granted, but explains them in a critical or self-reflective way."

5. Ecclesiology "from below" is more pneumatocentric, while ecclesiology "from above" is more Christocentric. One does not exclude the other, however, because neither Christ nor the Spirit can be absent from ecclesiology. The role of Christ in the perspective "from below" looks different. "Jesus is still the risen Christ, and the mediator of God to the Christian community. But the structure of an ecclesiology from below places more emphasis on Jesus as the historical source or head of the tradition, the Jesus movement, out of which the church emerged."

6. Ministry in the church has its source in community.[14] God enables ecclesial ministry through communities. Consequently, the dynamics of ministry comes "from below" and not "from above," i.e., not from any self-imposed non-communal authority.

7. In its social implications, ecclesiology "from below" is more flexible in accepting the realities of the world. It better explains the church to a modern person, and is more readily responsive to the challenges posed by globalization and pluralism, to the reality and value of other churches, other religions and the "world" beyond religions. It will be all the more able to hear and respond to the anguished cry of the unparalleled human suffering in the world today.[15]

A distinction between the concept and the historical reality of the church is an achievement mainly of the Roman Catholic ecclesiologists. This distinction forces Catholic theology to face some difficult questions, like papal infallibility, the origins and functions of the hierarchical orders, sources of authority, *etc.* Existing theories, even updated ones, do not fully satisfy the historical data and current realities of the Catholic church.

Eastern Christianity is not free from the dilemma between theory and reality, either. It faces it, however, in its own distinctive way. It obviously does not have to solve such problems as papal primacy. But it does have to solve other problems, such as for instance:

---

14. Ibid., 58–63.
15. Mannion, *Comparative Ecclesiology*, 21.

1. The incoherence between the theoretical canonical order and the real situation in the churches. The system of the local churches, as it has been institutionalized in the *diptycha*, was shaped in conformity with the administrative grid of the Roman Empire. The place of the churches in the diptychal rank corresponded to their real weight and importance, both political and ecclesial, in that time. Nowadays, these rankings reflect only the past of most local churches.

2. The coexistence of numerous ethnic communities in the "diaspora" is often perceived as another serious canonical anomaly, which contradicts the principle of one bishop in one city and undermines the universalist claims of Christianity.

3. The canons of the church are applied selectively, only when a synod or a bishop are interested in applying them; otherwise, they are ignored. In other words, there is no rule of law, which would be exercised in consistent way.

4. The Orthodox recently had the painful experience of the Panorthodox council (June 2016 in Crete), which has been in preparation since 1961. Four of fourteen unanimously recognized churches refused to attend it. This insulted conciliarity and became a challenge to the Orthodox identity, which holds conciliarity as its most important feature.

This list of the gaps between theory and practice in the life of the church can be continued and will be explored in more detail in the chapters that follow.

THE CHURCH FOR EVERYONE AND THE CHURCH FOR SOME

The distinction between the church as an historical phenomenon and an object of faith (i.e., what the Christians believe about it) is not a real division within the church. It is a matter of perception of the church. This distinction took various forms in the history of ecclesiology and sometimes led to real divisions within the church. It appeared first as a consequence of the persecutions during the second and third centuries, when the church faced a significant number of *lapsi*—those who renounced Christ—and had to figure out how they were related to the Christian community. In result, two interpretations of the church membership clashed with each other: the one included everyone professing to be a Christian; the other, only the Christians with marked morality and spirituality. Origen (c. 185–c. 254), who tried to reconcile the interpretation of the church as for everyone with the realty of mass apostasy, drew an imaginary line between a church full of unworthy Christians and a "heavenly church."[16] Many of those who wanted the church only for the worthy, ended up in the schisms such as Montanism. In his Montanist period, Tertullian (c. 155–c. 240), for instance, erected a dividing wall between the "church of the worldly" and the "church of the Spirit."[17] Schisms on the ground of such differentiations emerged because the early Christians were yet unprepared to concede with the idea that an invisible segregated church could exist within the visible church. The Christians who considered themselves particularly spiritual and moral often preferred to step away from the "common church," not to wait inside.

To avoid this unfortunate consequence and to accommodate in one church both those who felt themselves exceptionally spiritual and those who considered themselves sinners, Augustine (354–430) developed a sophisticated distinction between the visible and invisible aspects of the one church. He presented them as two cities that are mixed and entangled within the one church of God:

> But let this city bear in mind, that among her enemies lie hid those who are destined to be fellow-citizens, that she may not think it a fruitless labour to bear what they inflict as enemies until they become confessors of the faith. So, too, as long as she is a stranger in the world, the city of God has in her communion, and bound to her by the sacraments, some who shall not eternally dwell in the lot of the saints. . . . In truth, these two cities are entangled together in this world, and intermixed until the last judgment effect their separation.[18]

Augustine never used the words "visible" and "invisible" regarding the church. He explored the distinction between these two aspects of the church *en passant*. A thousand years later, the precursor movements to the Reformation and then the Reformation itself placed this distinction at the focal point of ecclesiology. The distinction was developed to counterbalance the "all too visible institution of the medieval Church, with its

---

16. Wiley, "Responding to God," 38.
17. Ibid., 37.
18. Augustine, *The City of God*, trans. Dods, I.35, 38.

spiritual and political empire."[19] It started with John Wycliffe (1324–84) and Jan Hus (1372–1415). In counterposition to ecclesial officialdom, which had become notorious for its abuses, they suggested considering the true church as one consisting of elect people who are distinguished by their purity.[20] Ulrich Zwingli (1484–1531) continued this line by counterposing the community of the elect as holy to the Roman institutions as sinful. He first coined the dichotomy of "invisible" and "visible" church.[21]

The protagonists in developing the idea of the "invisible church" were Martin Luther (1483–1546) and John Calvin (1509–64). They both in their early views considered the invisible church as the true and real one and contrasted it with the Roman ecclesial institutions. Later on, however, they drifted toward acknowledging the visible church and accepting its institutions. Thus Luther, who himself did not use the word "invisible," preferring instead *abscondita* or "hidden,"[22] identified a considerable number of the marks characterizing the visible church:

> First, the holy Christian people are recognized by their possession of the holy word of God.
>
> Second, God's people or the Christian holy people are recognized by the holy sacrament of baptism, wherever it is taught, believed, and administered correctly according to Christ's ordinance.
>
> Third, God's people, or Christian holy people, are recognized by the holy sacrament of the altar, wherever it is rightly administered, believed, and received, according to Christ's institution.
>
> Fourth, God's people or holy Christians are recognized by the office of the keys exercised publicly. That is, as Christ decrees in Matthew 18, if a Christian sins, he should be reproved; and if he does not mend his ways, he should be bound in his sin and cast out. If he does mend his ways, he should be absolved.
>
> Fifth, the church is recognized externally by the fact that it consecrates or calls ministers, or has offices that it is to administer.
>
> Sixth, the holy Christian people are externally recognized by prayer, public praise, and thanksgiving to God.

19. Küng, *The Church*, 34.
20. See Wiley, "Responding to God," 66.
21. See ibid., 68–69.
22. See ibid., 72.

Seventh, the holy Christian people are externally recognized by the holy possession of the sacred cross.[23]

Calvin also recognized visible marks of the church (*symbola ecclesiae dignoscendae*)[24] and required the Christian communities to have a "form of a church":

> When, in course of time, God has so prospered you, that you are, as it were, an ecclesiastical body maintaining the order already mentioned, and that there are some resolved to withdraw themselves from prevailing pollutions, then you may have the use of the sacraments. But we are nowise of the opinion that you should begin by them, or even that you should be in a hurry to partake of the holy Supper, until you have some order established among you. And indeed it is much better for you to abstain from it, so that thus you may be led to seek the means which will render you capable of receiving it. . . . Nay, it would not be lawful for a man to administer the sacraments to you, unless he recognized you as a flock of Jesus Christ, and found among you the form of a church.[25]

In England, Richard Hooker (1554–1600) developed further the insights of the continental Reformation. He drew a distinction[26] between "that Church of Christ which we properly term his body mysticall"[27] and the "visible Church."[28] The "mystical church" consists of all who are saved by God. The "visible church" includes all who are Christians "by externall profession"[29] of the one Lord. They belong to that church regardless of their relationship with God. That the church is invisible, for Hooker, does not mean that it is unreal. It is as real as "a real body there is."[30] It encompasses "God's transformative presence in the church" that stands behind "the visible body's mediating activity."[31]

For Luther, Calvin, and other magisterial reformers, as W. J. Torrance Kirby summarizes,

---

23. Luther, *Works*, ed. Pelikan et al. v. 41, 148–64.
24. See Wiley, "Responding to God," 107–31.
25. Bonnet, *Letters of John Calvin*, 2:433.
26. See Harrison, "The Church," 306.
27. Hooker, *Lawes* III.1.2; 1:194.27–28.
28. Ibid., III.1.3; 1:195.26–27.
29. Ibid., III.1.7; 1:198.17.
30. Ibid., III.1.2; 1.194.33–195.1.
31. Harrison, "The Church," 307.

> The Church is simultaneously supernatural and natural, invisible and visible, divine and human. Yet there are not two Churches, but rather one Church with "two natures," according to the analogy of the Christological paradigm. The union between Christ as mystical head and Church as mystical body is achieved through the union of the divine and human natures in Christ. The doctrine of the Church is to be interpreted on the basis of the Christological paradigm, namely the union of the divine and human natures in the person of Christ. The two aspects of the Church, like the two natures in the person of Christ, must never be confused, but remain wholly distinct, and yet, at the same time, unified and inseparable. Thus the Church in its external, visible aspect comes to be distinguished radically from the supernatural, invisible character of the true body of Christ.[32]

The Reformation carved within the church a space where only the elect and saved have a place, a holy and mystical place. The borderlines of this space will remain unidentifiable until the second coming of Christ. This place does not separate itself from the rest of the church, nor does it reject the common ecclesial environment. Rather, it makes the latter void and meaningless, thus welcoming a "dualist" approach to the church, in the words of Avery Dulles.[33]

In the nineteenth century, this approach took a step further under the influence of the German idealist philosophy. Friedrich Schleiermacher (1768–1834) made a particular contribution to the development of the binary visible/invisible church, which he

> reframes . . . as a function of a single predestination. For him, the invisible church is the self-identical element in a mutually reciprocal relationship with the visible, mutable element. The invisible church is thus the "totality of the effects of the Spirit," or "the peculiarly active element" of the visible church. The invisible church must be mediated through the visible.[34]

Emphasis on the invisible church in Protestantism pushed the Roman Catholic ecclesiology in the opposite direction, to promote the church as a perfect society. The protagonist of the Counter-Reformation, Robert Bellarmine (1542–1621), stated famously that the church is as much a "visible and palpable assembly of people as the assembly of the

---

32. Kirby, *Richard Hooker's Doctrine of the Royal Supremacy*, 66.
33. Dulles, "The Church, the Churches, and the Catholic Church," 203.
34. Wiley, "Responding to God," 31–32.

people of Rome, the kingdom of France or the republic of Venice."[35] This perception of the church was shared later on by many in the Roman magisterium. In a schema submitted to Vatican I (1869–70), those who "say that the Church of the divine promises is not an exterior and visible society, but is an entirely interior and invisible one" were suggested to be anathematized.[36] Pope Pius XII (from 1939 to 1958) in the *Mystici corporis* (1943) actually condemned those "who arbitrarily claim that the Church is something hidden and invisible."[37]

Till the end of the World War II, thus, two visions of the church—one with a strong emphasis on invisibility, the other with an even stronger emphasis on visibility—remained polarized. In the mid-twentieth century, they began moving closer to each other. Karl Barth (1886–1968) attempted to reconcile the two approaches from the perspective of the Reformed theology:

> If we say with the creed *credo ecclesiam*, we do not proudly overlook its concrete form; just as when we confess *credo resurrectionem carnis* we cannot overlook the real and whole man who is a soul and yet also a body, we cannot overlook his hope as though the resurrection was not also promised to him. Nor do we look penetratingly through this form, as though it was only something transparent and the real Church had to be sought behind it; just as we cannot overlook or look through the pleasing or less pleasing face of the neighbour whom we are commanded to love. We look at the visible aspect of the Church—this is the state of it. And as we look at what is seen—not beside it or behind it but in it—we see what is not seen. Hence we cannot rid ourselves in this way of the generally visible side of the Church. We cannot take refuge from it in a kind of wonderland. The *credo ecclesiam* can and necessarily will involve much

---

35. In Kingdon, "The Church: Ideology or Institution," 87.

36. "Si quis dixerit, divinarum promissionum ecclesiam non esse societatem externam ac conspicuam, sed totam internam ac invisiblem, anathema sit." Mansi, v. 51, col. 551, can. 3(52); English translation in Granfield, "The Church as *Societas Perfecta* in the Schemata of Vatican I," 438.

37. "Ex iis, quae adhuc, Venerabiles Fratres, vobis scribendo explanandoque persecuti sumus, omnino patet gravi eos in errore versari, qui ad arbitrium suum quasi latentem minimeque conspicuam fingant Ecclesiam; itemque qui eam perinde habeant atque institutum quoddam humanum cum certa quadam disciplinae temperatione externisque ritibus, at sine supernae vitae communicatione." Lora and Simionati, *Enchiridion delle encicliche*, v. 6, §212, pp. 188–9; English translation available on the website of the Holy See: http://goo.gl/yye9Ft [accessed October 19, 2015], §64.

distinguishing and questioning, much concern and shame. It can and necessarily will be a very critical *credo*. In relation to the side of the Church which is generally visible it can and necessarily will express what does not amount to much more than a hope and a yearning. But it does take the Church quite seriously in its common visibility—which is its earthly and historical existence. It confesses faith in the invisible aspect which is the secret of the visible. Believing in the *ecclesia invisibilis* we will enter the sphere of labour and conflict of the *ecclesia visibilis*. Without doing this, without a discriminate but serious participation in the historical life of the community, its activity, its upbuilding, its mission, in a kind of purely theoretical and abstract churchliness, no one has ever seriously repeated the *credo ecclesiam*.[38]

From the perspective of the Roman Catholic ecclesiology, Vatican II (1962–65) made a step forward to accept the church's invisibility to some extent. At the same time, as Douglas Koskela remarks, it "took great pains . . . to make clear the continuity of *Lumen Gentium* with Pius XII's encyclical."[39] Trying to balance between the new and the old ecclesiological paradigms, *Lumen Gentium* ended up with the following compromise formula:

Christ, the one Mediator, established and continually sustains here on earth His holy Church, the community of faith, hope and charity, as an entity with visible delineation through which He communicated truth and grace to all. But, the society structured with hierarchical organs and the Mystical Body of Christ, are not to be considered as two realities, nor are the visible assembly and the spiritual community, nor the earthly Church and the Church enriched with heavenly things; rather they form one complex reality which coalesces from a divine and a human element. For this reason, by no weak analogy, it is compared to the mystery of the incarnate Word. As the assumed nature inseparably united to Him, serves the divine Word as a living organ of salvation, so, in a similar way, does the visible social structure of the Church serve the Spirit of Christ, who vivifies it, in the building up of the body.[40]

38. Barth, *Church Dogmatics*, IV/1, 653–54.

39. Koskela, "Yves Congar's Vision of Ecclesiality," 19.

40. "Unicus mediator Christus ecclesiam suam sanctam, fidei, spei et caritatis communitatem his in terris ut commpaginem visibilem constituit et indesinenter sustentat, qua veritatem et gratiam ad omnes diffundit. Societas autem organis hierarchicis instructa et mysticum Christi corpus, coetus adspectabilis et communitas spiritualis, ecclesia terrestris et ecclesia coelestibus bonis ditata, non ut duae res considerandae

The ecumenical movement made a major contribution to the reconciliation of the two positions by promoting a "communion between the visible and the invisible," in the words of Jean-Marie Roger Tillard (1927–2000).[41] The ecclesiology developed in the framework of the WCC, distanced itself from the controversy between the ecclesiologies of the visible and invisible. The *Toronto Statement* (1950) made it clear:

> Membership in the World Council does not imply acceptance or rejection of the doctrine that the unity of the Church consists in the unity of the invisible Church. Thus the statement in the Encyclical *Mystici Corporis* concerning what it considers the error of a spiritualized conception of unity does not apply to the World Council. The World Council does not "imagine a church which one cannot see or touch, which would be only spiritual, in which numerous Christian bodies, though divided in matters of faith, would nevertheless be united through an invisible link." It does, however, include churches, which believe that the Church is essentially invisible as well as those, which hold that visible unity is essential.[42]

Two years later, at the third World Conference on Faith and Order in Lund (1952), the official ecumenical movement attempted to bridge the two poles: "We are agreed that there are not two Churches, one visible and the other invisible, but one Church which must find visible expression on earth."[43] The WCC substituted the binary invisible/visible church with the dynamics of moving from invisible to visible unity. For example, the WCC defines itself as "a community of churches on the way to visible unity in one faith and one Eucharistic fellowship."[44] In the words of the New Delhi Statement on Unity (1961), although this unity has not been

---

sunt, sed unam realitatem complexam efformant, quae humano et divino coalescit elemento. Ideo ob non mediocrem analogiam incarnati Verbi mysterio assimilatur. Sicut enim natura assumpta Verbo divino ut vivum organum salutis, ei indissolubiliter unitum, inservit, non dissimili modo socialis compago ecclesiae Spiritui Christi, eam vivificanti, ad augmentum corporis inservit (cf. Eph 4:16)." Alberigo et al., *Conciliorum Oecumenicorum Generaliumque Decreta*, vol. 3, cap. 1, §8, p. 301; English translation available on the website of the Holy See: http://goo.gl/QihaLC [accessed October 19, 2015].

41. Tillard, *Flesh of the Church, Flesh of Christ*, 92.

42. Chapter III: "What the World Council of Churches Is Not," § 5, available on the official website of the WCC: http://goo.gl/iLhAnn [accessed October 19, 2015].

43. Nelson, "Toward an Ecumenical Ecclesiology," 652.

44. Official website of the WCC: https://www.oikoumene.org/en/about-us [accessed October 19, 2015].

yet achieved, it needs a "recovery"[45] and "is being made visible."[46] In result, although the ecumenical movement helped the churches overcome the dilemma of invisible/visible church, in the process it introduced a new dilemma between the unity of the church as either given or to be achieved. This binary still bears an implicit dualist perspective.[47] At the same time, it is not as provocative as the earlier dilemma of the invisible/visible church.

The binary of the invisible/visible church has been criticized also from the perspective of the New Testament studies. In the words of George Lindbeck:

> An invisible Church is as biblically odd as an invisible Israel. Stories of the biblical realistic-narrative type can only be told of agents and communities of agents acting and being acted upon in a space-time world of contingent happenings. Thus to say that it was empirical churches in all their actual or potential messiness of which exalted concepts and images such as "holy" and "bride of Christ" were predicated is an analytic implicate of the primacy of narrative.[48]

Indeed, if the church is considered a set of concrete communities that consist of people who come together to share prayer and the eucharist and to care for each other, then the metaphysical juxtaposition of visible and invisible loses its sense. At the same time, these people have in mind a picture of what their community should be and realize that their community and they themselves are not as perfect as they want or as God wants them to be. This realization creates a powerful momentum for growth of both communities and individuals.

When the church is perceived as the dichotomy of visible and invisible, this creates a gap between the real and the ideal in the church. Its members do not have sufficient motivation to leap the gap. Polarization between the real and ideal in the church weakens the incentive for the Christians to grow and to become mature. It also reduces the presence of God in the real church, as his presence remains confined to the ideal church. It implies that God prefers to act on his own without human

---

45. §15, available on the website of the WCC: http://goo.gl/PgxZTI [accessed October 19, 2015].

46. Ibid., §1.

47. See Kinnamon, "Ecumenical Ecclesiology," 348.

48. Lindbeck, *The Church in a Postliberal Age*, 149. Bruce Marshall, Carl Braaten, and Reinhard Hütter make similar criticisms (see Wiley, "Responding to God," 21).

mediation. The church turns out to be simultaneously immanent and transcendent, in effect splitting into two churches. One is the church of God, and the other the church of human beings. The difference between them to a significant extent obliterates the results of the incarnation and eventually endangers the integrity of the church as a single human-divine organism. Such can be the consequences of a radical polarization between the visible and invisible aspects of the church. This happens when a theoretical, τῇ θεωρίᾳ μόνῃ, distinction between the present situation and the goal, between the real and the ideal, turns into a solid wall within the same church.

THE DUALISM OF THE SACRED AND PROFANE

Since the French sociologist Émile Durkheim[49] (1858–1917) and the German theologian Rudolf Otto[50] (1869–1937), it has become a commonplace in religious studies to affirm that any religion is based on the distinction between the holy and the unholy, the sacred and the profane. In the words of Otto, the idea of holiness is "the innermost essence of religion."[51] It is radically different from the idea of profane. As Durkheim put it, "In all the history of human thought there exists no other example of two categories of things so profoundly differentiated or so radically opposed to one another."[52] Forty years later, the Romanian historian of religion Mircea Eliade (1907–86) applied this distinction to the psychology of religion. He considered the sacred as an intrinsic element of the structure of the human consciousness.[53] He also stressed the radical difference between the holy and secular as an essential feature of the religious perception of the world. He spoke of "the abyss that divides the two modalities of experience—sacred and profane."[54] The idea that any religion is based on the binary holy-secular continues to be important in the modern religious studies.[55]

    49. Durkheim, *Les formes élémentaires de la vie religieuse*; English translation: Durkheim, *The Elementary Forms of the Religious Life*.

    50. Otto, *Das Heilige*; English translation: Otto, *The Idea of the Holy*.

    51. Otto, *The Idea of the Holy*, 177.

    52. Durkheim, *The Elementary Forms of the Religious Life*, 38.

    53. Randall Studstill, "Eliade, Phenomenology, and the Sacred," 183.

    54. Eliade, *The Sacred and the Profane*, 14.

    55. For instance, *The Brill Dictionary of Religion* defines "holy" as "an area completely bounded off from the everyday ('profane'), and simply never to be available

In the terms of ecclesiology, the binary of holy-profane would naturally translate to the counterposition of the church and non-church. The former would be then identified with sacred, and the latter, with profane. Many take this identification for granted. However, I would argue that the category of holy should not be identified with the church, as the church embraces both the holy and profane. This makes Christianity distinct from Judaism and polytheistic religions of the antiquity.

Indeed, the Old Testament draws a clear distinction between the holy and the profane. It warns against those who "do not distinguish between the holy and the profane, or recognize any distinction between the unclean and the clean" (Ezek 22:2). The Jewish Scripture applies the binary of holy-profane to places, times, objects, and people. Holy is everything and everyone touched by God and revelatory of his presence. Profane is used either neutrally as common and plain or negatively as desacrated, godless, and corrupt. Holy and profane are not only distinct but also remote from each other, even polarized. The Hebrew term *qadosh*, which is rendered "holy," means something that is set apart.

The Jewish perception of the holy as opposed to the profane developed in parallel and interaction with the surrounding cultures, which had their own perceptions of the holy. In the Near Eastern cultures, the category of the holy was closely related to space.[56] Thus, the whole land of Egypt was for its inhabitants a sacred space.[57] In Mesopotamia, the sacred geography was built on the contrasts between the center and the periphery. Cultivated lands and the wilderness of the steppes constituted the two poles of sacred and profane, which thus symbolized order versus disorder.[58] In coherence with the surrounding cultures of the Middle East, the Jews saw the people and land of Israel as holy and set apart of the rest of the world. As Martha Himmelfarb remarks, "Judaism is a religion deeply informed by geography. Its historical imagination is shaped by the contrast between other lands and the land of Israel; its stories move back and forth between those poles."[59]

---

to the human being." Von Stuckrad and Barr, *The Brill Dictionary of Religion*, vol. II: E-L, 876.

56. The Gale's *Encyclopedia of Religion* argues that the pair "sacred-profane" always applies to space. Jones, *Encyclopedia of Religion*, vol. 12, 7964.

57. See Johnston, *Religions of the Ancient World*, 244.

58. See ibid., 253.

59. Himmelfarb, "The Temple and the Garden of Eden in Ezekiel, the Book of the Watchers, and the Wisdom of Ben Sira," 63.

The polarization between the holy and the profane in Judaism was strengthened by the construction of the temple as the place of the ultimate presence of God. The temple epitomized the idea of the holy and became its utmost incarnation.[60] In comparison with the temple, everything else was profane. The very word "profane," after all, comes from the Latin *pro fanum*—"in front of the temple." The holiness of the temple had several gradations for the Jews that marked off the differentiated levels of access to its premises. The second temple, after Herod's reconstruction, had a court of Gentiles, a court of Jewish women, a court of Israel for Jewish males, a court of priests, and finally the holy of holies.

Picture 1: Sacred zones in the temple of Herod.

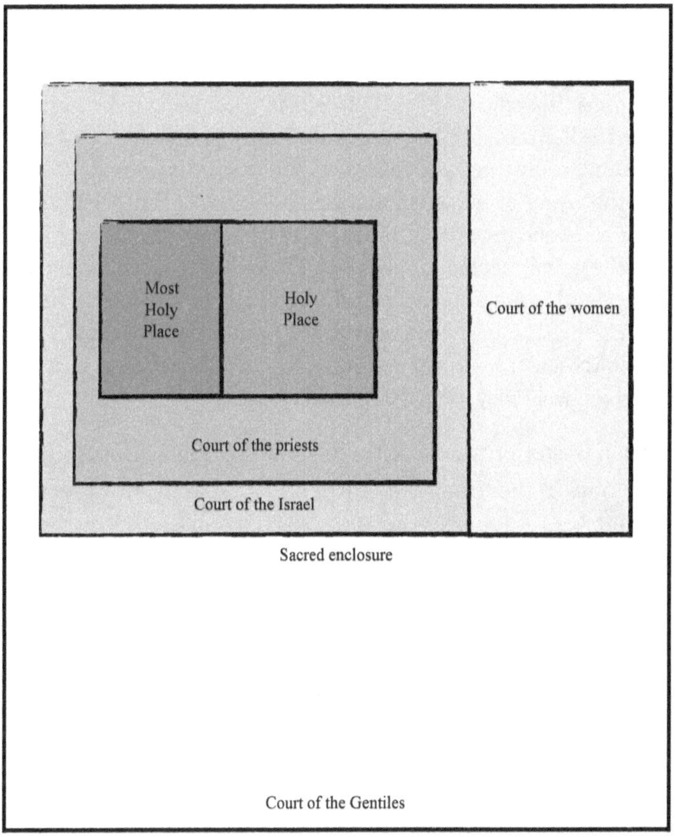

| Most Holy Place | Holy Place | Court of the women |

Court of the priests

Court of the Israel

Sacred enclosure

Court of the Gentiles

---

60. See Johnston, *Religions of the Ancient World*, 258.

The demolition of the temple in the first century after Christ and the further dispersal of the Jewish people changed their attitude to the holy. The holy became detached from place and migrated to the realm of ideas and of worship. This broader perspective allows a modern Jewish thinker to affirm that

> in Judaic thought the place is highly important, but it is always in resistance to as well as in compliance with the idea of the Divine. In fact, God himself is called Place.... In Judaic thought ... the place is never in place. The experience of being in place is conceived as a connection through the place to an abstract idea that points at the place but remains outside it. The Bible's sacred is unplaceable like voice, which is the figure of the divine, and which cannot be traced to its placeable origin. The voice is encountered out of place: whether on the boundary between places, in the desert, or on the way from one earthly place to another. Therefore, to be in place, and specifically to be in the land called variably Canaan, Zion, Judea, or Israel, cannot be automatically translated to nativity and cosmology. Unlike place as the center of the world, the Judaic notion separates between the place and the sacred. The place constitutes a prominent part in the grand theological plan, but it is not charged with sacredness, and is not a medium of the sacred, or of unification and harmony. The Jewish place is called upon to decenter itself at its own center, to imagine exile, to regard arbitrariness, and to disown what may seem as natural belonging.[61]

Such a posterior Jewish perception of the holy is closer to the early Christian one. In the time of the birth of Christianity, however, the Hellenistic Judaism cohered more with the Greco-Roman practices and theories of the sacred. The polytheistic world of antiquity was obsessed with pinning as many holy places as possible to its maps. The people's imagination was inexhaustible when it came to associating a landscape with the divine. An episode imagined by Béatrice Caseau could have happened anywhere in that world:

> In 201, when the newly-arrived Roman legionaries decided to build a military camp at Gholaia (Bu Njem, Libya), in the province of Tripolitania, their first move was to consecrate the place to divine beings. Their immediate concern was to conciliate the deity presiding over that precise spot, the genius of Gholaia. The Romans, although they brought their own deities with them,

---

61. Gurevitch and Aran, "Never in Place: Eliade and Judaïc Sacred Space," 135–36.

did not want to vex local gods ruling this part of the universe. They installed their own gods inside the camp, along with the genius of Gholaia. Around the camp, the Romans also built or maintained a circle of temples dedicated to romanized African gods—such as Jupiter Hammon, overseer of caravan routes—acknowledging the competence and power of these gods. Indeed, in the Roman mind, it was the duty of human beings to honor and not to offend those divine beings who had some power over a region.

. . . After the departure of the Roman legion from Gholaia around 260, the local inhabitants, now freed from Roman domination, took their revenge on the gods of the invaders. They carefully desecrated the religious spaces inside the Roman camp and destroyed the cult statues. This gesture was meant to prove the weakness of the Roman gods, already demonstrated by the retreat of the army. It was also a gesture of fear. By destroying the cult statues of Victory and Fortune, these people were making sure that the goddesses would not have any means of harming them.[62]

There was a dizzying variety of types of sacred places in the world of antiquity. They had complex hierarchies and hermeneutics connected with the ideas of space in general. Thus, the structure of the Greek habitat was triple.[63] *Polis* occupied the central place. In the center of this center, an acropolis dominated over the rest of the city as its holiest place. Outside of the polis was the countryside (*chora*, χῶρα) with cultivated fields (*agroi*, ἀγροί). Beyond that, the uncultivated borderlands constituted the most unholy space, where evil demons and ostracized convicts were sent. All three parts of the Greek space—cities, fields, and borderlands—contained *loci* devoted to the cult of gods or heroes. Each such space was surrounded by a wall or by border stones (*horoi*, ὅροι). These sanctuaries were called *temenos* (τέμενος), from the verb "to cut" (*temnō*, τέμνω). *Temenos* meant that the sacred place was cut off from the profane space.

The holiness of the sacred places had degrees, which were reflected in the structure and functions of the temples. Normally a temple consisted of an altar and a statue of a god or goddess. The sacred edifice was a casing around the statue. Inside it, there were spaces permitting different levels of access. The most common one was the *adyton* (ἄδυτον), reserved usually only to the priests. Sometimes other groups were allowed there

---

62. Caseau, "Sacred Landscapes," 21.
63. See Johnston, *Religions of the Ancient World*, 269–70.

too, like virgins. Some sanctuaries connected with the mysteries had special halls for initiation (*telestērion*, τελεστήριον). In the sanctuaries dedicated to Asclepius, for instance, there were special halls where those seeking healing slept in order to communicate with the gods in dreams and thus be cured. In the oracle sanctuaries, there were spaces reserved for mediums. There were also holy places regarded by the Greeks with special awe where no one was allowed. Spots where lightning had struck the ground were called *abaton* (ἄβατον), "not stepped over," separated from the rest of the area, and dedicated to Zeus *Kataibates*, "the one who comes down." In sum, the sacred spaces of the Greeks were structured hierarchically.

Even more structured was the Roman sacred space.[64] Its structure was enforced by laws. The basic territorial unit of the Roman holiness was *templum*. It was neither a building nor a sacred site but a piece of land released from divine charge by *auguri*. It could be further used by the city for public facilities, both civil and religious, after proper consecration or *inauguratio*. Only on *templa* could political assemblies, sessions of the senate, court hearings, *etc.* take place. Cultic buildings were also built only on *templa* and thus received from them their name. The entire city of Rome, the *urbs*, was regarded a sacred space. Its sacrality was demarcated from the adjacent territory (*ager*) by the *pomerium* or official boundary line, which had been established by an official ritual. Only within the limits of the *pomerium* could public cults, such as taking the auspices, be practiced. It was forbidden to bury within the boundary of the *urbs*. The military was also not allowed to cross the *pomerium* except on victory days.

The sacred grounds of the city contained a wide variety of sanctuaries ranging from simple altars to vast templar complexes. They had to be legal, i.e., inaugurated properly. Only those spots and buildings on them that were legally consecrated (the Romans used the word *constitutio* for the procedure) were regarded as *sacer*, sacred. Official consecration was a complex procedure; it was possible only on the *templum* and after official approval. Essential elements of the consecration were setting the borders of the place and putting down the first stone. The place was regarded as having been passed from the public domain to the god's possession after a special formula (*lex dedicationis*) was pronounced. A sanctuary that was not officially inaugurated was called *aedes*.

64. See ibid., 275–79.

Particular elements of the sacred places were also regarded holy. Such was *delubrum*, a paved area connected with a temple or an enclosure surrounded by porticos. Places in front of the temple, *areae*, were sometimes regarded sacred and sometimes partly secular, which made them accessible to the public. Near the temple or in the portico there were kitchens to cook offerings and sacrificial banquets. Some sanctuaries had banquet halls. Temple complexes could include wells, pools, and thermal baths for ablutions and purification procedures. In some cases, theatres and circuses were attached to the temples, as in certain cases worship was concluded by plays or chariot races. Some sacred buildings served as stores for dedicated objects; they were called *sacraria*. All these types of cultic premises and their elements had different degrees of sacrality that corresponded to the way in which they were consecrated, accessed, and used. Apart from the sacred buildings, there were also holy woods, grottoes, pools, and springs. They were places chosen by the gods for theophanies. Humans were supposed to recognize them and then to surround them with care and veneration. The ancient people attributed particular manifestations of the divine to groves, or *luci*. They used clearings in the sacred groves for worship and often built temples and porticos there.

An eloquent illustration of the hierarchy of sacred places in the ancient world is the island of Delos (Δῆλος) located in the center of the Cycladic archipelago in the Aegean Sea. The legendary birthplace of Apollo and Artemis, Delos became one of the most sacred and venerated places in the ancient Greek world.[65] The island itself was considered a holy place. No one could be born or die on it. The moribund were transported to neighboring Rheneia. Despite its sacrality, Delos was inhabited. It had secular buildings such as a market, an *ekklēsia* (a place of public meetings for citizens), a *bouleutērion* (council chamber), a *prytaneion* (town hall and treasury), *stoas* (public walkways), a *hyppodromos*, a gymnasium, a theatre, *etc*. The part of the *polis* with private accommodations has been preserved in exceptionally good condition. The secular buildings, however, were not mixed with the sacred edifices.

---

65. On this, see École française d'Athènes, *Exploration archeologique de Delos*; Laidlaw, *A History of Delos*; Themelis, *Mykonos-Delos: Archaeological Guide*; Rauh, *The Sacred Bonds of Commerce: Religion, Economy, and Trade Society at Hellenistic Roman Delos*; Papagiannes and Mallarach i Carrera, "The Sacred Dimension of Protected Areas."

The sacred precinct of the island was dominated by the sanctuary of Apollo, which contained three temples dedicated to the god. One of them, the *Poros*, was the oldest and most venerated. Another spot of particular veneration was the altar of horns, the *Keraton*, which according to legend was erected by Apollo himself and was situated in the center of the sanctuary. Apart from the temples of Apollo, there were sanctuaries of less importance dedicated to Artemis and Leto. There was also a "sanctuary of the bulls" located not far from the main sanctuary. It was home to a trireme (a kind of Greek ship), which was dedicated to Apollo in appreciation of naval victories. Nine lions from the island of Naxos can still be seen on Delos. They were sacred objects dedicated initially to Apollo and later to Leto. A distinct object of veneration was the "sacred lake," beside which, according to legend, Leto gave birth to Apollo and Artemis. Sanctuaries of the oriental gods were built on Mount Cynthus. The island has also a number of *abata*, places forbidden to step over, where lightning had struck the ground.

The message of Jesus Christ about the places of worship was radically different from both Jewish and Greco-Roman traditions. He relativized the religious importance and sacrality of the temple (Mark 13:1–2; John 2:19). This eventually became the main accusation against him that led to the death sentence (Matt 26:61–65; Mark 14:57–64). He shifted the epicenter of the sacred from the place of worship to worshipping in spirit and truth (John 4:19–24). In this vein, Paul instructed the Corinthian Christians that the temple of God is no longer a building but their own bodies, in which God's Spirit dwells (1 Cor 3:16–17; 6:19). At around 200 AD, the Roman Christian apologist Marcus Minucius Felix made even more clear the Christian attitude to the places and objects of worship, which contrasted with both Jewish and polytheistic views:

> When I, a man, dwell far and wide, shall I shut up the might of so great majesty within one little building? Were it not better that He should be dedicated in our mind, consecrated in our inmost heart? Shall I offer victims and sacrifices to the Lord, such as He has produced for my use, that I should throw back to Him His own gift? It is ungrateful when the victim fit for sacrifice is

a good disposition, and a pure mind, and a sincere judgment. Therefore he who cultivates innocence supplicates God; he who cultivates justice makes offerings to God; he who abstains from fraudulent practices propitiates God; he who snatches man from danger slaughters the most acceptable victim.[66]

For Minucius Felix and his contemporary Christian fellows, the holy was not to be found in the places where Christians worshipped God but in the worshipping human beings themselves. Therefore, they do not need specially designed and consecrated premises. Minucius Felix testified that the Christians in his time did not have "temples and altars."[67] Indeed, early Christians preferred to gather in their homes and celebrate the Lord's supper there. Neither the eucharist nor their gatherings as such added any special sacrality to the place where they came together. They regarded any place worthy for their meetings, as the entire world was God's place. Minucius Felix considered sacred not a particular place or edifice, but the mind and "inmost heart" of a human being.[68] Even Jerusalem in the first three centuries was not revered by the Christians the same way it was by the Jews. Only after Constantine did it become again a "holy land."[69]

The only "sacred" objects that early Christians venerated were the relics of martyrs. This veneration began with deacon Stephen, whose body was treated with special reverence after he was stoned to death (Acts 8:2). Such reverence increased during the persecutions. The places where the relics of the martyrs were buried were given special respect. Christians came to those places to celebrate the eucharist and wanted to be buried next to the martyrs. Thus, Christian worship became attached

66. *Octavius* (CPL 37): "Putatis autem nos occultare quod colimus, si delubra et aras non habemus? quod enim simulacrum Deo fingam, cum, si recte existimes, sit Dei homo ipse simulacrum? templum quod ei extruam, cum totus hic mundus eius opere fabricatus eum capere non possit? et cum homo latius maneam, intra unam aediculam uim tantae maiestatis includam? nonne melius in nostra dedicandus est mente? in nostro immo consecrandus est pectore? hostias et uictimas Deo offeram, quas in usum mei protulit, ut reiciam ei suum munus? ingratum est, cum sit litabilis hostia bonus animus et pura mens et sincera conscientia. igitur qui innocentiam colit, Deo supplicat, qui iustitiam, Deo libat, qui fraudibus abstinet, propitiat Deum, qui hominem periculo subripit, opimam uictimam caedit." *Corpus scriptorum ecclesiasticorum Latinorum* (CSEL), vol. 2, ch. 32. pp. 45.25—46.8; English translation: Roberts and Donaldson, *The Ante-Nicene Fathers*, vol. 4, 193.

67. Ibid.
68. Ibid.
69. See Caseau, "Sacred Landscapes," 40–41.

to the places that initially were graves. The earliest examples of such places were the catacombs. Remarkably, the relics of the martyrs made Christians more attached to a particular place of worship than the eucharist did.[70] Early Christians did not have any reserved space for eucharist as it is the case now when they come to church to take communion. There was no such thing as a "eucharistic place" to come to. The eucharist was celebrated wherever Christians gathered. At the same time, there were places where relics were venerated and consequently where the eucharist was often celebrated. This custom to combine veneration of relics with eucharist has survived to the present in the tradition of placing the relics of martyrs under the altar of new churches, as well as in *antimensia*, an altar cloth with a relic sewn into it, on which the eucharist is celebrated in the eastern churches. Gradually, from the third century on, Christians changed their attitude to the worship places. They adopted the Greco-Roman patterns of worship, which was attached to the holy places. After Constantine, Christian worship was confined to churches, which now were regarded as such holy places.

The Christian universalist way of worship also confronted various dualistic movements within the Christian community. These movements were inspired, on the one hand, by the eschatological mood of the early Christians who expected Christ to come back very soon. On the other hand, they were based on a dualistic outlook on the world. From the dualistic perspective, the world was seen as black and white, divided into evil parts and good parts. The faithful, if they wished to belong to the good part, had to separate themselves from the bad part and secure themselves in a place that would be as free as possible from the influences of the bad part of the world. This place would guarantee purity and proximity to God and would protect the faithful from the wild and evil winds of the world. Such an attitude was close to the perception of the sacred place in the Greco-Roman world. It featured, however, a stronger soteriological emotion in it. It was not just an occasional need that would be satisfied by the touch of the divine, as the Gentiles believed. For the Christians, their own salvation was at stake. This attracted thousands of them to specific "spaces of salvation."

---

70. R. A. Markus also argued that the Christian sacralization of space began with veneration of the martyrs and dramatically increased in the fourth century. He contested the idea that it started with the pilgrimages to Jerusalem. Markus, "How on Earth Could Places Become Holy?" 262.

Two recently discovered[71] settlements in ancient Phrygia (now the Turkish province of Uşak), Pepouza and Tymion, offer a clear visualization of such salvific spaces. The two cities constituted the spiritual and administrative center of the Montanist movement, which was active in the Roman Empire between the mid-second and mid-sixth centuries.[72] These cities were believed by the followers of the movement to be the descended "New Jerusalem," as it is referred to in Revelation 21. Montanism was a chiliastic and charismatic movement relying on prophetic gifts. Its founders were the "prophets" Montanus, Maximilla, and Priscilla. Montanists believed that prophetism was an essential part of the Christian life. They distinguished the true church and true Christians from nonspiritual Christians (*psychikoi*, ψυχικοί). This expression of Tertullian[73] resembles the gnostic category of sarkic (i.e., fleshly) people who did not have access to the special knowledge of the divine. The followers of the movement identified it as a "new prophesy."

For its adversaries, however, it was merely a "Phrygian sect." It was indeed a sect in a sense that it separated itself from the rest of the church, which it regarded as insufficiently spiritual and prophetic. In most of its doctrine, Montanism did not depart from the orthodoxy of its time. Its main difference was that it sacralized the place that it believed to be the New Jerusalem and confined itself to that very special *locus*. This attitude toward Pepouza and Tymion is reminiscent of the way in which the Cycladic Greeks venerated Delos with its sanctuary of Apollo. It is probably not a coincidence that, according to the *Dialogue of a Montanist and an Orthodox*, Montanus had been a priest of Apollo before his conversion to Christianity.[74]

The sacred structure of Pepouza, the more important of the two places that constituted the Montanists' "New Jerusalem," was built around the cathedral where the Montanist chief bishop, or "patriarch," resided. A shrine with the bones of the founders of the movement—Montanus,

---

71. The discovery in 2000 and the excavations were accomplished by the team of archeologists under the leadership of Peter Lampe from the University of Heidelberg and William Tabbernee from Phillips Theological Seminary in the US. They published together a book on their discovery: Tabbernee and Lampe, *Pepouza and Tymion*.

72. On Montanism, see: Trevett, *Montanism*; Tabbernee, *Montanist Inscriptions and Testimonia*; Butler, *The New Prophecy & "New Visions." Evidence of Montanism in the Passion of Perpetua and Felicitas*; Tabbernee, *Fake Prophecy and Polluted Sacraments*.

73. *Adv. Marcionem* (CPL 14) 4.22.5.

74. See Marjanen, "Montanism: Egalitarian Ecstatic 'New Prophecy,'" 189.

Maximilla, and Priscilla—was an important sacred spot. There was another church nearby as well as a hostel and houses for accommodation.[75] It was a self-sufficient sacred complex distinct from the rest of the profane world. It produced in those who stayed there a feeling of proximity to the divine and of being special and elected, different from others.

Montanism promoted a relatively soft version of dualism. There were more radical dualistic movements, primarily gnostic ones, which entertained various kinds of exclusivism: of place, of prophecy, of knowledge, of access to the divine, of membership, *etc*. The gnostics believed that their exclusivity was sacred. They counterposed it to the assumed "profane" common tenets of the church. In this regard, these movements were sectarian, non-catholic, or even anti-catholic. Their ecclesial structures were also introverted and exclusivist, uniform and uniforming. The religious, philosophical, and psychological matrix of these ecclesiological models was dualistic. They featured a black-and-white vision of the world, a belief that places can save and that saving places should be walled off from the rest of the bad world. The high and strong walls had to surround and protect the borders of the church. In the dualistic perception, they should separate the holy and sunlit hills of salvation from the dark valleys of profanity.

This dualistic ecclesiological matrix radically differed from the one held by the catholic church. This church was inclusive and extraverted. Its vision of the line between the sacred and the profane was not that of a wall to be safeguarded, because everyone received equal access to the revelation of God in Jesus Christ. All people are equal in this regard. The world is good because it is the creation of the good God. There are no places in the world that are exceptionally good or bad. The entire world is called to be reconciled with God through Jesus Christ.

This inclusive ecclesiological matrix was articulated by Irenaeus of Lyon (early second century—c. 202). He built on the Pauline tradition, for which God the Father had "revealed to us the secret of his will, according to his good pleasure that he set forth in Christ, toward the administration of the fullness of the times, to head up all things in Christ—the things in heaven and the things on earth" (Eph 1:9–10). The key word in this phrase, which Irenaeus took up, is *anakephalaiōsasthai* (ἀνακεφαλαιώσασθαι). The *New English Translation* (NET) renders it as "head up," the *New Revised Standard Version* (NRSV) as "to gather up,"

---

75. See Tabbernee and Lampe, *Pepouza and Tymion*, 20.

the *English Standard Version* (ESV) and the *Revised Standard Version* (RSV) as "to unite."

For Irenaeus, this word meant that the entire world regains its integrity and is united with Christ, who brings it back to the Father. The Son of God as the head of the invisible world gathered up the visible world as well by assuming human nature. Humanity in its entirety, the "whole flesh of the whole humankind," in Irenaeus's own words, came under the headship of Christ.[76] The Word who received human flesh covered all of humankind as if with wings.[77] Through human beings, the Son of God assumed also the whole world. This includes not only the empirical reality that we see now but also its past and future. The creation of the world, the history of the relations between peoples and Yahweh in the period of the Old Testament, the incarnation, crucifixion, and resurrection of Christ as well as his second coming, constitute for Irenaeus the entirety of the divine providence, which he called the *oikonomia* (οἰκονομία)[78] or *pragmateia* (πραγματεία).[79] Irenaeus placed at the center of this entirety the incarnation of the Logos. The teleology of the *recapitulatio*, for him, was concentrated in the salvation of humanity. Irenaeus developed his theology of the holistic salvation in response to the isolationist tendencies in the church that were induced primarily by gnostic dualism. He tried to pull down the walls of separation between the supposedly "good" and "bad" parts of creation, between the sacred and profane spaces. The entire world, for him, was called to be sanctified through the incarnation of the Word in Jesus Christ. The church was not to lock itself in the safety-deposit box of a particular locality, but to embrace the entire creation.

To overcome the problem of dualism, the church had to answer the question of evil and its nature. An answer was provided by the Christian Neoplatonists. The one who wrestled with this problem the best was the author who flourished from the late fifth to the early sixth century and wrote under the pseudonym of the first-century Christian Dionysios the Areopagite. Evil, for him, was not a part of the created world, but something non-material. Evil appears as a negation of the good, a lack of good. It is an emptiness that has to be filled with the good. Only good can be truly said to exist. The translator of Ps-Dionysius's works into English,

---

76. *Adv. haer.* (CPG 1306) 1.2.1.13–14; see also *Adv. haer.* (CPG 1306) 33.5–6.
77. *Adv. haer.* (CPG 1306) 11.43–44.
78. See *Adv. haer.* (CPG 1306) 1.2.1.8; 1.4.1.7; 1.8.7.12; 1.8.14.8; 11.59; 19.3; 16.4.
79. See *Adv. haer.* (CPG 1306) 1.4.1.7; 1.5.1.15; 1.11.1.6; 11.15; 11.44; 11.48.

C. E. Rolt, described the Dionysian concept of evil as being like zero in mathematics, "which is a non-entity (since, added to numbers, it makes no difference) and yet has an annihilating force (since it reduces to zero all numbers that are multiplied by it)."[80] Ps-Dionysius speaks best for himself:

> Evil hath no place either amongst things that have being or things that have not, yea it is farther removed than the Non-Existent from the Good and hath less being than it. . . .
>
> Evil (*qua* evil) causes no existence or birth, but only debases and corrupts, so far as its power extends, the substance of things that have being. . . .
>
> *Qua* evil it neither hath being nor confers it. . . .
>
> Evil is Non-Existent. Neither inhereth evil in existent creatures. For if all creatures are from the Good, and the Good is in them all and embraces them all, either evil can have no place amongst the creatures, or else it must have a place in the Good. Now it cannot inhere in the Good, any more than cold can inhere in fire. . . .
>
> In a word, evil . . . is weakness, impotence, and deficiency of knowledge (or, at least, of exercised knowledge), or of faith, desire, or activity as touching the Good.[81]

Ps-Dionysius thus offered a solution to the dilemma that fed the dualism, which contributed to the particularist, isolationist, and centripetal tendencies in the church of his time. He demonstrated that *all* things and beings are good in their nature. Evil does not exist as a thing or as matter. It is a result of the abuse of and deviation from nature, its dysfunction. The insights of Ps-Dionysius had immediate ecclesiological implications. They contributed to a vision of the church as an inclusive, all-embracing, and open reality. No part of the world can be excluded from the church because everything ontologically existent is good in its nature. This ecclesiological vision was in tune with the insights of Minucius Felix, Irenaeus of Lyon, and other authors who advocated a catholic, non-sectarian, and non-dualistic vision of the church. They were all adherents of what can be called an open ecclesiology.

The open ecclesiological vision counterbalanced the tendencies toward exclusivism and introversion, which dominated sectarian movements and existed in the catholic church as well, challenging its

---

80. Rolt, *Dionysius, the Areopagite, on the Divine Names and Mystical Theology*, 20.
81. *De divinis nominibus* (CPG 6602) 4.19–35 in ibid., 112–29.

universalist vision. In every epoch, both ecclesiological visions manifested themselves in the life of the church. Sometimes one had the upper hand, sometimes the other. Their dialectical coexistence can be illustrated by the ambivalent interpretations of what exactly the church is as a place of worship. As mentioned earlier, specially designated places of worship became the norm after the legalization of Christianity under Constantine. They certainly helped new crowds of Christians to be integrated into the church and facilitated their catechization, baptism, ongoing instruction in the Christian faith, and reception of communion. But at the same time, many converts to Christianity from paganism brought with them the same attitude to Christian places of worship as they'd had toward Greco-Roman temples, with their segregated sacrality and exclusivism.

The Christian buildings of worship after Constantine provided the possibility for a double interpretation of what they were. They fitted with both open and closed ecclesial visions. On the one hand, they could be regarded as the *imago mundi*, built with the idea of imitating the entire *kosmos*. Their walls were like the four sides of the world, and their cupola resembled the vault of heaven. In the description of the sixth-century Alexandrian monk and geographer Cosmas Indicopleustes, the world was very similar to the contemporary church architecture of the sixth century. It was cuboid with a downhill roof, just like basilicas, which were also popular at the time (Picture 2).

On the other hand, the churches could be interpreted as places of concentrated sacrality. From this perspective, the churches were seen to be like the sacred island of Delos, separated from the evil sea of the world, or like the promised city of Pepouza, which was supposed to be the "New Jerusalem." Such a vision was contrary to the initial Christian idea of space and sacrality.

In sum, the difference between sacred and profane is imagined, not real. Where a person draws the fine line between them depends very much on how Christian and open is her or his ecclesial vision. For the Christians with open views of the church, the entire world was good as a creation of God. For those with the dualistic mindset, however, the separation line between the sacred and profane was important. This mindset also leads to an undoubting trust in the structures of the church. Both mentalities, open and dualistic, found their place in the church. They continue wrestling with each other even now. Although the distinction between the sacred and profane is imagined, it has influenced the way in which some structures of the church were developed. It strengthened both internal and external borderlines of the church.

Picture 2: Cosmas Indicopleustes's pattern of the universe.[82]

THE CHURCH UNIVERSAL AND PARTICULAR

Another fine pencil line that was supposed to make a theoretical distinction within the church: between the categories of universal and particular, can also divide, and actually has divided the church.[83] Different interpretations of universality and particularity remain irreconcilable between

---

82. Based on the illustration from the *Codex Sinaiticus graecus* 1186, fol. 69r, eleventh century, probably from Cappadocia, now at St. Catherine's Monastery near Mount Sinai.

83. Theses of this sub-chapter appeared in Hovorun, "Universal and Particular in the Church," and Hovorun, "De regionale en universele kerk in de huidige orthodox-katholieke dialoog."

the Roman Catholic and the Orthodox churches. Because of their divergence in reading universality and particularity, the two churches cannot come to an agreement on the issue of primacy.

To understand universality and particularity in the church, one has to go as far back as to Aristotle and his commentators. In his *Categories*, Aristotle distinguished between individual things and their commonalities.[84] Substance (*ousia*, οὐσία) here means "individual thing" as, for example, individual man or individual tree. It is known also as a "primary substance." Species (*eidos*, εἶδος) and *genus* (*genos*, γένος) constitute the category of "secondary substance." They are related to the primary substance as a man and an animal are related to the individual man. Aristotle defined secondary substance as a "thing *said of* a subject" (*en kath hypokeimenou*, ἐν καθ' ὑποκειμένου). Aristotelian distinction between particular and common natures, through Porphyry (before 234–c. 305) and other Neoplatonic commentators,[85] became widely applied in the Christian theology. It helped, for instance, the Cappadocians to draw a distinction between the persons and the essence of the Trinity. It also constituted a framework for the Chalcedonian doctrine of the one hypostasis and two natures of the incarnate Logos. Among the theologians who explored the categories in the systematic way were Theodore of Raithu (flourished after 550, perhaps in the seventh century), Maximus the Confessor (c. 580–662), Anastasius of Sinai (died c. 700), and John of Damascus (c. 655–c. 750). There were also Christian philosophers who continued developing the Aristotelian categories in the vein with the earlier Neoplatonic commentators, such as Themistius (before 317–88) and the sixth-seventh century philosophers Elias, David, and Stephan.

In the terms of the Aristotelian dialectics, "particular churches" would mean communities. Communities, which consist of people who gather "in one place" (*epi to auto*, ἐπὶ τὸ αὐτό—Acts 2:1), are concrete ecclesial entities—the "first substances" or "hypostases" of the church. The ecclesial "hypostases" should not be interpreted as "persons" of the church—they are not the "who" but the "what" of the church, its "things." At the same time, all of them share some essential features, such as togetherness in prayer and life, baptism, eucharist ministry, *etc*. These

---

84. *Categories* 2a.11–19.

85. See Evangeliou, *Aristotle's Categories and Porphyry*; Sorabji, *Aristotle Transformed*; Barnes, *Porphyry*; Karamanolis, *Plato and Aristotle in agreement? Platonists on Aristotle from Antiochus to Porphyry*; Tuominen, *The Ancient Commentators on Plato and Aristotle*; Wilberding, *Porphyry*.

features make the individual communities sharing in the common nature of the church. This nature, which can be identified as "universal" church, does not exist apart from or beyond the communities, which are its concrete manifestations. In this regard Christopher O'Donnell is right when he says that "people *know* about the universal Church; they *experience* the local one."[86]

Maximus the Confessor added to the Aristotelian-Porphyrian dialectics some terms that made clearer the distinction between the individualities and commonalities of beings. He described the common essence of the individual beings as their *logos*. These beings individually have each a concrete way of existence (*tropos hyparxeōs*, τρόπος ὑπάρξεως),[87] which can be described as "how" (*pōs*, πῶς)[88] of the existence of their common nature. Maximus's language in application to ecclesiology would mean that the universal church is a common idea (*logos*, λόγος), while any given community is a concrete way (*tropos*, τρόπος) in which this idea actualizes itself. Communities substantiate the *logos* of the church as its concrete "how" (*pōs*, πῶς). The *logos* of the church is common for all the communities, while the way, in which it realizes itself, is unique to each of them.

The distinction between the particular and universal church, when interpreted in the Aristotelian terms, supports the ecclesiological formula of unity in diversity. Thus, each community as a hypostasis of the church realizes the common ecclesial nature in its own way. This should encourage the church to develop diversity of practices on the local level. However, when a concrete community alienates itself from the common *logos* of the doctrine, ethos, and rite—this happens, for instance, when it adopts its own understanding of baptism, eucharist, and ministry—it ceases to participate in the common nature of the church and becomes a sect. Equally harmful for the communities is when their unique way of participation in the nature of the church (the *tropos*/τρόπος or *pōs*/πῶς of participation) is forced to uniformity, as a result of the confusion between what is universal and what is particular in the church. This projection of the universal modality of existence of the church to its particular level constitutes a violation of the hypostatic character of

---

86. O'Donnell, *Ecclesia*, 272.

87. See *Ambiguum* 1 (CPG 7705).

88. See *Disputatio cum Pyrrho* (CPG 7698: PG 91, 292D–293A); *Opuscula theologica et polemica* 3 (CPG 7697: PG 91, 48A–B); Hovorun, *Will, Action and Freedom*, 125, 145.

the communities. Similar confusion has happened, when one concrete community (of Rome) identified itself with the common nature of the church (universal church).

If the Aristotelian categories of universal and particular were applied to the church in the patristic or scholastic era, they would probably conceptualize the church in the way described above. This did not, however, happen—probably because the idea of the church was not yet the focus of theological discourse. Nevertheless, the distinction between universal and particular in the church was not altogether missing in the early Christian literature. It can be traced back to the Scripture.

The idea of the universal church correlates closely to the concept of the people of God, *qāhāl Yahweh*,[89] which in the New Testament was rendered as "church of God" (*ekklēsia tou Theou*, ἐκκλησία τοῦ Θεοῦ, Acts 20:28). Even more frequently, the New Testament refers to the idea of the church as a particular community. This idea constitutes an essential part of the narrative of Acts, the communal ecclesiology of Paul, and the eschatology of John. Three New Testament books contain the greatest number of instances of the word *ekklēsia*: Acts (23 times), 1 Corinthians (21 times), and Revelation (19 times). These books deal with the particular Christian communities. Acts tells how they spread throughout the Roman world. 1 Corinthians deals with the problems of a particular community in Corinth. Revelation addresses seven local churches in Asia Minor. The most common meaning of the "church" in the New Testament appears to be a particular community of followers of Christ. Out of 114 references to *ekklēsia* in the New Testament, eighty-five clearly imply a particular community.[90]

The idea of the particular church in its biblical meaning continued to prevail in the subsequent Christian literature, though it did not cease to imply the universality of the church.[91] The two ideas, however, did

---

89. Deut 23:2; Judg 20:2; 1 Chr 28:8; Neh 13:1; Mic 2:5.

90. Acts 9:31; 11:22, 26; 12:1, 5; 13:1; 14:23, 27; 15:2, 3, 4, 22, 41; 16:5; 18:22; 20:17; Rom 16:1, 4, 5, 16, 23; 1 Cor 4:17; 6:4; 7:17; 11:16, 18, 22; 12:28; 14:4, 5, 12, 19, 23, 26, 28, 33, 34, 35; 16:1, 19; 2 Cor 8:1, 18, 19, 23, 24; 11:8, 28; 12:13; Gal 1:2, 22; Phil 4:15; Col 4:15, 16; 1 Thess 1:1; 2:14; 2 Thess 1:1, 4; 1 Tim 3:5; 5:16; Philm 1:2; Jam 5:14; 1 Pet 5:13; 3 John 1:6, 9, 10; Rev 1:4, 11, 20; 2:1, 7, 8, 11, 12, 17, 18, 23, 29; 3:1, 6, 7, 13, 14, 22; 22:16.

91. Christopher O'Donnell summarizes developments of the idea of particular church in the patristic era: "Immediately after the NT period we find in the letters of Ignatius Churches in cities presided over by a single bishop with presbyters and deacons. The *Didachè* is clearly descriptive of a local Church with its ordinances both

not receive any significant theological reflection. They were embodied instead in the ecclesial structures. By the end of the first millennium, western Christianity appeared to be more inclined to the idea of the universal church, while eastern Christianity headed toward privileging the particular church. Both West and East, however, departed quite far from the original meanings of the universal and particular.

The idea of the universal church became dominant in the western tradition simultaneously with the growing importance of the papacy. Historical circumstances modified the interpretation of the universal church as the one under the jurisdiction of the Roman bishop. The papacy at some stage over-emphasized the idea of the universal church and tailored it to historical expedience. The concept of the universal church in turn strengthened the papacy by providing theological justification for its claims.

In the East, the idea of the particularity of the church prevailed over the idea of universality. It did not produce, however, any significant "ecclesiology of particularity" parallel to the Roman theological reflections on universality. Particularity was incarnated in the structures and identities of the "local" eastern churches. The eastern inclination to particularity had its own historical reasons. One of them can be found in the rich apostolic traditions preserved in the East. Unlike the West with only the Roman see enjoying apostolic origin, many eastern churches claimed apostolic parentage, even when this was not always historically justifiable. Their traditions, which they correctly or incorrectly traced back to the apostolic times, preserved the significant diversity of the early Christianity, which survived the periods of careless unification. The second reason was the memories that many eastern communities kept from the times when it was common for them to be independent or effectively autocephalous. By the time of consolidation of the "autocephalous" churches

---

moral and liturgical. From the time of Irenaeus it is clear that the Ignatian model of Church order was to be found everywhere. In time the Church of Rome would become the touchstone for both unity and orthodoxy. As the Church expanded beyond the larger cities and towns, the parish structure began to emerge. Originally parish (Greek *paroikia* = a district) could mean diocese, but from late the 4th century it came to mean a subdivision of the diocese over which the bishop placed a resident priest. In the patristic period there was great autonomy in each diocese, but the notion of the universal Church was kept to the fore through councils and the exchange of correspondence, theological treatises, and by traveling. It is also important to note that a person excommunicated in one local Church was not admitted to communion in any other Church." O'Donnell, *Ecclesia*, 270–71.

into patriarchates, their local traditions had become sacredly ossified. In the process of merging into patriarchal structures, they gave up their jurisdictional independence but not their cultural and liturgical diversities. Local traditions in the East, thus, were valued more than in the West.

The East, however, migrated far from the original meaning of particularity. A *particular* church became identified with its *locus* and thus turned to *local*. This happened in the time when Christian communities became organized in conformity with the imperial territorial units. Communities became elements of the large supra-communal blocks (metropolises, patriarchates, *etc.*) that were measured to fit the territorial grid of the empire. Their original apostolic particularity was transformed into the locality of supra-communal ecclesial structures. Consequently, the idea of a particular church became disassociated from the community and identified with the supra-communal structures, which in turn were tied to territory. Territoriality substituted for particularity. A hierarchy of communities within the new supra-communal structures replaced their equality in sharing the same nature of the church in a unique hypostatic way.

The difference between the original and the eventual ideas of the particular church in the Christian East is therefore that the latter turned out to be territorial. It detached itself from the community. Communities ceased to be the "things/hypostases" of the church. This role passed to the administrative structures. These structures, based on administrative functions, are effectively ephemeral, not real manifestations of the ecclesial nature. They cannot be regarded "hypostases" of the church, even though they pretend to be ones. One can agree on this point with John Zizioulas, who remarks: "A metropolis, an archdiocese or a patriarchate cannot be called a *church* in itself, but only by *extension*."[92] The ecclesial nature and the administrative functions of the church should not be confused. The former is based on prayer, sacraments, and the common faith of the people who come together (*epi to auto*, ἐπὶ τὸ αὐτό). The latter deals mostly with the management of territory and the exercise of administrative authority. While the particularity of the church was initially connected with communities, the (ideal) task of the supra-communal structures is to facilitate the harmonious development of communities, not to substitute for them. Unfortunately, at some point the Christian East began identifying the particularities of the church with independent

---

92. Zizioulas, *Being as Communion*, 252, note 7.

hierarchical structures, first metropolises and later patriarchates. This new idea behind the particular church grew simultaneously with the enhancement of the patriarchates that gradually turned into strong monolithic structures. Patriarchs in the East began personifying the local churches and particularity in the church, just as the pope personified the universal church in the Christian West.

Eventually, eastern particularism became similar in many points to the Roman universalism. Both adopted a strict hierarchical logic, according to which authority is exercised from above, in one case by the pope and in the other case by the patriarch. Within their jurisdictions, the pope and the patriarchs adopted almost an absolute power, which often imposed uniformity. The patriarchs who represented particularism in the universal church, did not allow much particularism within their jurisdiction. The difference, however, was that, unlike the pope, the eastern patriarchs did not claim to exercise universal jurisdiction. Another difference was that the eastern bishops acted on their own behalf and not on behalf of their patriarch, as in the West. Nevertheless, their authority became significantly reduced, and a part of it was delegated to the patriarchs.

Nowadays the situation is changing. Although both East and West stick with their respective particular and universal self-identities, they both feel the deficiency of these identities. The western idea of universality sometimes remains a cold concept lacking the warmth of enculturation and domestication of the locality. It can be too abstract, too faceless, and too heartless. The eastern obsession with locality, in turn, often leads to noisy cantankerousness, to traditions-addicted autism, blindness and deafness to the universal Christian call. Both East and West need to restore the balance between universality and particularity, and both of them want this. The West tries to reconnect its universality with community and locality.[93] This was one of the main intuitions of Vatican II.

93. In the modern Roman Catholic ecclesiology, more emphasis is placed on local communities. See, for instance, Susan Wood's summary of the relationship between universality and locality in the Catholic church: "The relationship between the local churches and the universal church can be summarized by the following theses: 1. There is only one church of Christ. Catholics believe that this one church is present in the Roman Catholic Church although ecclesial elements are also found outside it. Vatican II stated: 'The church, constituted and organized as a society in the present world, subsists in the Catholic Church, which is governed by the successor of Peter and by the bishops in communion with him.' This represents a development from Pius XII's *Mystici Corporis*, which identified the church of Christ with the Catholic Church. 2. The particular churches are formed in the likeness of the universal church; in and from these particular churches there exists the one unique Catholic Church. This means

In an effort to overcome its existent deficiencies, the West encourages cultural, liturgical, and even theological diversities in the body of its church, redefining the role of the bishops and the significance of parishes. The East, in turn, struggles to reinforce the universal dimension of its own particularities. It tries to correct the hierarchy of Christian values by downgrading ethnicism and etatism to the bottom of the scale of values. The Orthodox churches struggle to overcome their disagreements on the territorial issues and to witness to the world with a common voice. An impressive degree of rapprochement has been achieved between the two ecclesiological traditions, western and eastern, in their understanding of what universality and particularism are in the church. Some points of this rapprochement have been reflected in the document *The Nature and Mission of the Church* prepared by the WCC commission on Faith and Order (2005). This document states, concerning relations between local and universal dimensions of the church,

> The communion of the Church is expressed in the communion between local churches, in each of which the fullness of the Church resides. The communion of the Church embraces local churches in each place and all places at all times. Local churches are held in the communion of the Church by the one Gospel, the one baptism and the one Lord's Supper, served by a common ministry. This communion of local churches is thus not an optional extra, but is an essential aspect of what it means to be the Church.[94]

Both East and West agree on this statement. In practice, however, neither of them is successful enough in its efforts to reconcile particularity and universality. Synods of bishops in the Catholic church, for instance, remain in the perception of many merely an imitation of conciliarity

---

that the universal church does not have more than a notional existence unless it exists in and out of the local churches. The mystery of the church is present and manifested in a concrete society. The many churches are not churches except in the one church; the one church does not exist except in and out of the many churches. 3. The universal church is not a federation of particular churches. 4. A particular church is not a subunit or branch office of the universal church. 5. A particular church is wholly church, but not the whole church. 6. The universal church exists only as the communion of the particular or local churches. . . . The only place in which one can encounter the universal church is in the particular church." Wood, "Continuity and Development in Roman Catholic Ecclesiology," 168–69.

94. §65, available on the website of the WCC: http://goo.gl/NNJsmm [accessed October 19, 2015].

without real power and influence. Roman universalism continues to absorb many responsibilities that can and should be exercised by dioceses and parishes. This was a point of the letter to the bishops from the Congregation for the Doctrine of the Faith (CDF, 1992). For the author of the letter, the primacy of the universal church "is a reality ontologically and temporally prior to every individual particular Church."[95] This letter ignited a famous discussion between Walter Kasper, then bishop of Rottenburg-Stuttgart and later the president of the Pontifical Council for Promoting Christian Unity (1999), and Josef Ratzinger, then the prefect of the CDF. Kasper, in particular, insisted that the local communities have ontological priority over the idea of the universal church, which remains largely an idea. He in particular accused the CDF of reversing the communal ecclesiology of Vatican II.[96]

The Orthodox have their own shortcomings in living and witnessing to the universality of the church. In many cases, they are still unable to sacrifice their local interests to the universal Christian or at least pan-Orthodox aspirations. An illustration of this are the difficulties faced by the Pan-Orthodox Council held in June 2016 in Crete. Attempts to have in the modern era a venue that would match the ecumenical councils go back to the 1860s. At that time, the patriarchate of Constantinople dealt with the issue of Bulgars, who wanted church autonomy. To solve this issue, the Phanar decided to summon a Pan-Orthodox council. However, the Ottoman and Russian governments opposed these plans, and the council did not happen. After the fall of both empires, the patriarch of Constantinople Meletios (1871–1935) made another attempt to summon a "Pan-Orthodox Congress" (*Panorthodoxon Synedrion*, Πανορθόδοξον Συνέδριον) in 1923. However, some local churches did not participate in it because they regarded its agenda to be exceedingly liberal and politicized. A Pan-Orthodox council, which had been scheduled for 1932 in the monastery of Vatopedi, could not even commence its sessions, because some churches did not send their delegates. In 1948, the Russian church celebrated five centuries of its autocephaly. On this occasion, it called for a Pan-Orthodox Council. As in the previous cases, some churches did not come, because this time its agenda was for them too conservative and also politicized. In the early 1960s, Vatican II inspired the Orthodox to try again to have their own council. This time the mistakes of the

95. §9, available on the official website of the Holy See: http://goo.gl/KiiVTk [accessed October 19, 2015].

96. See McDonnell, "The Ratzinger/Kasper Debate," 230.

past were taken into consideration, and the preparation process began in advance, with all local Orthodox churches invited to contribute to its agenda. This process was inaugurated at the Pan-Orthodox Consultation at the Greek island of Rhodes in 1961. Several other consultations towards what had been called "Holy and Great Council of the Orthodox Church" took place on the regular basis in the period from 1961 to 2016. The only break in this process was from 1999 to 2009; it was caused by the quarrel of the churches of Constantinople and Moscow over the small Orthodox community in Estonia. Since 2009, however, the process of preparation of the Pan-Orthodox Council has been speeded up. All the churches eventually agreed on its agenda and format at the meeting of the primates (*Synaxis*) in January 2016. The council was scheduled for the Pentecost 2016 (June 19–26) in Crete. However, a few weeks before this date, some churches unexpectedly decided not to attend the council.[97] As a result, a Pan-Orthodox council did not happen in the form it has been envisaged since the 1960s.

---

97. See more on the reasons why some churches did not participate in the Pan-Orthodox council in Hovorun, "As Pan-Orthodox Council Approaches, Conflicts and Uncertainty Intensify," and Hovorun, "A Blessedly Unpredictable Council."

2

Partition Walls: Territory and Administration

AT ITS "ZERO POINT," the church fitted the Upper Room (Acts 2:1–6), which did not have any partition wall in it. So the earliest church had neither structures nor hierarchies. The church was only Jesus Christ, the Holy Spirit, and the disciples. Probably the only ecclesial structure that can be distinguished at this point was two circles of apostles, the twelve and the seventy. The difference between the two circles was not that of superiority, but of the degree of interest and engagement in the mission of Christ. After Christ's death and resurrection, both circles, together with other disciples, including women, constituted one community that came together in one place in Jerusalem. They as a community received the Holy Spirit in common. Community, thus, became the initial structure of the church.

Most references to *ekklēsia* in the New Testament speak about local communities. These communities emerged as replicas of the apostolic community in Jerusalem. The latter was the archetype for other communities outside of Jerusalem. The first community in Jerusalem was basically a group of disciples of Jesus who came together in one place to share their faith and memories about Christ. They did so through thanksgiving and meal. These features were replicated in other communities and constituted their nature. In this sense, Paul used the word *phyrama* (φύραμα, Rom 11:16; 1 Cor 5:6–7; Gal 5:9)[1]—which means something mixed or

---

1. See Pascuzzi, "Ethics, Ecclesiology and Church Discipline," 151–55.

kneaded, like bread dough—as a synonym of *ekklēsia*.² To Paul, church was about meeting together and worshiping.³ He stressed the intrinsically *communal* character of the first churches (1 Cor 11:18).

Although the early Christian communities shared the same core features such as discipleship of Christ and remembering him at the gatherings through common thanksgiving and meals, they adopted diverse forms of organization. These forms were built on the common social models at their time. These models were of Jewish, Greek, and Roman origins and can be epitomized as the synagogue, the *ekklēsia*, and the *collegium*.

It took some time for the early Christian communities to disassociate themselves from Judaism and develop a distinct identity. Before that happened, the Jewish synagogue constituted a basic pattern for Christian gatherings.⁴ "Synagogue" meant primarily a place where the Jewish community came together to read the Torah. After the destruction of the temple (AD 70), it also became a place for prayer and rituals. Gradually it developed into the center of religious, social, and political life for the Jewish people. It became a place of study, a courthouse, a place for collecting taxes, and a guesthouse. In the diaspora, the synagogue additionally served as a connecting link with Jerusalem. Synagogues had their own administration. The synagogue's special representative, *ḥāsān*, had responsibilities for a variety of tasks and acted in the capacities of a scribe, executor of court decisions, tax collector, *etc*. All members of the community were in full charge of their synagogue. The community owned it and managed its business. The synagogue provided an initial structural setting for the first Christian communities and could easily lend its name to Christian gatherings. The Greek word *synagōgē* (συναγωγή) meant "bringing together" and thus perfectly reflected how the Christian communities understood themselves. However, Christian communities gave preference to another Greek word to describe themselves, namely *ekklēsia* (ἐκκλησία).

The word *ekklēsia* for many centuries before Christ was connected with the Greek political culture. Primarily in Athens, but also in other ancient Greek states-*polises*, this word meant an assembly of free adult male citizens who were entitled to make decisions in the matters relevant

2. Liddell et al., *Greek-English Lexicon*.
3. 1 Cor 14:19, 23, 28, 33, 34, 35; also Philm 1:2.
4. See Burtchaell, *From Synagogue to Church*, 272–338.

to the community that they represented. The *ekklēsia* was not identified with the place where it met. Sometimes the *ekklēsia* met in a special place, an *ekklēsiastērion* (ἐκκλησιαστήριον), like in Olbia or Delos. Athenians met first at the hill of Pnyx, and from the fifth and fourth centuries BC onward they moved to the theatre of Dionysus. Theatres often served as meeting places for *ekklēsia*.

During the centuries of its semantic evolution in the period of antiquity, the word *ekklēsia* accumulated many, one might say too many, connotations. Most of them were related to political life. The word implied debates and divisions. Much less was it related to the religious life of the Greek states. The word *synagogē*, on the other hand, was more religiously charged. We can now only guess why the word *ekklēsia* attracted early Christians more than the word *synagogē*. Probably it was the idea of the call, which is coded in the root of the word, *ek-klēsis*, and which is missing in *synagogē*. Possibly, it also implied the idea of liberation, because the ancient *ekklēsia* was a gathering of free people only. It is also plausible that the foundational principles of the ancient Greek *ekklēsia*, such as *isēgoria* (ἰσηγορία), the equal right of every citizen to speak publicly, *isonomia* (ἰσονομία), equality under the law, and *isopoliteia* (ἰσοπολιτεία), equal right to exercise political power, also mattered for the Christians, who lived through the experience of overcoming the old social divisions (Col 3:11) and of embracing equality for all in Christ (Gal 3:28). Apparently, by calling their community *ekklēsia* and not *synagogē*, the early Christians stressed their openness to the Roman world.

In Rome, during the period of the birth and initial development of Christianity, the most popular form of professional or religious community was *collegium*.[5] It was more popular in the western part of the Roman Empire but also spread to the East. Diasporal synagogues, for instance, functioned largely as *collegia*. *Collegia* were independent self-organized bodies. Each had its own goal. Often they united people of the same profession, like later medieval guilds did. Even in this case, however, they practiced cults. Practically all *collegia* were to a greater or lesser extent religious. They took care of their dead and poor, shared communal meals, and together participated in rituals and other public events. Organizationally, *collegia* followed the model of the Roman civic municipalities with magistrates, councils, and *plebs*. They often met in the halls known

---

5. See Scheid, "Graeco-Roman cultic societies"; Kloppenborg and Ascough, *Greco-Roman Associations*.

as *curia*. Usually *curia* were the places of public and governmental offices, primarily of the Roman senate. Many early Christian communities, especially in the West, were established and functioned as *collegia*.

Another structure of the Roman society that became popular among early Christians was an urban household.[6] This structure spread throughout the empire to its eastern borders. It was distinct from the other structures mentioned so far. It was private, compact, and easily manageable. It incorporated all the people living together in one house, including members of the family, servants, and slaves. Relatives and friends could also join the household. This social structure was confined to one place, the home. It was not public or accountable to any authority outside the household. At the same time, it was hierarchical, more so even than other contemporary social structures.[7] The *paterfamilias* was the unconditional master of it.

This social structure became a model for many communities established by Paul.[8] It turned out to be popular and survived until quite late, along with the other types of communities. "A portrait of small, close-knit, and yet diverse" community[9] of the household type can be best painted on the basis of the archaeological findings at Dura-Europos. A Christian household with a built-in baptistery excavated in the Mesopotamian city of Dura-Europos[10] is probably the only surviving exemplar of the pre-Constantinian places of worship of the type referred to in the epistles of Paul. This particular community flourished in the middle of the third century. Typologically it is similar to the early Christian households that spread in Syria under Paul and evolved through the third century. The archaeological findings in Dura-Europos, excavated and explored jointly by the French Academy of Inscriptions and Letters and Yale University, tell a lot about how such communities functioned.

---

6. See Meeks, *The First Urban Christians*, 29; see about the social structure of household in Antiquity in Bodel and Olyan, *Household and Family Religion in Antiquity*.

7. See Schillebeeckx, *The Church with a Human Face*, 66–67.

8. See Meeks, *The First Urban Christians*, 29, Haight, *Christian Community in History*, vol. 1, 78.

9. Prusak, *The Church Unfinished*, 75.

10. On this see Hopkins and Baur, *Christian Church at Dura-Europos*; Rostovtzeff, *Dura-Europos and Its Art*; Perkins, *The Art of Dura-Europos*; Hopkins and Goldman, *The Discovery of Dura-Europos*; Weitzmann and Kessler, *The Frescoes of the Dura Synagogue and Christian Art*.

Dura-Europos was a city situated in the territory of modern Syria. It was established around 300 BC on the Greco-Roman frontier and at the crossroad of diverse cultures, including the Greek, Roman, Syriac, Palmyrene, Parthian, Jewish, *etc.* Its architecture reflects the rich cultural and religious diversity of the region. The religious life of the city was pluralistic. Archaeologists have found altars dedicated to the Roman and Greek gods, a Mithraïc sanctuary, a synagogue, and a Christian chapel (Map 1). The Christian site in its size and decoration is the humblest among the cultic places of the city, located on the outskirts of the city next to the outer walls. This means that the Christian community in Dura-Europos constituted a small minority and kept a low profile. At the same time, it did not hide itself from the rest of the city, but gathered openly. The big persecutions were yet to come. In the meanwhile, it had to coexist in peace with the non-Christian majority. In its neighborhood were the temples of Zeus Kyrios and Adonis, and a synagogue. It is noteworthy that the Mithraïc and Jewish places of gathering in Dura-Europos were also set in private households. It means that this type of organization was common for religious communities of small sizes regardless of their beliefs. Christians in this regard simply followed a common practice of the time.

In the description of Clark Hopkins, the Christian house in Dura Europos "shared common walls with the adjacent buildings. The early Christian of Dura entered the open court by an entryway in the northeast corner, which shielded observation of the court from the street."[11] It was typical for Mesopotamia of that time[12] and did not differ from the majority of other houses in the city.[13] According to Hopkins, the house initially served as a private residence. Later it was used for Christian gatherings, but the house as a whole did not change. Only its interior was redesigned. A wall between two rooms was demolished to make a larger assembly hall, and one room was rebuilt to make a baptistery. Symbolically, the inner wall between the baptistery and the common hall implies the only partition wall in the early Christian community—between those baptized and non-baptized. Archaeological data indicate that the baptistery was used for both baptisms and the eucharist.[14] Worship places were em-

11. Hopkins and Goldman, *The Discovery of Dura-Europos*, 94.
12. Kraeling, "The Church Building," 138.
13. See Hopkins and Baur, *Christian Church at Dura-Europos*.
14. Hopkins and Goldman, *The Discovery of Dura-Europos*, 115–16.

bellished with wall paintings on biblical themes.[15] A room adjacent to the baptistery was used for studies and preparation for baptism (Picture 3).[16]

Map 1: Plan of Dura-Europos.[17]

15. Ibid., 94.
16. Ibid., 96.
17. Source: Yale University Art Gallery: http://media.artgallery.yale.edu/duraeuropos/dura.html [accessed August 12, 2016].

Picture 3: Plan of the Christian household in Dura-Europos.[18]

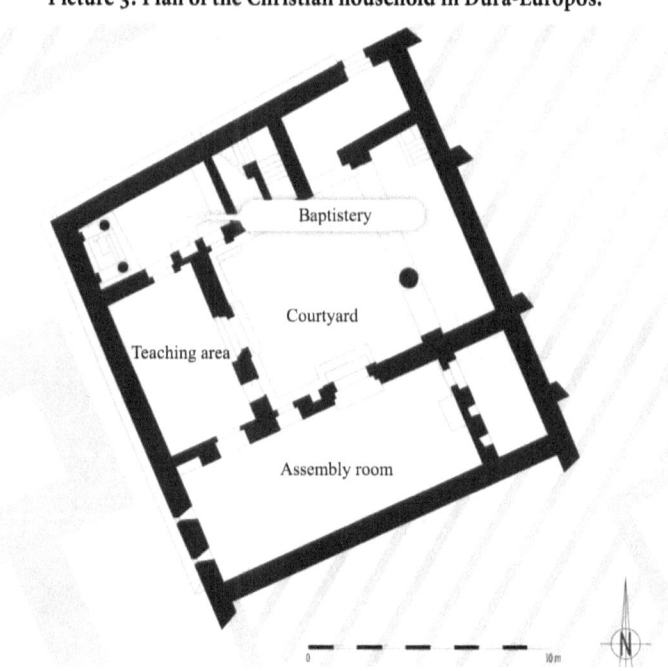

Among other artefacts, the archaeological expedition under Clark Hopkins discovered in Dura-Europos a significant number of papyri and parchments. Among them they found a papyrus with fragments from the *Diatessaron* of Tatian, now kept at the Beinecke Rare Book and Manuscript Library at Yale University.[19] This is the earliest Greek manuscript of the Gospels' compendium, which was widespread in Syria at the time. It is possible that Tatian's compendium of the Gospels was the main scriptural text for the Christian community in Dura Europos. It also served as a source for the paintings on the premises of the "chapel."[20] Themes for the paintings were selected to edify both those being baptized and the members of the community.

The early church was not only a community. From its very beginning, it was also a movement. Christ gathered disciples, taught them, and sent them to disseminate his teaching. At his death, the community of his

---

18. Source: Yale University Art Gallery: http://media.artgallery.yale.edu/duraeuropos/dura.html [accessed August 12, 2016].

19. Dura Parchment 24 (Uncial 0212 in the Gregory-Aland numbering).

20. Hopkins and Goldman, *The Discovery of Dura-Europos*, 109.

followers was ready to dissolve. However, Christ's resurrection restored the fellowship. His rising from the dead created a powerful momentum for the disciples to spread the good news about resurrection and the kingdom of God. No less powerful was the momentum that they received at Pentecost. The resurrection of Christ and outpouring of the Holy Spirit became the main driving force of the Jesus movement.

The movement from its beginning featured two vectors: one centrifugal and the other centripetal. The former indicated the community's dynamic to go out preaching, while the latter represented the conservative force that cared about integrity of the community. These two dynamics often clashed in conflicts, as, for instance, in the discussions about whether to open up to the Gentile world or to stay within the Jewish setting. When balanced, however, the two dynamics helped the church expand without losing its integrity.

By the year 50, the Jesus movement had spread throughout Palestine and reached the coast. At this stage, it remained mostly Jewish. It radically changed its character in Antioch. There, non-Jews joined it. This was a radical shift in the way that the church organized its mission and structure—one of the most radical in the history of the church. It became possible owing to the Greek-speaking Jews of the early Jesus movement, who were more open to the non-Jewish world. As Roger Haight remarks, "Jewish Hellenist followers of Jesus, in translating his gospel message into Greek, opened Christianity to a 'universal' and 'universalizing' culture."[21] This allowed Christianity, Haight continues,

> to spread with a rapidity proportionate to the prevalence of this culture and language; it provided a medium of elementary comprehensibility and transferability. No matter what one's assessment of "Hellenization" might be, one has to recognize the profound impact of this linguistic and cultural "translation."[22]

Antioch became an epicenter of the shift. It provided an urban and cosmopolitan environment for the growing movement, boosting it further. Soon there appeared a man who used the environment of Antioch to give a new momentum to the movement, namely Paul. It was in Antioch that Christianity was put on a global track and began spreading throughout the *oecumene*.

---

21. Haight, *Christian Community in History*, vol. 1, 143.
22. Ibid., 144.

Gerd Theissen has distinguished four basic currents in the Christian movement of the first century: 1) the Pauline, as reflected in the most letters under his name; 2) the Jewish, of James, Matthew, and Hebrews; 3) the Synoptic, represented by these Gospels as combining both Jewish and Gentile dimensions; and finally 4) John's, with his distinct interpretation of prehistory and Christology.[23] Different currents often passed through the same communities. Some communities emerged from or adopted one or another of the currents. They formed alliances and networks along these lines, and in this way, the first supra-communal structures were set.

At the initial stage, communities were loosely affiliated to each other[24] and relations between them are hardly identifiable. As Paula Gooder put it:

> The task of tracing the history of the earliest Christian communities is a little like trying to describe, in a single narrative, the path of twenty rubber balls thrown into the air and left to bounce wherever they come down. . . . The New Testament provides us numerous snapshots of life in early Christian communities but what is unclear is what, if anything, connects these snapshots.[25]

Nevertheless, some inter-communal connections can be suggested. The earliest known communal network was established by Paul. It featured a particular connection with Paul through the people he installed as community leaders, his narrative about Christ, and the correspondence, through which he kept in touch with his communities.

Although there is no sufficient evidence, the earliest Christian networks might have followed the intercommunal models common in the Greco-Roman world.[26] By analogy with the social types of communities, such as synagogue, *ekklēsia*, and *collegium*, the social patterns of intercommunal relations can be identified as stemming from the models of diaspora, *polis*, and empire. Those early Christian communities that adopted the pattern of Jewish diaspora[27] were orientated to the "metropolis" in Jerusalem. They were communities that consisted mostly of the Ara-

---

23. See Theissen, *The Religion of the Earliest Churches*, 254–56; Haight, *Christian Community in History*, vol. 1, 83.

24. Haight, *Christian Community in History*, vol. 1, 87.

25. Mannion and Mudge, *The Routledge Companion to the Christian Church*, 16.

26. Theses of this description appeared in Hovorun, "Evolution of Church Governance: From the Diaspora-Model to Pentarchy."

27. See Schwartz, "Ancient Jewish Social Relations."

maic-speaking Jews living in Palestine. We may suggest that the Greek-speaking communities that followed the model of *ekklēsia* did not feel the same connection with Jerusalem. They maintained their autonomy and had loose relations with other churches, similar to how the Greek cities related to each other. The model that influenced the Christian intercommunal structures most was that of *imperium*.[28] Roman *collegia* were not isolated but related to each other in various ways and had complex hierarchical structures.[29] The Roman hierarchical pattern eventually dominated in the Christian church over the horizontal patterns of networking.

Before that, however, the Jesus movement featured an impressive variety of types of intercommunal relations. Actually, as the recent scholarship suggests, there was not only one Jesus movement. Apart from the mainstream movement that stemmed from the community of the twelve in Jerusalem, there were movements of Jesus's followers elsewhere in Palestine, each with "quite different relationships to Jesus."[30] Even though some preset patterns of relations between and inside these movements could be discerned, they remained unorganized and spontaneous.

When the early Christian networks had developed enough, intercommunal relations could not be regulated *ad hoc* anymore. In result, an overarching model of these relations emerged that helped the church addressing the issues that it faced repeatedly, such as when a care-taker of the community had to be tried or a new one had to be installed. In both cases, the internal resources of the community often did not suffice to address these issues. Primates from other communities, now called *episkopoi* (ἐπίσκοποι), had to participate in order to handle such situations. Most convenient were those *episkopoi* who were near at hand. The participation of neighbor *episkopoi* in solving the problems of a local community shaped the model of the neighborhood in administering the church's affairs. This model became the first commonly accepted throughout the entire Christian network.

There were other problems that the local communities had to solve together, namely deviations from what it believed to be the apostolic norm in teaching and practice, like heresies, schisms, *etc*. These problems affected not just one community but clusters of them. Therefore,

---

28. See Brent, *The Imperial Cult and the Development of Church Order*.

29. See Scheid, "Graeco-Roman Cultic Societies."

30. Haight, *Christian Community in History*, vol. 1, 73; see Cameron and Miller, *Redescribing Christian Origins*, 20.

communities had to face them in common.³¹ This also meant that *episkopoi* needed to meet together at councils. The meetings of the *episkopoi*, however, were not regular. There were also no criteria for who could participate in them. As Vlasios Pheidas remarks, "the activation of the conciliar system was occasional or an emergency."³²

In the model of neighborhood, all local communities were equal, as at any moment any community could be called to serve as a neighbor church for the benefit of another community that asked for help. At the same time, there were communities that were regarded as especially authoritative, either because they were planted by apostles, or had charismatic leaders. Among them were the communities of Rome, Alexandria, Antioch, Jerusalem, Ephesus, Caesarea in Cappadocia, Corinth, Philippi, Carthage, and so on. These communities enjoyed what could be called the "primacy of honor."³³ This kind of primacy was not in any sense institutional or obligatory. It was freely recognized by those churches that wanted to. It did not introduce any sort of hierarchy in the relations between the communities.

Such a hierarchy was introduced with the "metropolitan model." The metropolitan model made the model of the neighborhood more ordered. It was legalized by canons 4, 5, and 6 of the council of Nicea.³⁴ However, it did not spread evenly throughout the church. It was implemented more in Asia Minor and Syria, and less in the West and North Africa.³⁵ Features of this model were as follows:

1. It clearly defined what kind of neighborhood was required to try a bishop or to install a new one for the community. The neighborhood was tailored to the administrative unit of the Roman Empire, the province (*eparchia*, ἐπαρχία).

2. All bishops of the province, if it was possible of course, had to participate in the required procedures.

3. Actions of the bishops of the neighborhood had to be approved by the one who resided in the capital of the province, called the

---

31. See Prusak, *The Church Unfinished*, 128.
32. Φειδᾶ, Ἐκκλησιαστική Ἱστορία, 805.
33. Ibid.
34. See ibid., 457.
35. See more Говорун, "Исторический контекст 28-го правила"; Hovorun, "On Formation of Jurisdictional Limits of Eastern Churches in 4–5th Centuries."

"metropolitan bishop" (*mētropolitēs episkopos*, μητροπολίτης ἐπίσκοπος). Without his approval, the decisions of the bishops of the neighborhood were void.

The metropolitan model implied four radical shifts in the arrangement of the Christian church. First, communities were considered to belong to the imperial administrative territory. The church thus adopted the Roman principle of territoriality. This principle would become dominant in the later history of Christianity. The model of neighborhood also had implied some kind of territoriality, but it was different. The territoriality of neighborhood served the good of the community. In the metropolitan model, territoriality became a self-sufficient principle of administration that changed the way in which community functioned.

Second, for the first time the hierarchy among the bishops and among the communities became institutionalized. Before that, there were only bishops who had responsibility for their own communities. Now some bishops were also endowed with supervision over other bishops, apart from their responsibilities for their own communities. Although this supervision was limited, it affected important and sensitive issues of the installation and removal of other bishops. Metropolitans thus became "first among equals" (*primi inter pares*). They enjoyed a sort of primacy, which had become institutionalized. This inevitably led to conflicts between the bishops who enjoyed the old-fashioned primacy of honor and the metropolitans who received a new kind of primacy that stemmed from their administrative position.[36] In these conflicts, initially the administrative sort of primacy won over the honorary one.[37] Later on, primacy of honor was partially reintroduced, as in the case of the church of Jerusalem. Jerusalem's political significance was next to nothing. Nevertheless, its church received a place in the line with such important political centers as Alexandria and Antioch.

These two shifts introduced a new rationale to the office of bishop, who became an official governing his territory. The focus of the bishop's

---

36. Such conflicts were reported in the provinces of Palestine (between Caesarea and Jerusalem), Caria (between Tralleis and Aphrodisias), Pamphilia (between Side and Perge), Paphlagonia (between Pompiioupolis and Gangra), Lycia (between Patara and Myrrha), Cyprus (between Paphos and Konstantia), Mesopotamia (between Nisibis and Edessa), Pisidia (between Sagala and Ikonion), and others. See Φειδᾶ, Ὀ θεσμὸς τῆς Πενταρχίας τῶν Πατριαρχῶν, vol. 1, 53–54.

37. See Φειδᾶ, Ὀ θεσμὸς τῆς Πενταρχίας τῶν Πατριαρχῶν, 53.

office was relocated from community to territory, from pastoral care of the people of God to administering the ecclesial structures.[38] As Bernard Prusak puts it: "The notion of a bishop presiding at his church assembled for the Eucharist was no longer the principal focus. The bishop's primary function had become administration."[39]

The third shift in the metropolitan model was that the council of bishops became a regular institution. According to canon 5 of Nicea, councils had to be summoned twice a year.[40] All bishops of a province had to take part in them. Conciliarity or synodality became a regular function in the church.[41] These venues of bishops became an ultimate authority in the matters related to the communities belonging to the same ecclesial province. No other community from outside the province could intervene or change the decisions of the provincial council.

This, fourth, constituted a network of the communities within one province as a kind of "super-church." Autocephaly or self-governance was delegated by the local communities to the super-church or metropolis. Theodore Balsamon (d. 1199) testified to that: "In old times, all metropolitans of the provinces were autocephalous and consecrated by their own councils."[42] Speaking more generally, the notion of the church was transferred from a community to the network of communities.

The shift to the metropolitan model was one of the most dramatic in the development of the church structures. This model introduced and legalized the principles that shaped the church as we know it now. Like any other model, however, the metropolitan one early on demonstrated its vulnerability. In particular, this model helped the civil authorities in Constantinople and their ecclesial counterparts to introduce state-sponsored Arianism quickly to the majority of the newly established metropolises. It would have been more difficult to disseminate this doctrine to cell-communities if they had not been organized into larger structures connected with civil centers. On the plus side, in the struggle with Arianism, the Nicenes in both East and West managed to open up the closed structures

---

38. See "Vescovi e pastori in epoca teodosiana," (Incontro di studiosi dell'antichità cristiana, Rome: Institutum Patristicum Augustinianum, 1997).

39. Prusak, *The Church Unfinished*, 210.

40. Alberigo, *Conciliorum oecumenicorum generaliumque decreta*, 22.

41. Hans Küng in his elegant theology of the church councils has enthusiastically argued that the church *per se* is a council, and particular councils represent the church (Küng, *Structures of the Church*, 15, 19).

42. Ῥάλλη καὶ Ποτλῆ, Σύνταγμα τῶν θείων καὶ ἱερῶν κανόνων, 171.

of metropolises and made them accountable to other churches. This was particularly accomplished by the councils in Antioch (341) and Sardica (343).[43] The former approved the institution of a "major council" (*meizōn synodos*, μείζων σύνοδος), which in addition to the bishops of metropolis would include the bishops from other provinces as well.[44] The council of Sardica introduced the possibility of appealing to the authoritative sees.[45]

In addition, the council of Constantinople, which was convened in 381 to handle the neo-Arian reactions to Nicea, along with the theological instruments developed by the Cappadocian fathers, introduced what can be called a "diocesan model" of church administration.[46] This model was called upon to correct the abuses of the metropolitan system that had been committed in the period of the anti-Nicene reaction. Constantinople I continued the councils of Antioch (341) and Sardica (343) in constructing a supra-metropolitan model. This model was supposed to establish control over the metropolises. But unlike Antioch and Sardica, which tried to settle the problem within the same metropolitan paradigm, Constantinople I "upgraded" the model. It applied the Nicene logic of employing civil models and projected onto the church administration

---

43. See Stephens, *Canon Law and Episcopal Authority*.

44. "Εἴ τις ἐπίσκοπος ἐπί τισιν ἐγκλήμασι κρίνοιτο, ἔπειτα συμβαίη περὶ αὐτοῦ διαφωνεῖν τοὺς ἐν τῇ ἐπαρχίᾳ ἐπισκόπους, τῶν μὲν ἀθῶον τὸν κρινόμενον ἀποφαινόντων, τῶν δὲ, ἔνοχον· ὑπὲρ ἀπαλλαγῆς πάσης ἀμφισβητήσεως, ἔδοξε τῇ ἁγίᾳ, τὸν τῆς μητροπόλεως ἐπίσκοπον ἀπὸ τῆς πλησιοχώρου ἐπαρχίας μετακαλεῖσθαι ἑτέρους τινάς, τοὺς εὐκρινοῦντας, καὶ τὴν ἀμφισβήτησιν διαλύσοντας, τοῦ βεβαιῶσαι σὺν τοῖς τῆς ἐπαρχίας τὸ παριστάμενον." "If a bishop shall be tried on any accusations, and it should then happen that the bishops of the province disagree concerning him, some pronouncing the accused innocent, and others guilty; for the settlement of all disputes, the holy Synod decrees that the metropolitan call on some others belonging to the neighbouring province, who shall add their judgment and resolve the dispute, and thus, with those of the province, confirm what is determined." Canon 14, in Fulton, *Index Canonum*, 240–41.

45. In my earlier publication (Hovorun, "Apostolicity and Right to Appeal"), I have argued that the canons of Sardica (primarily canon 3) did not constitute the basis for the recognition of the Roman right to entertain appeals for the eastern church. The eastern bishops considered them either as a canonical basis for the western churches to appeal to Rome—on the ground that Sardica belonged to the Roman jurisdiction, and bishop Hosios of Cordoba, who initiated the canons, was a western bishop himself. Alternatively, they saw them as a temporal right, which was bestowed personally upon pope Julius under the harsh circumstances of the suppression by the Arians. See also Hess, *The Early Development of Canon Law and the Council of Serdica*, 179–200.

46. Vlasios Pheidas calls it an "exarchic system": Φειδᾶ, Ἐκκλησιαστικὴ Ἱστορία, vol. 1, 821; see also Φειδᾶ, Ὁ θεσμὸς τῆς Πενταρχίας τῶν Πατριαρχῶν, 146–67.

the diocesan structure of the Roman state. Civil dioceses (*dioikēseis*, διοικήσεις) were established during the administrative reforms of Diocletian in the 290s. They were organized into four praetorian prefectures (*praefectura praetorio*, ἐπαρχότης τῶν πραιτωρίων or ὑπαρχία τῶν πραιτωρίων) and included the smaller provinces (Map 2).[47]

Canons 2 and 6 of Constantinople I made metropolises more accountable to the dioceses. As Peter L'Huillier put it, Constantinople I proposed considering imperial dioceses as "coherent entities in which the bishops ought to assume common responsibilities."[48] Independence in managing church affairs, including the most important canonical procedures of consecration and trial of bishops, was expanded from the level of the civil province to the higher level of diocese. This model of church administration, which was attempted to be built on the level of civil dioceses, did not stand for long. Soon it was replaced with a new model that proved to be more viable. This model survives, in a modified form, to the present day. It is a patriarchal model.

The patriarchal model emerged in parallel to the metropolitan and diocesan models and was eventually substituted for them. This process lasted from the council of Constantinople I (381) to the council of Chalcedon (451). This model did not exactly follow the pattern that had been adopted by the council of Nicea and did not reflect only the civil divisions of the Roman Empire. Although the number of the patriarchates was almost equal to the number of the civil prefectures (five against four), their territories did not coincide. The rationale behind dividing the church into five patriarchates was not only political. It also included ecclesial and historical reasons: apostolicity, primacy of honor, theological importance, *etc*. A synthesis of political and historical criteria helped the church to relieve the tensions between the newly emerged administrative and the traditional centers of ecclesial governance.

---

47. See Appendix 1.
48. L'Huillier, *The Church of the Ancient Councils*, 117.

Map 2: Administrative divisions of the Roman Empire in the fourth century AD.[49]

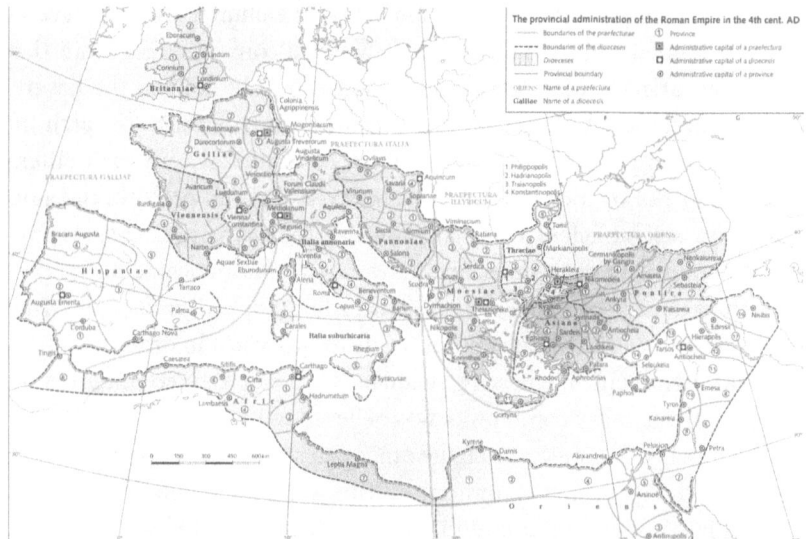

The patriarchal model continued the process of evolution of the supra-metropolitan systems. Although metropolises did not cease to play a key role within the patriarchates, they lost for good their self-sufficiency or autocephaly. They became accountable to the five patriarchal centers: Rome, Constantinople, Alexandria, Antioch, and Jerusalem. The only exceptions were the metropolis of Cyprus, which secured its full independence at the council of Ephesus (431), and the metropolis of eastern Illyria, which became a subject of the fight between Rome and Constantinople. All metropolises were distributed among the patriarchates in the following way:[50]

Rome: dioceses of Gallia, Vienna, Hispania, Italia I and II, Africa, Pannonia, and Moesia.

Constantinople: dioceses of Thracia, Asiana, and Pontica.

Alexandria: parts of the diocese of Oriens, including Libya I and II, Thebai, Aegyptus I and II.

Antioch: the rest of the diocese of Oriens.

Jerusalem: the provinces of Arabia Nova and Palaestina.

---

49. Source: Wittke et al., *Historical Atlas of the Ancient World*, 225.
50. Source: Wittke et al., *Historical Atlas of the Ancient World*, 228.

The institution of the patriarchate proved to be the most effective instrument for securing communion across the church on all its levels. First, it framed communion between the local communities within the same patriarchate. Metropolitans and sometimes bishops in the lower-level communities had to commemorate the name of their patriarch in public prayer. In this way they sustained communion with each other. Second, in the relations between themselves, the patriarchates did not turn into self-sufficient ecclesial monads. They struggled to preserve communion with each other. In the words of Elias, a legate of the patriarch of Jerusalem to the council of Constantinople II in 869–70: "The Holy Spirit established patriarchal heads in the world in order to eliminate through them all emerging scandals."[51] Through the communion of the patriarchs, every community was believed to be in communion with all the other communities in all the other patriarchates. The patriarchates functioned as proxies of communion. This was a reduction of the initial idea of intercommunal communion, but it turned out to be an effective and easy way of securing communion throughout the entire church.

The mechanism of securing the unity of the patriarchates has been called "pentarchy." The Byzantines themselves did not use this word. It was introduced to the modern vocabulary of canon law from Aristotle's *Politica*.[52] Nevertheless, pentarchy existed even before it was called such as an instrument of managing the matters relevant to the entire church. Among other tasks, it ensured that the councils of the church, including the ecumenical ones, functioned properly. Thus, the iconoclastic council in Hiereia (754), which claimed to be ecumenical, was not received by the church largely because it was not approved by the pentarchy—not one patriarch participated in it. The patriarchs were expected to correct each other when the positions of some of them deviated from the norms of the tradition. In the words of Theodore the Studite (759–826), "If someone from the Patriarchs stumbles he should receive correction . . . from the same rank."[53] Through the mechanisms of pentarchy, the patriarchs tried to protect their relative independence from the civil authorities. This was especially important for the patriarchs of Constantinople, who were permanently threatened by the interventions of emperors. Thus, patriarch

---

51. Mansi, *Sacrorum conciliorum*, vol. 16, coll. 317–20.
52. Ross, *Aristotelis politica*, 1273a, line 13.
53. *Epistolarum liber* 2 (PG 99, 1420B).

Nikephoros (805–15), when forcefully removed from his office by the emperor, appealed to other patriarchs.[54]

As with any other institution in the church, the pentarchy was abused from time to time. For instance, when emperor Heraclius (610–41) promoted monenergism and later on monothelitism, he confirmed them with the consent of all five patriarchs: Honorius of Rome, Sergius of Constantinople, Cyrus of Alexandria, Macedonius of Antioch, and Sergius of Jerusalem. Only an ecumenical council (Constantinople III, 680–81) corrected the failure of the pentarchy.[55]

The rise of the institution of the patriarchate led to the flattening of the ecclesial diversity within each one of them. Liturgical, linguistic, and other cultural varieties were eventually forced into uniformity as well. The lack of diversity *within* the patriarchates was compensated for, however, by the increasing diversity *between* them. Although the institution of the pentarchy was called upon to safeguard the unity between the patriarchal sees, the unifying tendencies within the patriarchates made it harder to preserve unity between them. The more the patriarchates consolidated structurally, liturgically, and culturally within, the harder it was for them to tolerate the differences of other patriarchates. The history of the largest schisms shows that the division lines within the church in most cases ran along the borders of the patriarchates. The first great schism around Chalcedonian theology left the patriarchates of Rome, Constantinople, and Jerusalem on the one side and the largest parts of the patriarchates of Alexandria and Antioch on the other. The schism between the East and West in the eleventh century was also essentially a conflict between two patriarchates, those of Rome and Constantinople. Now one can only guess what would have happened if the church had chosen another model of supra-metropolitan organization, not as large as the patriarchates. Maybe the divisions within it would be not as wide-scale as they are now.

In the early medieval period, the churches in the East and West simultaneously adopted similar monarchical models. They each had, however, their own reasons for that. In the West, the political consolidation of the Carolingians and the controversies about the practice of investiture[56] contributed to the rise of the monarchical model of papacy, which

54. *Vita* (PG 100, 121–24).
55. See Hovorun, *Will, Action and Freedom,* 74.
56. See Wallace-Hadrill, *The Frankish Church.*

continued to develop until the twentieth century.⁵⁷ In the East, the nature of the ecclesial monarchy and its later transformations were different.

Byzantium's territorial losses to the Persians, Arabs, and Turks led to the situation that many bishops and even patriarchs were unable or did not want to stay with their flocks. They either preferred or had no choice but to spend most of their time in safe Constantinople. These circumstances changed the model of decision-making in the church. The old institution of the *endēmousa* synod (ἐνδημοῦσα σύνοδος),⁵⁸ i.e., a gathering of all the bishops that by chance found themselves in the capital, became the most important instrument of the church's synodality. Not only the hierarchs under the jurisdiction of Constantinople but also bishops and even primates of other patriarchates participated in such councils, which now managed ecclesial matters related not only to the church of Constantinople but to the entire empire. In this situation, "the jurisdiction of the East Roman Emperor and the Oecumenical Patriarch," according to Arnold Toynbee, became "geographically coextensive."⁵⁹

Besides this, the new churches of the peoples that joined the eastern Christian commonwealth as result of the efforts by the Byzantine missionaries, primarily the Slavic churches, came under the jurisdiction of Constantinople. This extended the reach of Constantinople beyond the borders of the empire. This contributed to the process of the eastern church becoming monarchical in its structure, with the role of the patriarch of Constantinople the dominant one. The tendency of monopolization of the patriarchal authority was symptomatically manifested in the conflict between the prominent late-Byzantine ascetic Symeon the New Theologian (949–1022) and the patriarchal office in Constantinople.⁶⁰

This monarchical tendency in the East repeated similar developments in the West, where the pope had become a church monarch for all of western Christianity and had designs even on its eastern part. The eastern monarchy of the patriarchs of Constantinople, however, was more flexible than the monarchy of the popes. On the one hand, it was balanced by the emperors. On the other hand, the old patriarchal structures in Egypt, Syria, and Palestine, as well as the new ambitious churches

---

57. See Morris, *The Papal Monarchy*.
58. See Φειδᾶ, *Ἐνδημοῦσα σύνοδος*.
59. Toynbee, *A Study of History*, vol. 4, 388.
60. See Louth, *Greek East and Latin West*, 329.

in the Balkans urged the patriarchs of Constantinople to maneuver and to prefer soft power in dealing with other jurisdictions.

The difference between the western and eastern models of ecclesial monarchy can be illustrated by the modern theory of U- and M-hierarchies. These two types of hierarchy were identified first in economics[61] and later on in political science.[62] The U-hierarchy is a unitary form of management that implies high centralization and integration of the administrative structures. It organizes these structures according to their function. The expansion of the structures with the U-hierarchy always adds new levels of management to the existing structure, and thus increases the hierarchy.[63] The M-hierarchy means multidivisional. It replicates the structures with the same functionality in different places without adding new levels of hierarchy. The structures, thus, become territorial and autonomous.[64] The church of Rome developed a classical U-hierarchy, while the eastern churches, the M-hierarchy. At the same time, in building their inner structures, the eastern patriarchates also followed the U-model of hierarchy.

The monarchical model received further development after the collapse of the Byzantine empire. Under the Ottoman rule, the see of Constantinople preserved many of the rights that it had had in Byzantium. There is an early testimony by Kritovoulos of Imvros about the meeting between Mehmet II el-Fātiḥ (1444–46; 1451–81) and Gennadios II Scholarios (1454–56; 1463–65) soon after the conquest of Constantinople. According to Kritovoulos, Mehmet confirmed the privileges that the patriarchs had enjoyed in Byzantium:

> In the end, he made him patriarch and High Priest of the Christians, and gave him among many other rights and privileges the rule of the church and all its power and authority, no less than that enjoyed previously under the emperors. He also granted him the privilege of delivering before him fearlessly and freely many good disquisitions concerning the Christian faith and doctrine. And he himself went to his residence, taking with him the dignitaries and wise men of his court, and thus paid him great honor.

61. Chandler, *Strategy and Structure*.
62. Cooley, *Logics of Hierarchy*.
63. Ibid., 21.
64. Ibid., 22.

Thus, the sultan showed that he knew how to respect the true worth of any man, not only of military men but of every class, kings, and tyrants, and emperors. Furthermore, the Sultan gave back the church to the Christians, by the will of God, together with a large portion of its properties.⁶⁵

The Ottoman policy towards the Jewish and Christian population on the territories they had captured was based on the idea that they were the "people of the Book" (*ahl al-Kitāb*). They were "protected people" (*ahl al-dhimmah*) who, in return for taxes (*cizye*), were allowed to practice their religion and live in autonomous and religiously homogeneous communities known initially as *tâ'ifse* and later on, *millet*. The communities of Jews (*Yahud milleti*), non-Chalcedonians (*millet-i Ermeniyan*), Chalcedonian Orthodox (*millet-i Rûm*), and Roman Catholics (*Katolik millet*) enjoyed significant independence and had to rely on themselves.⁶⁶ They had their own courts and taxation systems. The religious leaders of these groups were endowed by the Ottomans with political leadership. They became heads of their own *millets* (*millet başı*).

The patriarch of Constantinople, for his part, became both religious and political leader of the entire Orthodox population of the Ottoman Empire. Now all Orthodox, regardless of their background or the patriarchate to which they had belonged, were subject to him in both religious and civil matters.⁶⁷ Only with the patriarch's permission could the Ottoman authorities arrest a bishop.⁶⁸ The patriarch judged his clergy and lay people in the matters of marriage, parentage, testaments, and successions. In his court he could even hear commercial cases, when both sides of the argument were Orthodox. The patriarch could tax the members of the *millet-i Rûm* for his own benefit. In carrying out his duties, he could

---

65. Kritovoulos, *History of Mehmed the Conqueror*, trans. Riggs, 94–95.

66. The mainstream scholarship holds that the millet system existed from the beginning of the Ottoman rule (see Gibb and Bowen, *Islamic Society and the West*). There is also an alternative point of view that criticizes the millet system as a later Ottoman construction, which should be not anachronistically extrapolated to the earlier period (see Braude, "Foundation Myths of the Millet System," 69). Tom Papademetriou in his study (*Render Unto the Sultan*) has suggested that scholars replace the theory of millet with the theory of the church institutions (including the patriarchate of Constantinople) as "tax farms," which were to collect and pay taxes (*pişkeş*) to the budget of the Ottoman Empire. This view, however, is not necessary alternative to the millet system, but rather supplements it.

67. See Karpat, "The Balkan National States and Nationalism," 332–33.

68. See Runciman, *The Great Church in Captivity*, 171–72.

always rely on the enforcement of the Turkish militia. The authority of the patriarch applied to all Orthodox subjects of the Ottoman Empire, regardless of the patriarchate to which they belonged. As a result, even those dotted demarcating lines between the patriarchates that survived to the end of Byzantium lost their meaning and were largely obliterated in the Ottoman period.

The patriarch of Constantinople had never enjoyed in Byzantium as many rights over his flock as he received from the Ottomans. He also had more responsibilities. As a recognized high-ranking Ottoman official, he had to play the role of a mediator between his people and the High Porte. He was responsible for the loyalty of his *millet* to the sultans and had to cultivate this loyalty. Otherwise he had to pay dearly as, for instance, Gregory V (in office 1797–98, 1806–8, and 1818–21) did, paying with his life for the Greek revolution of 1821.

The election of a new patriarch was supposed to be an internal matter of the local community; the Ottoman authorities would just have to approve it. However, in practice the patriarchs were treated by the Ottomans as "tax farmers" (*mültezim*). The High Porte encouraged the hopeful for the patriarchal throne to compete by bidding more for the sultan's approval. After they received the approval, the patriarchs were supposed to replenish regularly the state treasury. If they failed, they were immediately dethroned. In result, the fees increased and elections took place more and more often. According to the calculations of Tom Papademetriou, "between 1453 and 1500, the office of the Patriarch of Constantinople changed hands eighteen times with an average of one patriarch every 2.4 years. Between 1500 and 1600 it changed thirty-two times with an average of one patriarch every 3.1 years, and between 1500 and 1600 it changed fifty-three times with an average of one patriarch every 1.9 years."[69] This situation led to tremendous corruption in the patriarchate, which spread to other dioceses as well.

At the same time, to survive financially, the dioceses throughout the Ottoman Empire had no other choice but to rely on the support of communities, while the priests were completely dependent on their parishioners. As a result, the circumstances of Ottoman rule reversed the Byzantine hierarchical paradigm and re-introduced more solidarity and communality to the relationship between the ecclesial orders and laity.[70]

---

69. Papademetriou, *Render Unto the Sultan*, 214.
70. See Karpat, "The Balkan National States and Nationalism," 333.

Under the Ottomans, the church in its majority was forced to come back to community as the basic unit of its structure. Owing to the *millet* system, communities and lay people became important in the church again.

In the nineteenth century, the *Tanzimât* reforms of the Ottoman Empire enhanced the logic and structure of the *millet* system. *Millets* became the structures with more distinguishable social and ethnic identities. This eventually resulted in the revolts of the Balkan nations against their Turkish rulers and the creation of independent national states. In the Ottoman Empire, Serbs, Bulgars, Romanians, and Greeks had felt that they all belonged to one religious *genus* (γένος) with one head, the patriarch-*başı*, who guaranteed their unity. In the national states, however, they turned into distinct nations, (*ethnoi*, ἔθνοι). Each nation pursued its own interests and conducted politics for its own good. The mentality of national sovereignty deeply affected the Orthodox churches in these new states. Just as independent nations had to safeguard their sovereignty against possible intrusions and violations from the outside, the churches began implementing the same pattern in relations with each other. This made the churches consider relations with other sister churches in the categories that had been applied in the interstate relations. Interchurch relations became increasingly political and turned into "church diplomacy."

3

Ditches: Sovereignty

THE TERRITORIAL SOVEREIGNTY OF the national states that emerged in the nineteenth century inspired the local Orthodox churches to develop their own sovereignty, which was branded "canonical territory." This was a new term, but not a new idea. As early as through the process of coalescing with the Roman Empire, the church had adopted some of the civil concepts and mechanisms of political territoriality.

Pax Romana, within which Christianity emerged and shaped its structures, did not foresee any geographical limitations for itself. A constitutional element of the Roman imperial self-understanding was that the *Imperium Romanum* was the only empire in the world. There could not be two empires. The Roman Empire alone was called to cover the entire *orbis terrarum/oikoumenē* (οἰκουμένη). If some parts of the world remained not yet under control of Rome, this was only a temporary situation. Eventually those parts were supposed to come under the Roman dominance. The Roman world did not have borders therefore; it had frontiers—*syn-ora* (σύν-opα) rather than *horia* (ὅρια).

The frontiers of the empire were both visible and invisible: walls, ditches, and rivers, as well as military zones and client states. The latter reached far beyond the direct political control of Rome. They surrounded the empire like cushions and softened barbarian attacks. Rome created a belt of client states in Britain, Germany, territories beyond the Danube, the northern shore of the Black sea, Mesopotamia, and the Arabian lands.[1] It also developed partnership with the tribes in Africa.[2]

The Roman frontiers did not function as borders in the modern sense of the word. Their purpose was not to separate one sovereign territory from another sovereign territory. Demarcation lines like the Antonine[3] and Hadrian's[4] walls in Britannia and the Germanic,[5] Dacian, Arabic, Mesopotamian, Pontic, and other *limes*[6] were built not with the idea of *limiting* Roman territory, but to protect this territory from external threats. They were meant to be departure points for further expansion into "barbarian" lands. Thus, just twenty years after Hadrian's wall had begun construction in 122 AD, Rome moved its frontiers over a hundred kilometers further to the north, deeper into the lands of Picts, and constructed the Antonine wall.

Roman frontiers were not only movable but also porous. They allowed new peoples to settle in imperial territory. People who decided to come under the Roman protection were given certain rights, though often limited, and were expected to contribute through military recruitment and taxation.[7] The way in which the frontiers of the *Imperium Romanum* functioned sheds light on the Roman ideology of territory. It was not centripetal but centrifugal, directed beyond its actual boundaries. Roman territories were never sufficient and self-sufficient. They had to grow and to move their limits further constantly. The only obstacles to this dynamic of expansion were enemies. The Roman world struggled ceaselessly to expand and thus to realize the vision of its own endlessness.

Christianity was born with a similar perception of its own universality and endlessness. The universalist thinking of the early Christians

---

1. See Lee, *Information and Frontiers*, 49–78.

2. Wittke et al., *Historical Atlas of the Ancient World*, 208.

3. The *Vallum Antonini* was a defensive rampart with military road running alongside its 60 km, constructed in the period between 142/145–166/167 AD.

4. The *Vallum Hadriani* was a defensive rampart and wall with a military road running alongside its 118 km, protected by fourteen forts, constructed in the period between 122/128–410 AD.

5. A network of embankments, ditches and walls 548 km long, with approximately 900 turrets and 120 forts.

6. See Wittke et al., *Historical Atlas of the Ancient World*, 208–13.

7. See Cameron, *The Mediterranean World in Late Antiquity*, 33–56.

was coherent with the universalist Roman ideology and the dynamics of Rome's expansion. The *Pax Romana* secured a relatively homogeneous cultural, communicational, and infrastructural environment that helped the Christian communities to spread like wildfire. Christianity did not see any limits for itself and was eager to conquer the entire world, just like Rome.

It is possible that the church became interested in Roman methods of organizing the newly acquired territories even before it was recognized by the state. Particularly attractive for the church could be the way in which Rome "established in each province centers of jurisdiction, then assigned to those centers contiguous territories and subordinated all settlements in those territories to the *conventus*, the assize-city at its center."[8] This was an effective method of expansion, which the church might have wanted to employ. If so, then it was the first engagement of the church with territory in the Roman way.

The Christian church as a universalist movement with closely-knit communities became a new phenomenon in the Roman world. Polytheistic religious communities in the Roman Empire were not organized into a "church." They were independent. Each had its priest who was not accountable to any higher authority. Even the *pontifex maximus* in Rome could not dictate his will to other members of the Roman *collegium pontificum*. The Christian church was different. In its structure, even before the edict of Milan, it resembled more the civil administrative system of the Roman Empire than the Roman cults. This structural similarity between the church and the empire facilitated the church in adopting the Roman philosophy of territoriality.

Adoption of this philosophy helped the church to solve many of its managerial problems and gave it mechanisms to regulate the intercommunal relations. In result, for instance, the church adopted the principle "one bishop in one city,"[9] which certainly improved the coordination between communities on the local level. The church had to pay, however, for these facilities. It began losing communities from its sight and concentrated its attention on the administrative structures. The unity of the church came to be secured not by communality but by administrative control and territory.

---

8. Ando, "The Administration of the Provinces," 183.
9. See Stewart-Sykes, *The Original Bishops*, 4.

When the Romans conquered new lands, they assigned settlements to the territories, which were divided into big blocks. This eliminated cultural differences between the peoples who happened to find themselves in one such block. As Strabo complained on the eve of the Christian era, it had not been easy to distinguish Phrygian, Carian, Lydian, and Mysian communities in central Asia Minor before the Romans came. After they took those lands, they divided the regions into large districts regardless of the races that inhabited them and thus made the differences between those peoples even less distinguishable.[10] "Forcibly deprived of contact and connection with the social fabric that had constituted and nurtured their identities, provincials found themselves reassigned to new and different places in the social and geographic reality of the Roman Empire."[11] Many Christian communities, which because of the administrative reforms in the fourth century were incorporated into the territorial units, came to experience something similar. The shifting of the weight of the church structures from community to territory had, as one of the consequences, the unification of structures at the expense of the richness of the traditions.

Administrative reforms of the church created new supra-communal administrative bodies like metropolises and, later, patriarchates. Their emergence marked a shift of the ecclesial paradigm from community to territoriality. Canon 4 of the council of Nicea (325) was one of the earliest signals of the change:

> It is by all means desirable that a bishop should be appointed by all the bishops of the province. But if this is difficult because of some pressing necessity or the length of the journey involved, let at least three come together and perform the ordination, but only after the absent bishops have taken part in the vote and given their written consent. But in each province the right of confirming the proceedings belongs to the metropolitan bishop.[12]

---

10. Strabo, *Geography*, 13.4.12.

11. Ando, "The Administration of the Provinces," 183.

12. "'Ἐπίσκοπον προσήκει μάλιστα μὲν ὑπὸ πάντων τῶν τῆς ἐπαρχίας ἐπισκόπων καθίστασθαι· εἰ δὲ δυσχερὲς εἴη τοῦτο ἢ διὰ κατεπίγουσαν ἀνάγκην ἢ διὰ μῆκος ὁδοῦ, ἐξάπαντος τρεῖς ἐπὶ τὸ αὐτὸ συναγομένους, συμψήφων γινομένων καὶ τῶν ἀπόντων καὶ συντιθεμένων διὰ γραμμάτων, τότε τὴν χειροτονίαν ποιεῖσθαι· τὸ δὲ κῦρος τῶν γινομένων δίδοσθαι καθ'ἑκάστην ἐπαρχίαν τῷ μητροπολίτῃ ἐπισκόπῳ." Tanner, *Decrees of the Ecumenical Councils*, vol. 1, 7.

This canon describes a new situation, in which the consecration of bishops was connected with territory and its civil center. A bishop who resided in this center was endowed with the authority to approve consecrations on the territory under his control. According to Peter L'Huillier, "This decision implied that the civil provinces (ἐπαρχίαι, *provinciae*) constituted the geographical boundaries on which the territorial organization of the Church was henceforth to be modeled."[13]

The fixation of the churches on territory soon caused first tensions between territorial structures. One of the earliest examples of the territorial controversy was the dispute between the churches of Constantinople and Rome over the eastern part of Illyria (*Illyricum orientale*).[14] This province comprised the Balkans and had its capital in Thessalonica. Initially, it was under the authority of the western emperors. After it was separated from western Illyria (after 395), the eastern emperors took it over. Ecclesiastically, however, it remained under the bishops of Rome. Pope Innocent I (401–17) had the bishop of Thessalonica for his vicar.[15] After emperor Theodosius II (reigned 402–50) ordered in 421 that the church disputes in eastern Illyria should be heard by the archbishops of Constantinople,[16] Rome continued regarding the province as its own territory. Thus, during the dispute over the election of the bishop of Corinth, some Illyrian bishops appealed to the archbishop Attikos of Constantinople (406–25). Then pope Boniface I (418–22) contested this move and claimed the right to entertain appellations exclusively for himself. It is noteworthy that while the emperor in his decision came from the administrative rearrangement of the territory, Boniface appealed to the authority of Peter.[17] This authority, thus, was initially employed to counterweigh the political rationale of the distribution of territory between the churches.

---

13. L'Huillier, *The Church of the Ancient Councils*, 38.

14. Rennie, *The Foundations of Medieval Papal Legation*, 42.

15. See Dunn, "The Church of Rome as a Court of Appeal in the Early Fifth Century."

16. *Codex Theodosianus* 16.2.45, in Mommsen and Meyer, *Theodosiani libri XVI*, 352.

17. See Dunn, "Boniface I and the Illyrian Churches on the Translation of Perigenes to Corinth"; also his presentation at the conference of the Canadian Society of Patristic Studies in June 2015: "Boniface I's Theology of Papal Authority in *Manet beatum*."

Meanwhile, outside the Roman world, where the territories were not structured by the empires, the bishops for a long time continued to be connected with their communities rather than territories. For instance, German bishops for a long time were nomadic, without being attached to a permanent place.[18] The same nomadic were the bishops that served the Arabic Christian communities before the establishment of the Caliphate.[19] In the Anglo-Saxon and Celtic lands, bishops were also more tribal than territorial until the times of Bede.[20] At the same time, according to the testimony of Bede, after the council of Hertford (673), the episcopal governance of the church on the British Isles began changing from communal to territorial.[21]

That the church developed all its structures in the homogeneous environment of the *Pax Romana* implied that its intraecclesial administrative divisions were still not as deep as we know them now. Thus, the quarrel between Rome and Constantinople over eastern Illyria was quickly resolved with the political intervention.[22] Pope Boniface then addressed the western emperor Honorius (418–22), while the archbishop of Constantinople appealed to the eastern emperor Theodosius II. The two emperors easily found a solution, which the churches were more unlikely to achieve. During the iconoclastic period, however, the same imperial authority exacerbated the relations between the two churches by forcefully transferring Illyria, Calabria, and Sicily under the ecclesiastical jurisdiction of the patriarchs of Constantinople. One of the reasons of this move was polarization between the political centers of Byzantium and the Frankish kingdom.[23]

Another example of how the ecclesiastical quarrels over territory became dramatically sharper and more divisive when the church found itself on two separate imperial platforms happened in the late fifth–early

---

18. See Godfrey, *The Church in Anglo-Saxon England*, 240.

19. See Fisher, *Arabs and Empires Before Islam*, 355; Evans, *The Age of Justinian*, 185.

20. See *Historia ecclesiastica gentis Anglorum* III.21; Wright, *A Companion to Bede*, 75.

21. Wright, *A Companion to Bede*, 94.

22. This has been the main point of the presentation of Geoffrey D. Dunn at the 17th International Conference on Patristic Studies at Oxford (August 2015): "Ecclesiastical Conflict between Rome and Constantinople in the Early Fifth Century: Diplomatic Efforts to Resolve the Dispute about Perigenes of Corinth."

23. Brubaker and Haldon, *Byzantium in the Iconoclast Era*, 87, 175.

seventh century, when the rivalry between the Roman and Persian empires[24] largely contributed to the split between the Ephesian Orthodoxy and the Persian "Nestorianism."[25] After the 630s, the rapidly expanding Arab caliphate harbored and framed those pieces of the church in Syria and Egypt that did not accept the council of Chalcedon. Clashes between the antagonistic imperial platforms caused deep schisms in the church. By comparison, the Arian controversy had not led to schisms of the same scale as those caused by the later christological controversies. One of the reasons for that was that Arianism and Nicene orthodoxy argued standing on the same terrain. If they had fought each other from two different imperial platforms, then with a high degree of probability the great schism would have happened not in the fifth but in the fourth century.

In the meantime, the political philosophy of territory and borders in Byzantium went through dramatic transformations. In the seventh century, Byzantium lost huge territories, first to the Persians and then to the Arabs. It also had been stripped of most of its client states. A radical shrinking of territory and depravation of geopolitical influence forced the Byzantines to re-evaluate their habitat.[26] Territory became more precious than it was in the time of Justinian (527–65), when the Christian Roman Empire was dynamically expanding. In response to the territorial losses, and in the spirit of the new perception of territory, emperor Heraclius (610–40) initiated a dramatic reorganization of the administrative structures of the state, which became more tightened[27] and militarized. The old system of prefectures and dioceses was replaced with a new system of military provinces—*themas* (*themata*, θέματα), which were administered not by civilians but by generals (*stratēgoi*, στρατηγοί). These administrative changes became reflected in the ecclesial legislation. The council in Trullo (692), which was convoked soon after these administrative reforms, adopted an unprecedentedly long list of canons that addressed the relationship of the church to territory.[28] These canons locked the ecclesial structures to the territorial grid of the empire even more firmly than the

---

24. See Dignas and Winter, *Rome and Persia in Late Antiquity*; Bowersock, *Empires in Collision in Late Antiquity*

25. See Hovorun, *From Antioch to Xi'an*.

26. See Kaegi, "Reconsidering Byzantium's Eastern Frontiers in the Seventh Century."

27. See Wittke et al., *Historical Atlas of the Ancient World*, 238.

28. See canons 8, 17, 18, 20, 25, 31, 37, 38, and 39.

canons of the earlier councils, thus strengthening further the concept of "canonical territory."

During the Ottoman rule, the connection of the church with territory weakened. Even the borders between the patriarchates became relativized, to say nothing of the boundaries of the dioceses. Now it was not the administrative grid of the empire but belonging to one *millet* that framed relations between the bishops. Many of them did not live in their dioceses but moved to Istanbul. Even the patriarchs of Alexandria, Antioch, and Jerusalem preferred to spend their time in the capital, helping the patriarch of Constantinople to rule the entire church in the Ottoman lands.

The relationship between the church and territory was strengthened again in the nineteenth century, when new national states emerged from the decaying Ottoman Empire. New autocephalous churches in those states came to be connected with the concept and mentality of national sovereignty. A brief inquiry into the idea of political sovereignty will help us to understand what "canonical territory" meant then and how it has developed up to the present day.

The idea of political sovereignty oscillated widely depending on the historical circumstances.[29] In the late Middle Ages, princes in Europe fought for sovereignty over the territory that they ruled, battling for some political freedom from the pope and the emperor. In the sixteenth century, some of them, like in Germany and Britain, went so far in their struggle for political emancipation from Rome as to establish "autocephalous churches." In some sense, the churches of the Reformation were "autocephalous." Their canonical status reflected the idea of political sovereignty and, at least for the rulers behind them, had priority over theological issues. The churches of Reformation developed their own concepts of "canonical territory," which did not stray far from the contemporary concepts of the political emancipation of territory.

The idea of the political sovereignty of the European states was dramatically upgraded by the Peace of Westphalia (1648). This package of agreements influenced not only the European political system, but also the ecclesial systems both in the West and in the East, though not immediately and directly. The Peace of Westphalia, on the one hand,

---

29. "Sovereignty is the most glittering and controversial notion in the history, doctrine and practice of public international law. Its meaning has oscillated throughout the history of law and of the State since medieval times." Steinberger, "Sovereignty," 500–501.

strengthened the sovereignty of the European states within their territorial boundaries and introduced the principle of non-intervention. On the other hand, it gave full freedom to the European states to act in the lands not yet declared by any state, namely the colonies.

There is a striking resemblance between the Westphalian principles of sovereignty and the modern model of interchurch relations that have been adopted in the Orthodox world since the emergence of the national autocephalous churches in the nineteenth century. According to this model, the Orthodox churches, on the one hand, respect sovereignty and the principle of non-intervention within the traditional borders of a local church. On the other hand, they enjoy full freedom of action in the "diaspora." The latter, according to this model, appears to be equivalent to the colonies in the period of active colonization of the New World. The Westphalian model thus became a prototype for the system of the Orthodox churches after they were multiplied in the nineteenth century and spread to the New World in the twentieth century.

The modern system of interchurch relations also encompasses some further developments of the Westphalian model of sovereignty. In the nineteenth century, many states in Europe became national. Orthodox churches, especially those that received national autocephaly, adopted nationhood as the pivot of their identity. Additionally, the national states redistributed their sovereignty from the personalities of rulers, like kings, to the people. This coincided with the growing conciliarity and participation of laity in the life of many local churches. According to Helmut Steinberger, the model of a national state implied a

> state's general independence from and legal impermeability in relation to foreign powers, and the State's exclusive jurisdiction and supremacy of governmental powers over the State's territory and inhabitants. Such supremacy was seen as entailing a monopoly over fundamental political decisions, as well as over legislative, executive, and judicial powers, based on consolidated, durable institutional, organizational, economic and financial means and structures capable, as a rule, of maintaining law and order and providing the ways and means for the external assertion of liberty of action indispensable for acceptance as a structurally reliable entity of an international legal order.[30]

Many Orthodox churches, especially the new ones, adopted the same idea of independence—from the patriarchate of Constantinople.

30. Ibid., 507.

According to the new developments in international law, the principle of sovereignty was extended to all states, including the so-called "non-civilized" and "semi-civilized" ones. All states were equated in their sovereignty. Some churches also became supportive of the idea of the absolute equality of all autocephalous churches, regardless of their size and history. This idea has been particularly promoted by Moscow. It is contested, however, by Constantinople, which advocates the idea of a "hierarchy of equalities."[31] According to this standpoint, certain of the "old patriarchates" (*ta presbygenē patriarcheia*, τὰ πρεσβυγενῆ πατριαρχεία) constitute an elite group: Constantinople, Alexandria, Antioch, and Jerusalem. They belong to this group because they are older and were given their privileges by the councils of the early church. The other group consists of the "newer patriarchates" (*ta neopagē patriarcheia*, τὰ νεοπαγῆ πατριαρχεία): Moscow, Serbia, Romania, Bulgaria, and Georgia. After them, the "mere" autocephalous churches, which do not have status of patriarchate, follow: Cyprus, Greece, Poland, Albania, the Czech lands and Slovakia. Finally, the so-called autonomous churches conclude the list: Finland and Estonia.[32] According to one interpretation, the autonomous churches are not quite independent and constitute an integral part of the Ecumenical patriarchate. According to the other interpretation, they are independent like autocephalous churches, with the only exception that their primates are elected with the consent of Constantinople.

The period from the mid-eighteenth century through World War I is often regarded as an age of the "absolute" concepts of sovereignty.[33] These concepts shaped a framework in which the modern idea of ecclesial sovereignty was born. This was a new idea, which was, nevertheless, branded with the traditional term "autocephaly." This rebranded autocephaly implied a new concept of the "canonical territory." The latter concurred with the new developments in the national sovereignty of states. "Canonical territory" in most Orthodox churches came to coincide with the national borders of their states.

The crisis of the Peace of Westphalia as a result of the World War I, and the collapse of the Russian and Ottoman Empires, deeply affected

---

31. There is no official document that would confirm this classification of the churches. It is practiced as an unwritten tradition.

32. The autonomy of the Estonian church under the Ecumenical patriarchate is disputed by the Russian Orthodox church, which regards it as a mere diocese under the jurisdiction of Constantinople.

33. Steinberger, "Sovereignty," 510.

inter-Orthodox relations and changed their pattern. Some churches took it as an opportunity to revise their "canonical borders" and set their foot in the "territories" of other churches. This was the case, for instance, with the church of Constantinople, which actively embraced communities or granted autocephaly to the churches on the territories of the former Russian and Austro-Hungarian empires: in Finland (1923), Estonia (1923), Czechoslovakia (1923), and Poland (1924). These and other violations of the "Westphalian order" in inter-Orthodox relations became a source of conflict between the churches all through the twentieth century.

Another source of the conflicts between the Orthodox churches during the twentieth century was the situation in the so-called "diaspora." Two irreconcilable approaches clashed over this issue. One can be called "colonialist." It sees Western Europe and the new world as a "no-church's-land," which every church has right to colonize. No one church can claim this land as its canonical territory. According to the other approach, the non-Orthodox parts of Europe and the new world constitute a "canonical territory" that belongs to Constantinople. Constantinople argues that its right to the territory of the "diaspora" is based on the canon 28 of the council of Chalcedon (451).[34] However, this canon implies just the opposite of this interpretation. It is focused on the communities, not on the territory; and it establishes a direct control by Constantinople over the "barbarian" communities, surpassing the heads of the metropolitans

---

34. "Following in every way the decrees of the holy fathers and recognising the canon which has recently been read out—the canon of the 150 most devout bishops who assembled in the time of the great Theodosius of pious memory, then emperor, in imperial Constantinople, new Rome—we issue the same decree and resolution concerning the prerogatives of the most holy church of the same Constantinople, new Rome. The fathers rightly accorded prerogatives to the see of older Rome, since that is an imperial city; and moved by the same purpose the 150 most devout bishops apportioned equal prerogatives to the most holy see of new Rome, reasonably judging that the city which is honoured by the imperial power and senate and enjoying privileges equalling older imperial Rome, should so be elevated to her level in ecclesiastical affairs and take second place after her. The metropolitans of the dioceses of Pontus, Asia and Thrace, but only these, as well as the bishops of these dioceses who work among non-Greeks, are to be ordained by the aforesaid most holy see of the most holy church in Constantinople. That is, each metropolitan of the aforesaid dioceses along with the bishops of the province ordain the bishops of the province, as has been declared in the divine canons; but the metropolitans of the aforesaid dioceses, as has been said, are to be ordained by the archbishop of Constantinople, once agreement has been reached by vote in the usual way and has been reported to agreement has been reached by vote in the usual way and has been reported to him." Tanner, *Decrees of the Ecumenical Councils*, vol. 1, 99–100.

in the three dioceses under the general supervision of Constantinople: Pontus, Asia, and Thrace. According to the canon, bishops for the "barbarian" communities were to be installed not by their metropolitans but directly by the archbishop of Constantinople.[35] What counted as a "barbarian" community often changed; the notion was not restricted to any single territory. Therefore, the jurisdiction of the archbishops of Constantinople over the mobile "barbarian" communities was moveable and not locked to the territory where those communities found themselves located—it remained connected with the communities. Therefore, canon 28 did not establish the jurisdiction of Constantinople over any territory beyond Pontus, Asia, and Thrace, and Constantinople's modern claims for "ecclesial colonies" cannot be justified by this canon.

The church of Constantinople was never supportive of the "Westphalian" model of the interchurch relations because it lost much of its territory as a result of the implementation of this model. Therefore, it did not betray its own standpoint when it attempted to reshape the ecclesial landscape in Europe in the 1920s by acquiring pieces of other churches or granting them independence in a unilateral way. Other churches, which initially were proponents of the "Westphalian" model and supported the new churches in the Balkans during the nineteenth century, corrected their positions in the twentieth century and put less emphasis on the national sovereignty of the churches. For instance, Moscow, which in the nineteenth century had supported national Slavic churches splitting from Constantinople, refused to recognize the independence of the churches that emerged in the national states after the collapse first of the Russian Empire and then of the Soviet Union. It still claims jurisdiction over the territories that belonged to either of them, even if for a short while. In the same manner, Belgrade claims jurisdiction over the territories of the former Yugoslavia, particularly Macedonia (FYROM) and Montenegro.

According to this territorial mentality, all communities in a certain territory, regardless of their previous ecclesial affiliation, their ethnic or other identity, regardless of the state to which they belong, and regardless of their own wish about where they'd like to belong, automatically belong to the church that claims the territory where the communities are situated. This mentality has established the strongest connection with territory in the history of the church. It appears to be stronger than the connections of the church with the administrative grid in the Roman Empire, or

---

35. On this, see my earlier article: Говорун, "Исторический контекст 28-го правила"; it is available online: http://goo.gl/J6jbpF [accessed October 20, 2015].

even with the national states in the nineteenth century. It constitutes an apogee in the evolution of the idea of territoriality.

It is noteworthy that in the period of the Cold War, the global antagonism between the communist East and the "capitalist" West influenced the policies of the churches.[36] Constantinople and Moscow developed alliances that can be called "canonical orbits" of influence. There were local Orthodox churches in the "orbit" of Moscow and others in the orbit of Constantinople, just as there were NATO countries and the Warsaw Pact countries.

The category of the "canonical territory" continues to develop. In its present form, it differs not only from the situation a century ago, but also from the situation twenty years ago. Changes like globalization and regional integration, of which the most remarkable instance is the European Union, urge the Orthodox churches to rethink the concept of "canonical territory." In the new situation, the old paradigms of "canonical territory" often do not work. An example of failure of the principle of canonical territory in organizing church life and solving its problems is Ukraine, where this principle works not toward overcoming the divisions between the churches but toward strengthening them. This principle also seems to fail in the case of Macedonia (FYROM). In both cases, the churches that used to cover the now independent states, the Moscow Patriarchate and the Serbian Church correspondingly, claim exclusive rights over the territory of these states. "Canonical territory" in these cases is utilized in attempts at neo-imperial projects. In the frame of these projects, the above-mentioned churches do not allow any mediating interference from outside and deprive the autochthonous churches that do not recognize these rights of any recognition. An even more striking example is the one of the Orthodox diaspora in Western Europe and the new world. The patriarchate of Constantinople claims these territories as its exclusive dominion. This claim is contested by some other churches, which consider them as "colonial" lands, where every church has equal rights. In this situation, the voices of the "diasporal" churches remain unheard, and their criticism of the concept of "diaspora" is ignored.

At the same time, there are examples where the principle of territoriality in its modern sense works well. For instance, the patriarchate of Alexandria in the twentieth century extended its jurisdiction over the entire continent of Africa, even though the rights of this church were

---

36. See Filo, *Christian World Community and the Cold War*.

traditionally confined to the northeast edge of the continent only. However, its claims over the entire continent as its exclusive canonical territory helped the mission of the Orthodox church there and prevented the problems of jurisdictional fragmentation that the churches face in Europe and the Americas.

The idea of "canonical territory" should not, therefore, be rejected altogether. It was adopted and developed by the church during its historic journey because it proved to be helpful in organizing the life and mission of the church. At the same time, it should not be taken as dogma. It is *not a sacred institution* but *a historic convenience of relative value*. It should not substitute for more important values, like the unity of the church. When it does not serve the ends of the unity it can and should be ignored. The principle of "canonical territory" should be applied with the interests of the communities, not jurisdictions, in mind. One should remember that the idea of territoriality during the historical journey of the church often forced the community away from the center of the church policies. Community should be placed back at the heart of these policies and be reinstalled at the center of the administrative paradigms, including the ones that build on canonical territories.

There are instructive examples in modern history of how the church pushed aside the principle of territoriality and instead paid attention to the well-being of communities. During the exodus of the Greek population from Asia Minor in the 1920s, the communities of emigrants established themselves in new places in the independent Greek state. They brought with them their identities and even the names of their home places. Thus, new districts surrounded big cities in Greece like New Smyrna, New Ionia, New Philadelphia in Athens, or Neapolis in Thessalonica. These communities preserved not only their identities but also their ecclesial structures. To accommodate them, the church of Greece established new dioceses for immigrants, like for instance the metropolises of New Smyrna or Neapolis. These dioceses were diasporal within the boundaries of the local church. Although they looked like a canonical anomaly, they preserved the integrity of the relocated communities. With the passage of time, the communities of immigrants lost their original identities and gradually assimilated with other communities. This happened naturally, not because the mainland Greek church blindly followed the principle of territorial homogeneity and crushed the identities of the immigrants for the sake of this principle.

If we look at the situation in the "diaspora" from the same communal perspective, the current situation does not appear as tragic as it would if seen from the territorial point of view. If communities, not territories, are considered to be the cells of the church body, then moving a community to another place where it still preserves its integrity does not distort the texture of the church structures. The communities should certainly cooperate better in the "diaspora," but they should not be required to realign to the new territory, at least not by force. The current diversity of communities in the "diaspora" should not be treated as a mere canonical challenge but should be regarded as something to be appreciated. Their diversity resembles the diversity that the church enjoyed in its first centuries before the processes of unification turned them into territorial blocks.

4

Strongholds: Autocephaly

THESE TERRITORIAL BLOCKS HAVE become independent from each other and "self-headed"—autocephalous. Autocephaly is one of the oldest institution of the church and the most viable one. More than any other institution, it has gone through multiple historical transformations without getting lost.

Initially all communities, as a rule, were in some sense autocephalous—not that they were autarkic, but that they were not accountable to other communities by obligation.[1] With the growth of the church, most communities became accountable to the superior communities and thus were deprived of their autocephaly. Independence was left only to chosen communities that were put in charge of other communities, primarily in matters of consecration and trial of bishops. Thus autocephaly was transferred from a community to supra-communal structures.

The autocephaly of supra-communal structures was intended as a canonical institution to help the church in maintaining order and unity. With the passage of time, however, autocephaly often turned out to be manipulated by political authorities, with consent of their ecclesial counterparts, and directed to serve political ends rather than ecclesial unity. Autocephaly survived many transformations and crises. In some periods of its history it almost vanished and in some it gained an extreme

1. Theses of this chapters appeared in Hovorun, "Autocephaly as a Diachronic Phenomenon and Its Ukrainian Case."

power. It took different forms and interpretations during its long historical journey.

In spite of its importance, this institution remains understudied. Those scarce studies that exist[2] offer rather reductionist accounts of autocephaly. Many of them praise autocephaly of particular churches[3] without offering a critical and whole picture of this phenomenon. Autocephaly is often presented from the canonical perspective, as a category of the canon law.[4] Some see it as an administrative institution.[5] There is also a popular view of autocephaly that identifies it with nationhood.[6] All these approaches are correct and should be taken into consideration by anyone who undertakes a serious study of autocephaly. However, they are not sufficient. The case studies below will explore other aspects of autocephaly as they emerged in history. During the centuries of its evolution, autocephaly was a factor that strengthened the political independence of states, a vessel for *transitio imperii*, an instrument of building the cultural and national identities of people, and finally a symbol of deimperialization and indigenization of the church. Before proceeding to these aspects of autocephaly, we will consider it from the standard viewpoints of canon law and church administration.

Canon law regards autocephaly an instrument of administering a local church. Literally, "autocephaly" means that a local church is "self-headed." This is to say that an autocephalous church elects its own primate who, with the consent of the local synod, consecrates bishops for his own church without being accountable to any external ecclesial authority. In the canons of the church, this initial idea of autocephaly is best expressed in the resolution of the council of Ephesus (431) "that the bishops of Cyprus may themselves conduct ordinations" (canon 8).[7]

---

2. See Russell and Cohn, *Autocephaly*.

3. See Dadeshkeliani, *The Autocephaly of the Orthodox Church of Georgia*; Öörni, "Autocephaly and Its Meaning for the Finnish Orthodox Church"; Γλαβίνα, *Το αυτοκέφαλο της Ορθόδοξης Εκκλησίας της Αλβανίας*; Hadjiioannou, "A Study of the Helladic Autocephaly (1821–1852)"; Mojanoski, *Avtokefalnosta na Makedonskata pravoslavna crkva*, etc.

4. See "Die Kirche und die Kirchen, Autonomie und Autokephalie."

5. See Sanderson, "Autocephaly as a Function of Institutional Stability and Organizational Change in the Eastern Orthodox Church."

6. See Walters, "Notes on Autocephaly and Phyletism"; Meyendorff, "Ethnophyletism, Autocephaly, and National Churches."

7. "The most reverent bishop Rheginus and with him Zenon and Evagrius, revered bishops of the province of Cyprus, have brought forward what is both innovation

The case of the church of Cyprus constituted a precedent that made the most important contribution to the formation of the institution of autocephaly in its initial form. The reason this case emerged was a conflict between the church of Cyprus and the church of Antioch about the election of a new metropolitan for the former. Cyprus at that time belonged administratively to the civil *dioecesis Oriens*, which had its capital in Antioch. The church of Antioch took this as an opportunity to extend its control over the church of Cyprus. For this purpose, it even engaged a high military official who resided in Antioch. This official, whose name was Dionysius, sent two letters to Cyprus, one to the governor of the island and the other to the local church. He ordered the postponement of the elections of the new metropolitan. His orders, however, were ignored. The church elected a metropolitan, Rheginus, who together with his two assistant bishops came to Ephesus and presented there his petition concerning the insinuations of Antioch. He asked the council to confirm his election as metropolitan and to validate the right of the church of Cyprus to elect and install its own metropolitans. The council, after having considered the matter, decided to take the side of Cyprus. Contrary to the tendencies of the time that favored reshaping the church structures in accordance with the civil administrative grid, the council exempted Cyprus from this rule and confirmed its independent *status quo*. The fathers of

---

against the ecclesiastical customs and the canons of the holy fathers and concerns the freedom of all. Therefore, since common diseases need more healing as they bring greater harm with them, if it has not been a continuous indent custom for the bishop of Antioch to hold ordinations in Cyprus—as it is asserted in memorials and orally by the religious men who have come before the synod—the prelates of the holy churches of Cyprus shall, free from molestation and violence, use their right to perform by themselves the ordination of reverent bishops for their island, according to the canons of the holy fathers and the ancient custom.

The same principle will be observed for other dioceses and provinces everywhere. None of the reverent bishops is to take possession of another province which has not been under his authority from the first or under that of his predecessors. Any one who has thus seized upon and subjected a province is to restore it, lest the canons of the fathers be transgressed and the arrogance of secular power effect an entry through the cover of priestly office. We must avoid bit by bit destroying the freedom which our lord Jesus Christ, the liberator of all people, gave us through his own blood. It is therefore the pleasure of the holy and ecumenical synod to secure intact and inviolate the rights belonging to each province from the first, according to the custom which has been in force from of old. Each metropolitan has the right to take a copy of the proceedings for his own security. If any one produces a version which is at variance with what is here decided, the holy and ecumenical synod unanimously decrees it to be of no avail." Tanner, *Decrees of the Ecumenical Councils*, vol. 1, 68–69.

Ephesus warned against the involvement of the civil authorities in the redistribution of the ecclesial jurisdiction.

This story conveys three important messages about what autocephaly was in the period of its formation as a canonical institution. First, autocephaly was not related to the way in which the church was administered. It addressed a narrower issue of the election and consecration of the primate of an autocephalous church. Second, autocephaly secured the relative independence of the church from the civil administration and territorial pattern of the state. This aspect was contrary to the idea of autocephaly that evolved later, which was best expressed in the famous dictum of Patriarch Photios (810–91): "The ecclesial rights and particularly those related to the borders of dioceses should change together with the civil domains and administration."[8] The third aspect of autocephaly in the case of Cyprus was manifested through the history of this church which followed Ephesus. Emperor Justinian (527–65) transferred Cyprus from the political jurisdiction of Antioch to a new territorial formation with its center in Odessos (now Varna in Bulgaria). Apart from Cyprus, this formation included Lower Moesia, Scythia, Caria, and the Aegean islands. Later on, Justinian II (685–95) relocated the majority of Cypriots from their homeland to Hellespont. The primate of the church of Cyprus moved there, too. His new see became the city of Nova Justiniana. When there, he had the highest rank among the bishops of that province and retained all the rights that he had enjoyed in Cyprus. This situation demonstrates that the autocephaly of a local church could be detached from a particular territory and developed into a self-sufficient canonical institution, which became more important than some other institutions, including that of canonical territory.

The initial idea of autocephaly as related to the procedures of election and consecration of new primates gradually expanded to other administrative matters. It particularly modified the character of authority that the primates of the autocephalous churches exercised within their own churches. This authority became more direct and "authoritative." In interjurisdictional relations, the primates of the autocephalous churches assumed all responsibility for maintaining communion between the local

---

8. "Τὰ ἐκκλησιαστικά, καὶ μάλιστά γε τὰ περὶ τῶν ἐνοριῶν δίκαια, ταῖς πολιτικαῖς ἐπικρατείαις τε καὶ διοικήσεσιν συμμεταβάλλεσθαι εἴωθεν." Letter 290, in Laourdas and Westerink, *Photii patriarchae Constantinopolitani epistulae et amphilochia, vol. 3*, 406–8.

churches. Autocephaly, thus, evolved into an instrument of church administration, both inside and outside a local church.

Charles Sanderson undertook an insightful analysis of autocephaly from the point of view of modern organization theories. He particularly dwelt on the theories of two American economists and Nobel Prize winners, Douglass North (1920—2015) and Oliver Williamson (b. 1932).[9] Sanderson considers autocephaly a kind of organization that undergoes constant change and therefore constitutes an eligible subject for analysis in terms of organization theories. The factors that exercise decisive influence on the changes of this institution, for him, are an "institutional framework" and "enforcement."[10]

The "institutional framework" for autocephaly consists primarily of canonical legislation, but also includes unwritten traditions and "rules of the game."[11] Canons regulate the shared arrangements[12] between the churches and function as constraints for the agents that seek to change the *status quo* in the system of the autocephalous churches. These agents interact on the basis of making contracts:

> Particular churches . . . are aligned in contractual relationships governed by an institutional framework, which with credible enforcement makes defection from those institutional rules costly. The interrelations between particular churches, as with any other organization, can be considered contractual because they include the exchange of goods and services, which comprise a web of interdependent linkages. These relationships may be either hierarchical—as with parent-subsidiary relationships—or horizontal—as between self-governing autocephalous churches. In all cases and at all levels, however, the relationships are contractual: clergy—needed by the bishop to perform sacramental functions locally in the bishop's stead—cannot legally perform those functions without the bishop's authorization, and should the priest fail to discharge his duties in the prescribed manner that authorization can be withdrawn. A subsidiary bishop is dependent upon a patriarch for the myrrh used to anoint laity and, historically, consecrate emperors, and this could be withheld

---

9. North, *Structure and Change in Economic History*; North, *Institutions, Institutional Change, and Economic Performance*; Williamson, *The Mechanisms of Governance*.

10. Sanderson, "Autocephaly as a Function of Institutional Stability and Organizational Change in the Eastern Orthodox Church," 28.

11. Ibid., 34.

12. Ibid., 33.

should the patriarch see the need to censure a subordinate. A subsidiary church is dependent upon its parent, at least initially, for funds, clergy, and organizational support, while the parent eventually may come to rely upon the subsidiary as a source of revenue, resources, and influence. A nascent autocephalous church requires official recognition from its parent and/or other autocephalous churches to validate its own autocephaly. In all cases and at all levels, an institutional framework binds the contracting "parties" (ecclesiastical organizations) together according to rules that provide incentives for both enforcement and compliance.[13]

Organizational change, in this case through the introduction or exclusion of autocephalous churches to or from the network of local churches, in most cases presupposes a breach of the existent contracts. It "usually occurs 'illegally,' which is to say through the breaking of (defection from) the contractual relationship."[14] Such a change causes an "exogenous shock"[15] to the system. Organizational change of this sort is practically impossible without the state. The state thus is an important part of the institutional framework, which is most capable of promoting changes in the system of autocephalous churches. The state functions in the capacity of "enforcement."[16]

Indeed, it is commonly accepted that in eastern Christianity the state played and continues to play a crucial role in shaping the administrative borderlines within the church. These borderlines were redrawn by the state and together with the states. In this regard, Sanderson is right when he remarks:

> Where we observe changes in political boundaries, the dissolution or consolidation of states, or other political reconfigurations, we should expect to see efforts to implement corresponding organizational changes in the church, within institutional limits, subject to enforcement by a third party (usually the state)....
>
> The organizational form of the church at any given time is intimately related to the political geography, meaning the political boundaries of the state in which a particular church is embedded. The reconfiguration of that geography—the devolution

13. Ibid., 35.
14. Ibid., 38.
15. Ibid.
16. Ibid., 2.

of an empire into discrete states, for example—prompts corresponding changes to the church's organizational form.[17]

The degree of the influence of state on the church in the matters of autocephaly was historically even greater than that. The state conditioned not only the *quantitative* parameters of autocephaly, i.e., the number of independent churches, but also the *quality* of their autocephaly. Thus, in the framework of the eastern Roman Empire, the autocephaly of the local churches was a matter of the church's administrative convenience. It did not exceed the sphere of the canon law. The political or cultural significance of this institution was minimal.

The situation changed when some neighbors of Byzantium, after having joined the fellowship of the Christian peoples, began employing the autocephaly of their newly established churches as a factor that, as they believed, would help them to secure political self-sufficiency. This happened primarily in Bulgaria. Apart from becoming an instrument of political independence, autocephaly, from the end of the first millennium to the middle of the second millennium, evolved into a factor of identity for states and peoples that pursued it. It was a borrowed identity, one originally held by Constantinople. In the eyes of the Orthodox, Constantinople was the archetypical capital, *the* City (*hē Polis*, ἡ Πόλις). Bulgaria, Serbia, and later Muscovy at some stage began pursuing autocephaly for their churches as an attribute that allowed them to imitate Constantinople and the Roman (Byzantine) empire. Autocephaly thus became an agent of *transitio imperii*, a vehicle to transfer the imperial identity of Constantinople to other political centers that emerged in the course of history. It was thus used to build new identities: ecclesial, political, and cultural.

THE CASE OF BULGARIA

The ruler who created the precedent of using autocephaly as a political instrument was Bulgarian khan Boris (reigned 852–89).[18] Soon after he was

---

17. Ibid., 28–29.

18. James Lindsay Hopkins in his monograph on the Bulgarian church has argued, in a rather reductionist and generalizing way, that this church from its beginning was always a political arm of the state: "The [Bulgarian Orthodox] church forged a role for itself in Bulgarian foreign and national affairs by willingly becoming an instrument of Bulgarian geopoliticism, allowing itself to get used by the government, as a necessary medium toward the realization of its goal of national unification." Hopkins, *The*

baptized in the mid-860s and had officially introduced Christianity to his people, he decided that the newly established church of Bulgaria had to be independent from Constantinople. Boris believed, not without good reason, that the canonical dependence of his church would weaken the independence of the Bulgarian state. He wanted to get a ticket to the club of the Christian nations without paying for it with political dependence. This was a difficult goal to achieve, given the lack of historical precedents. Boris's efforts shaped a new paradigm of the state-church and church-church relations. Basic elements of this paradigm have survived till the present. They are: 1) an independent state should have an independent church, 2) the state can serve as an enforcement for the autocephaly of its church, and 3) the state can be a mediator in the relations between autocephalous churches.

In pursuing the independence for the Bulgarian church, Boris, whose kingdom belonged to the much disputed eastern Illyria, made use of the political contradictions and tensions between Constantinople and the western political powers—primarily the Franks, but also Rome, which stood behind the German rulers. Before accepting Christianity for himself and his people, Boris began negotiating with Constantinople and the Franks. He initially inclined to accept the western proposals, which made Constantinople nervous. In the last months of 863, the Byzantines attacked Bulgaria to prevent it from accepting Christianity from the Germans. They insisted that Boris accepts Christianity from them. Under the military pressure, Boris had to yield. The two sides concluded a "deep truce" for thirty years. In the late autumn 863, a mission from the patriarch of Constantinople came to the capital of the Bulgarian state, Pliska, and baptized Boris with his family and high-ranking dignitaries.

Boris's affiliation to Constantinople, however, did not last for long. After the patriarchate of Constantinople refused to grant the newly-established Bulgarian church autonomy, Boris turned to the Roman pontiff. In the end of August 866, a Bulgarian mission arrived at Rome. Their task was to ask the pope questions from Boris about various aspects of the Christian life. More importantly, they inquired how the newly established Bulgarian church could function, under the jurisdiction of Rome. On November 13, 866, Boris received the pope's answers, which he found suitable for what he was seeking. He ordered the Byzantine missionaries to leave Bulgaria and thus switched his ecclesial affiliation

---

Bulgarian Orthodox Church, 8.

from Constantinople to Rome. Byzantine emperor Michael III (reigned 840–67) became angry about Boris's decision. He was also angry with Rome. Relations between the two centers of Christendom became even more tense. As a result, the council that was held in the summer of 867 in Constantinople anathematized Pope Nicholas I.

In the meantime, Boris continued building an independent church. He soon realized that the pope would not support him to the extent he wanted. When, for instance, he asked the pope to appoint one of his candidates for archbishop in Bulgaria, the pope refused to satisfy his request. Having seen that Rome did not want to grant the Bulgarian church independence, Boris came back to Constantinople. He resumed communications with it, expecting that this time Constantinople would be more cooperative in meeting his requests. In September 867, Emperor Michael III was murdered by his close acquaintance Basil, who started the Macedonian dynasty. Patriarch Photios was replaced by Ignatius (847–58; 867–77). In 869–70, a large council was convened in Constantinople with the purpose to find ways of reconciliation with the Roman see. A high-ranked delegation from Bulgaria came to the capital of the eastern Roman Empire. In front of the members of the council, they were asked what ecclesial center they consider their own. To the surprise of the Roman legates, who were unprepared for such interrogations, the Bulgarians confirmed their association with the patriarchate of Constantinople. The protests of the pope's legates were ignored. With the approval of the council, the Bulgarian church became an autonomous archbishopric, with its archbishop to be elected from among the Bulgarian bishops and approved by the ruler of Bulgaria, together with the patriarch of Constantinople. Thus, although Boris's oscillation between the East and West dramatically worsened relations between the two parts of the Christian world, he managed to secure an unprecedented degree of independence for the Bulgarian church and, consequently, for his state.

To protect and strengthen the political independence of Bulgaria, Boris recruited not only the church but also culture and language. He and his successors took care that the Bulgarian people used their own language, Slavonic (also called Old Bulgarian). This language was officially introduced for both civil and church use. Numerous Greek and Latin texts were translated into Slavonic and then spread throughout Bulgaria and far beyond it to other Slavic peoples. Language and culture thus were instrumentalized, together with the church, and mobilized to serve the political purposes of the state.

The independence of the Bulgarian church was not a once-and-forever constant to be assumed. It evolved, sometimes dramatically. It started with an "enhanced autonomy"[19] granted to the Bulgarian church by the council of Constantinople in 879-80. This autonomy presupposed that the archbishop of the Bulgarian church was to be installed in Constantinople, but bishops under his jurisdiction were not listed as hierarchs of Constantinople in the catalogues (*ta taktika*, τὰ τακτικά) of this church. Soon, under the tsar of Bulgaria Simeon (893-927), the church assumed the rights of archbishopric, similar to the rights of the church of Cyprus.[20] It meant that the primates of the church were elected and enthroned in Bulgaria; they did not have to go to Constantinople. Under Simeon's successor Peter (927-70), the archbishopric of Bulgaria was elevated to patriarchate.

The independence of the Bulgarian church in the status of patriarchate continued to fluctuate. During the first Bulgarian state (681-971), the Bulgarian patriarchate did not have to give an account of itself to any other church. When the patriarchate was reestablished in 1235, during the second Bulgarian state (1186-1396), the patriarchs were required to meet certain requirements from Constantinople. In particular, they had to commemorate other "old" patriarchs, who were not, however, obligated to commemorate the Bulgarian primates. They also had to receive holy myrrh from Constantinople, pay taxes to Constantinople, and be accountable to Constantinople in cases of violation of the above conditions. Bulgaria's new patriarchal status was honorary (*psilō onomati*, ψιλῷ ὀνόματι)[21] rather than equal to the "old" patriarchates. This initial form of "new" autocephaly was similar to modern ecclesiastical autonomy.

By the fourteenth century, the Bulgarian patriarchate, now situated in Tirnovo (presently Veliko Tarnovo, Велико Търново), stopped keeping to these conditions. There is an eloquent testimony about the situation in the autocephalous Bulgarian patriarchate during the mid-fourteenth century to be found in a letter that a group of Bulgarian monks wrote to the patriarch of Constantinople Kallistos I (1350-53, 1355-63/64). They drew a picture, possibly exaggerated, of a church that had come to be

---

19. Γόνη, Ιστορία των Ορθοδόξων Εκκλησιών Βουλγαρίας και Σερβίας, 23-24.

20. In one of the *Notitiae* of the patriarchate of Constantinople, dating to the tenth century, the church of Bulgaria together with the church of Cyprus were placed after the five patriarchates and before the metropolises under Constantinople. See Darrouzès, *Notitiae episcopatuum Ecclesiae Constantinopolitanae*, no 8, p. 290.

21. See Γόνη, Ιστορία των Ορθοδόξων Εκκλησιών Βουλγαρίας και Σερβίας, 67.

completely unaccountable to any other church. They reported that the Bulgarian patriarch in Tirnovo did not commemorate the primates of the rest of the Orthodox churches at the liturgy; that the Bulgarian priests baptized by sprinkling only once; and they used holy myrrh not from Constantinople and not prepared from fragrant components but from the relics of saints.[22] This letter serves as testimony that autocephaly at that time was not only a canonical matter but also a liturgical issue.

Granting the status of patriarchate to the Bulgarian church during the first Bulgarian kingdom was an unprecedented *political* act. In formal terms, it was accomplished by a decision of the senate of Constantinople in response to the request of Emperor Romanos I Lekapenos (920–44), who in turn was officially asked for it by the tsar of the Bulgars, Peter. The church of Constantinople was only consulted on this matter. It is not a surprise, in consequence, that when the Bulgarian state was occupied by the Byzantine emperor, John I Tsimiskes (969–76), he annulled by his own act[23] the status of patriarchate of the Bulgarian church, as if it were a mere political attribute of Bulgarian statehood. In a sense, it was.

The independence of the Bulgarian state was not the only political rationale of the church's autocephaly and patriarchal status. At some stage, this status became an instrument for transferring the idea of the universal Christian *imperium* from Constantinople to Bulgaria. Tsar Simeon (reigned 893–927) made Bulgaria the most powerful state in southern Europe at his time. Simeon dreamed of his state becoming the center of the Roman Empire. He began thinking of himself as a Roman emperor and called himself *tsar*, which derived from "caesar." Moreover, he wanted to be an autocrat not just for the Bulgars but for the Romans as well. He adopted for himself the title of "tsar of the Bulgars and Romans" (*Basileus Boulgarōn kai Rōmaiōn*, βασιλεὺς βουλγάρων καὶ ῥωμαίων).[24] Autocephaly in its highest manifestation, the patriarchate, turned to serve this imperial dream, evolving into an imperial identity. This side of autocephaly was not promoted only by the state but was also accepted by the church. One of the illustrations of such a reception can be found in the Bulgarian translation of the Byzantine chronicle of Constantine Manasses (c. 1130–c. 1187). The translation was accomplished

22. See ibid., 95–100.

23. The sources testify that the patriarchate "καθηρέθη παρὰ Ἰωάννου τοῦ Τζιμισκῆ." See ibid., 49.

24. On the Bulgarian political titles, see Wolff, "The 'Second Bulgarian Empire,'" 170.

in the circles of Patriarch Evtimiy of Tirnovo (1375–93). When rendering Manasses's description of the fall of Rome in the fifth century, the Bulgarian translator opposed not Constantinople, as the Greek original had, but Tirnovo to the old Rome:

> This happened to Old Rome, but our new imperial city [= Tirnovo] flourishes, thrives, is strong and young. It will remain so to the end of time because it is under the dominion of the high Tsar of the Bulgars, the generous, the noble, the friend of the monk, the great Tsar, Asen Alexander, whose lordship cannot be outshone by numberless suns.[25]

Thus, Bulgarian rulers in cooperation with the church leaders radically changed the initial idea of autocephaly. Autocephaly became an instrument to serve political independence and imperial ideology. It was also connected with culture. Language and literacy were instrumentalized and subjected to political purposes, together with the church through the institution of its autocephaly.

THE CASE OF SERBIA

Autocephaly in the same modified form was also employed by the Serbs, though in a more moderate way. The southern Slavic tribes that would later form the Serbian people were in touch with Christianity since the times of the Byzantine Emperor Heraclius (610–41). However, Christian faith did not take root among them until they settled under the grand *župan* of Serbia, Mutimir (reigned c. 850–91/93). Unlike the Bulgarian tsars, the Serbian *župans* did not pursue immediate independence for their church. Mutimir chose to acknowledge the supremacy of Emperor Basil I (reigned 867–86). Considerably later, under Stefan Nemanja (reigned 1166–96), the Serbs started claiming more political and ecclesial independence from Byzantium.

A key figure in the process of the autocephalization of the Serbian church was Nemanja's son, Ratko (c. 1175–1235). After having spent several years at Mount Athos, in 1207 Sava (as Ratko was named when

25. In Wolff, "The Three Romes," 300. The original text of Manasses reads: "This is what happened to Old Rome. Ours, however [= Constantinople], flourishes, thrives, is strong and young. May it continue to grow eternally, O Lord of all, since it has so great an Emperor, whose light shines far abroad, victor in a thousand battles, Manuel, the golden glowing scarlet rose, with whose brilliance a thousand suns cannot compare." Ibid.

tonsured at the Holy Mountain) came back to Serbia, which had gone through a crisis caused by the struggle between his two brothers, Stefan and Vukan. Stefan had been named by his late father upon the latter's abdication as grand *župan*, but Vukan launched a campaign against him. When he came back to Serbia, Sava helped his brothers to reconcile and stopped the civil war.

After order was restored, Serbia regained its strength. At the same time, Byzantium had been dramatically weakened by the fourth crusade (1202–4). Emperor Theodore I Laskares (reigned 1204–21) and Patriarch Manuel I (1216–22) found refuge in Nicea. Sava came to Nicea in 1219 and negotiated there an independent status for the Serbian church. Remarkably, his partner in the negotiations was the emperor and not the patriarch, who would be only consulted later on. Sava was persuasive and won the consent of the emperor. The Serbian church received the status of archbishopric, and its first primate became Sava himself.

It is impossible to identify the conditions of granting the Serbian church autocephaly, as there are no surviving documents. It is only possible to guess that they were not much different from those that the Bulgarian church had received from the council in Lampsakion (1235): the archbishop had to commemorate the name of the patriarch of Constantinople at liturgy, to receive the holy myrrh from him, and to pay taxes to Constantinople.[26]

It remains an enigma why the Byzantines granted autocephaly to the Serbs so easily, given how much effort the Bulgars had had to apply to win their own autocephaly. One of the explanations is that the Serbian and Byzantine rulers at that time were married to two sisters, who were daughters of the late Emperor Alexios III Angelos (reigned 1195–1203). More important, however, is that Byzantium was much weaker and troubled by the Bulgars. To counterbalance the latter, the Byzantine emperor decided to elevate the *political* importance of his allies the Serbs by granting them autocephaly. The Bulgarian church would thus lose its monopoly over ecclesial and cultural identity in the Slavic world. Among the direct impacts of this was that the Serbs would claim for their autocephalous church the territories belonging to the archbishop of Ochrid Demetrios Khomatianos (1216–35), who politically supported the rival of the Nicene kingdom, the despotate of Epirus. Finally, Serbian autocephaly would weaken the position of Rome in the Balkans, as some

---

26. See Γόνη, *Ιστορία των Ορθοδόξων Εκκλησιών Βουλγαρίας και Σερβίας*, 189.

Serbian dioceses belonged to the Roman jurisdiction. Grand *Župan* Stefan, who had been crowned as king (*kral*) by Pope Honorius III, now could be crowned by his own Orthodox archbishop, something that happened indeed after Sava came back home.

Serbian autocephaly had some similarities and some differences in comparison with the Bulgarian case. Similar was its political character. It was negotiated with the emperor and granted as a political attribute. The difference is that while in Bulgaria autocephaly was a project of the state (with the protagonistic role played by Tsar Boris), in Serbia it was a project of the church (with the protagonistic role played by Archbishop Sava), even though Sava acted in consent with and to the benefit of Grand *Župan* Stefan. In Serbia, autocephaly became closely connected with the name of Sava and, as such, constituted a more sacred institution than in Bulgaria, where it was perceived more as a political institution. Another difference was that Bulgarian autocephaly from the very beginning was hostile to Byzantium, while the Serbian one was initially friendly.

In the mid-fourteenth century, however, the situation changed. Serbia reached one of the highest points of its development and territorial expansion. It grew mostly at the expense of Byzantium, which was going through a series of civil wars. After Stefan Dušan (reigned 1331–55) conquered most of Macedonia, in 1346 he proclaimed himself "basileus and autocrat of the Serbs and Romans." This was an ultimately hostile action toward what remained of the eastern Roman Empire. Just like the Bulgarian rulers earlier, he took advantage of the weakness of Byzantium and tried to grab Roman imperial identity. He strove to create a new empire on the platform of Serbia from the pieces of Byzantium, which would combine both Serbian and Roman identities. In the terms of that time, such was impossible without converting the Serbian archbishopric to a patriarchate.

Stefan did not expect that the change in the status of the Serbian church would be blessed by the patriarch of Constantinople. He decided to act unilaterally and convened a council in Skopje, where he invited the Bulgarian patriarch Simeon, the archbishop of Ochrid Nicholas, a Byzantine metropolitan, and the *protos* of the Mount Athos. All key participants in the council were dependent on Stefan. The council declared the archbishopric of Serbia a patriarchate and elevated archbishop Joanikije to the dignity of patriarch. This happened on Palm Sunday 1346. One week later, on the day of Easter, Joanikije crowned Stefan Dušan as tsar. The selection of the dates for the two ceremonies—the enthronement of the patriarch on Palm Sunday and the coronation of the emperor on Easter day—indicates that the institution of the patriarchate was seen, at least by Stefan, as instrumental to the institution of the tsar: the former was supposed to imitate the latter. Therefore, it is no surprise that the successor of Joanikije, Sava IV (1354–75) adopted the title "patriarch of the Serbs and Greeks." This means that the Serbs did not just *copy* the patriarchal office of Constantinople but actually tried to *replace* it, an act of extreme hostility to the church of Constantinople.[27] This act was followed by the annexation of a number of dioceses under Constantinople by the Serbian church.

Constantinople did not react immediately. Only seven years later, the new patriarch, Kallistos I (1350–53, 1355–63/64), anathematized Stefan, the patriarch, and all bishops and clergy of the Serbian church.[28] Many scholars believe that Kallistos was urged to proceed to such a severe action by Emperor John VI Kantakouzenos (1347–54), who was at war with Stefan. In this war between Byzantium and Serbia, the patriarchs were soldiers and the emperors were generals.

This story best illustrates that, during the Middle Ages, autocephaly in the eastern church functioned largely as a political instrument used by the states to strengthen their own power and to reduce the power of their rivals. Autocephaly had become an imperial attribute. The states that pursued imperial status simultaneously struggled to gain autocephalous status for their churches, a vehicle of *transitio imperii* from Constantinople to the new ambitious Slavic states. Having turned into a political instrument, autocephaly was often manipulated by the civil authorities. In the situations of war between the Orthodox states, autocephaly caused deep splits between the churches, up to the point of schism. Schism, in this regard, became a projection of the state of war between rival political centers. Autocephaly looked like a projection of the imperial and hegemonic ambitions of the state.

THE CASE OF MOSCOW

The case of the autocephaly of the Russian church exactly fits the medieval paradigm of autocephaly established by the churches of Bulgaria and

---

27. See Obolensky, "Byzantium, Kiev and Moscow," 40.

28. The anathema was lifted in 1375. Simultaneously, the patriarchate of Constantinople recognized the patriarchal dignity of the Serbian church.

Serbia. After the people of Kyiv, the capital of Rus', were baptized under Grand *Knyaz* Volodimer (Volodymyr-Vladimir, reigned 980–1015) in 988, the newly established metropolis of Kyiv was included in the jurisdiction of the patriarchate of Constantinople. The *knyazes* had either to send their own candidates to Constantinople to be approved and installed as metropolitans or to receive appointees of the patriarch. With a couple of exceptions, the rulers of Rus' did not attempt to violate this order or to emancipate the church of Kyiv from Constantinople. The first exception occurred under Grand *Knyaz* Yaroslav (reigned 1016–54), who promoted Hilarion (d. c. 1055) as metropolitan of Kyiv without the consent of Constantinople. This attempt to assert the ecclesial independence of Kyiv failed. The second attempt was undertaken by Izyaslav II (grand *knyaz* 1146–49 and 1151–54), who independently of Constantinople installed his protégé Clement (in the metropolitan office 1147–55) to the Kyivan see. This was an "open revolt"[29] against Constantinople, which placed the Kyivan church in a state of schism for eight years. Constantinople soon reestablished its control over Kyiv and supervised it without further problems. Unlike their Slavic brothers in the Balkans, the civil rulers of Kyiv did not pretend to imitate the Byzantine emperors.[30]

The situation changed with the decline of Kyiv as the capital of Rus' when it was pillaged by *Knyaz* Andrew of Vladimir in 1169 and then destroyed by the Mongols in 1240. The political and ecclesial legacy of Kyiv was divided between two centers that claimed succession to Kyiv. In the southwestern part of the Kyivan state, its successor claimed to be the principality of Galicia-Volhynia, while in the northeast, the principality of Vladimir-Suzdal. The former was absorbed in the fourteenth century by the grand duchy of Lithuania and the kingdom of Poland, which united in 1385 by the act of Krewo. The principality of Vladimir-Suzdal, at approximately the same time, was absorbed by the grand duchy of Moscow or Muscovy. Both polities claimed Kyiv's legacy. They tried to secure it by having the metropolitan of Kyiv in their own domain. This led to "cloning" the Kyivan see. One "clone" moved to southwestern Rus' and had its residence at various times in Galych, Novgorodok, Vilno, and then again Kyiv. The other one moved to the northeast and resided in Vladimir-upon-Klyazma and then in Moscow. This split of the Kyivan see led to confusions and collisions between the two parts of the formerly

---

29. Obolensky, "Byzantium, Kiev and Moscow," 67.

30. "Kiev did not borrow extensively from the Byzantine imperial ideology." Wolff, "The Three Romes," 297.

single church and became a permanent headache for Constantinople, who had to satisfy rulers of both polities on the one hand and to maintain some appearance of canonical order on the other.[31]

Eventually, one of the Kyivan sees, the one that Constantinople supported most, managed its own autocephaly. The events developed as follows. Most probably in 1436, the patriarch of Constantinople enthroned a prominent theologian and diplomat from his own environment, Isidore (1380/90–1463), as the new metropolitan of Kyiv, and had him reside in Moscow. Before that, Constantinople had satisfied the request of the grand duke of Lithuania, Švitrigaila (c. 1370–1452, reigned 1430–32) and approved for him Bishop Gerasim of Smolensk as metropolitan of Kyiv. The patriarch did not satisfy a similar request of the grand *knyaz* of Moscow, Basil III (reigned 1505–33), when he chose the bishop of Ryazan, Jonas, for the Kyivan see after death of Gerasim. Jonas, who had been sent to Constantinople for enthronement, had to return to Moscow not as a metropolitan but as a bishop accompanying Isidore. Although it was with some hesitations, Basil received Isidore.

A plausible explanation as to why Constantinople insisted on Isidore is that the latter was expected to play an important role in the upcoming negotiations with Rome. The subject of the negotiations would be theological differences between East and West and the possibility of the restoration of unity between the two churches. Through these negotiations, Constantinople also expected to secure the military assistance of the West. That is why they were of crucial importance for the patriarch, who took proper care to choose appropriate members to the delegation.

---

31. As John Meyendorff remarked, "Nineteenth-century Russian historiography—and particularly the ecclesiastical historians—tended to understand the transfer of the metropolitan's seat from Kiev to Vladimir and Moscow as a natural and organic development and to present the attempts at establishing separate metropolitanates in Galicia and Lithuania as flagrant usurpations, initiated by "foreign" Polish and Lithuanian rulers and supported by the corruption and venality of the Byzantines. This view may give the partial explanation of some concrete incidents, but it certainly does not provide any adequate description of the historical situation as a whole. It suffers from an obvious anti-Byzantine bias and presupposes that, for all practical purposes, the borders of the Muscovite Grand-principality corresponded to the limits of 'Russia,' as such. In fact, for Byzantium, the situation in Russia presented a difficult choice between 'two Russias,' and if . . . the Muscovite grand-princes may occasionally have been quite generous in replenishing the empty treasury of the Greek emperors and of ecclesiastical officials, there is no sufficient reason to believe that Byzantine support was given always and only to the highest bidder." Meyendorff, *Byzantium and the Rise of Russia*, 270–71.

Before his election to the see of Kyiv, Isidore showed himself to be a skillful diplomat in the mission of Emperor John VIII Palaiologos (reigned 1425–48) to the council of Basel (convoked in 1431), which continued in Ferrara and then in Florence. He was one of the persons from the side of Constantinople who contributed to the council of Basel-Ferrara-Florence at all its phases, which formally lasted from 1431 to 1445. By electing him as metropolitan of Kyiv, Constantinople expected to strengthen Isidore's position and to engage the church of Rus' as an additional argument in the negotiations with Rome.

When Isidore came to Ferrara, now as metropolitan of Kyiv, he showed himself a strong advocate for union. His advocacy, now enhanced with his high hierarchical status, contributed significantly to the position of the Orthodox delegation, which in its majority accepted the union. After the council, Isidore became a devoted promoter of the union, particularly in southwest Rus', where he spent over a year on his way back to Moscow. In Moscow, however, where he returned in 1441, he was met with hostility. After he celebrated a liturgy in the Kremlin, in which he commemorated the pope and proclaimed the act of the union, he was asked by a council, summoned by Grand *Knyaz* Basil, to reject the union. He disagreed and was first arrested, then allowed to flee to the West. Bishop Jonas was installed to Isidore's place (1448), now without the consent of Constantinople. This move on the part of Moscow was a *de facto* proclamation of autocephaly by the Muscovite part of the Kyivan church.

Moscow elaborated a sophisticated argumentation in support of its self-proclaimed autocephaly. This argumentation was based on the assumption that, as the Russian historian of the church Yevgeny Golubinsky put it, the Greeks had ceased to be Orthodox enough and true Orthodoxy was now kept only by the Russians.[32] In a fourteenth-century text originating from Pskov, those who tried to say something in favor of the Greeks were rebuked by the following argument: "Now one can expect from Jerusalem only the antichrist with his harmful teaching." Therefore, it "does not fit us to receive a new teaching from the Greeks and to get corrupted by the Greek land."[33] The idea of the corruption of the "Greek faith," and of Russian superiority in the matters of piety and doctrine, became extremely popular among the Muscovites and is still

---

32. Голубинский, *История Русской Церкви*, vol. 2, 459.
33. In ibid., 463.

kept by many Russians. It implied, according to Golubinsky, that "Christianity in Russia is higher and its Orthodoxy is bigger than in Greece, and that we, the Russians, are a better and a more pious people than the Greeks."[34]

The idea of superiority found its proof, in the eyes of Moscow, when Constantinople was captured by Turks in 1453, just a few years after the council of Basel-Ferrara-Florence. For the Muscovites, this was a token of God's revenge for the union. In the eyes of Moscow, the deprivation of imperial support and of external grandeur made the church of Constantinople deficient even after it had denounced the union with Rome. John IV "the Terrible" (reigned 1547–84) reasoned later in one of his letters that because "the Turkish tsar turned big churches of God to mosques; and those churches, which were left to the patriarch, have no crosses on them and bells . . . , the Orthodoxy of the Greeks has been corrupted."[35]

The events of the union accelerated the realization of the Balkan scenario in Muscovy. The two main acts of this scenario were the autocephaly of the church with its promotion to the patriarchal status and *transitio imperii*. This scenario became attractive for Moscow even before the council of Basel-Ferrara-Florence. As early as in 1339, the grand *knyaz* of Moscow was already being compared with Emperors Constantine and

---

34. Ibid., 464. Golubinsky used harsh words criticizing this arrogant stereotype: "The Russians, as people without real education, formed specific views on the purity of true Orthodoxy. . . . Given the absence of real education among us, we were destined to slip into the extremity of ascribing an exaggerated meaning to the rituals by equating them with dogmas of faith. . . . In the first period [of Kiev] we did not reach such an extremity as to consider rituals to be dogmas and did not accept their pluriformity from this perspective. In consequence, in that period, the pluriformity of rituals that passed to us from the Greeks did not confuse anyone. After the invasion of the Mongols, when the influence of the Greeks weakened, as well as through other influences, when in the Muscovite north we became a people that hid themselves away from other peoples behind the mountains and walls and isolated ourselves to the extent that we began looking like a European China, the development of the radical views escalated without restrictions and reached its extreme. . . .

Having ascribed an exaggerated importance to the rituals and having equated them with dogmas, our ancestors . . . gave more weight to superficial piety and external worship. They were attracted by the false piety that was favored among the Jews by the Pharisees and condemned by the Savior. We demonstrated a great devotion to the external prayer and to the places of the external public prayer, the churches. In this regard, we indeed became higher than the Greeks. . . . However, we did not understand our piety in the way that the prophet Isaiah described (chapter 1 and 58), as a simple nothing." Голубинский, *История Русской Церкви*, vol. 2, 460–65.

35. In ibid., 511.

Justinian.³⁶ After the council, the second and most important part of the scenario, *transitio imperii*, began developing rapidly. In 1461–62, a collection of treatises was published on the installation of a new metropolitan, Feodosiy (1461–64), in Moscow. The Moscow court sponsored this publication, which means that it fitted the political agenda of the grand duchy. The first treatise in the collection was about the council of Ferrara-Florence; the second one was about the heresies of the Latins; and the third was an *encomium* to the great *knyaz* of Moscow, with an emphasis on his Orthodoxy. The collection was built around two ideas that became central in the *transitio* ideology: 1) the *knyazes* of Moscow had taken over the office of Constantine and 2) the Muscovites are better Christians than the Greeks.³⁷

These ideas were developed further and shaped the core of the ideology of Moscow as the third Rome.³⁸ This ideology was articulated by a monk from Pskov named Filofey.³⁹ In his epistle on the "unfortunate days and hours," addressed to *Dyak* Mikhail Misyur'-Munekhin, he referred to the grand *knyaz* of Moscow, Basil III, as a ruler who

> in the entire world is the only tsar for the Christians and the ruler of the holy God's thrones, of the holy catholic and apostolic church, which emerged instead of the Roman and Constantinopolitan [churches] and which exists in the God-saved city of Moscow.... [It] is the only in the world that shines brighter than the sun.... All Christian kingdoms reached their end and came together in one single kingdom of our sovereign. According to the prophetic books, this is the Roman kingdom, because two Romes fell and the third one stands still, while there will be no fourth one.⁴⁰

---

36. See Wolff, "The Three Romes," 297.

37. See Голубинский, *История Русской Церкви*, vol. 2, 466–67.

38. See Кириллов, *Третій Римъ*; Zernov, *Moscow, the Third Rome*; Оглоблин, *Московська теорія III Риму в XVI–XVII стол.*; Strémooukhoff, "Moscow the Third Rome: Sources of the Doctrine"; Toumanoff, "Moscow the Third Rome"; Wolff, "The Three Romes"; Haney, *Moscow-Second Constantinople, Third Rome or Second Kiev*; Meyendorff, *Byzantium and the Rise of Russia*; Meyendorff, *Rome, Constantinople, Moscow*; Poe, "*Moscow, the Third Rome*"; Синицына, *Третий Рим*; Успенский, *Царь и патриарх*.

39. See on him Лихачев, *Словарь книжников и книжности древней Руси*, vol. 2, 471–73.

40. Синицына, *Третий Рим*, 345.

Filofey repeated himself in a direct address sent to Basil III: "All Christian kingdoms came together in your kingdom, after which we expect a kingdom that will have no end."[41] In some sense, the ideology articulated by Filofey was no different from the imperial ideologies behind the Bulgarian and Serbian states. It is in effect the same ideology of *transitio imperii*. The difference is that according to Filofey, the new Roman kingdom of Moscow is the chiliastic one—the last kingdom in human history.

The monks might have seen the Muscovite state eschatologically, but the rulers saw it in terms that were more practical. With the assistance of the church, they began actively constructing a new political identity for their statehood, employing for this purpose the symbols of the eastern Roman Empire. When grand *knyaz* of Moscow, John III (reigned 1462–1505), married in 1472, he used the title "tsar," a Slavic derivative from "Caesar" borrowed from the Balkan "emperors." His wife, Zoe Palaiologina, who took name Sophia, signed her letters as "Empress of Byzantium," though she was only a niece of the last Byzantine emperor Constantine XI. They built the Kremlin, which was a Muscovite version of the Byzantine sacred palace.

John IV "the Terrible" (reigned 1547–84) was enthroned officially with the title "tsar." His title was confirmed by the patriarch of Constantinople. Metropolitan Makary of Moscow (1542–63) composed a rite of anointing John as a "tsar,"[42] in imitation to the similar rite applied to the Byzantine emperors. John nevertheless was not anointed himself. The first tsar who was anointed was Theodore (1584–98). The idea of anointment to tsardom in Moscow took a different path than in the West and in Byzantium. In Moscow, it was identified with the sacrament of chrism. Moreover, at some stage it came to be regarded as the highest degree of chrismation. As Boris Uspensky remarked, "While in Byzantium and in the West through anointment a monarch imitated the kings of Israel, in Russia the tsar imitated Christ himself."[43] The office of tsar in Russia became more sacred and more remote from the common people than in Byzantium. Tsars were regarded as bearers of special charisma of power, which Christ himself bestowed upon them. Those who doubted this were

---

41. Ibid., 360.

42. On the role of Makary in the development of the new state ideology of Moscow, see Bogatyrev, "Reinventing the Russian Monarchy in the 1550s."

43. Успенский, *Царь и патриарх*, 20.

anathematized.⁴⁴ Thus, in the view of the Muscovites, their tsars exceeded even the Byzantine emperors in their sacrality.

The unique place of the Russian tsars was reflected in the office of the primates of the church of Moscow. The first independent metropolitan of Moscow, Jonas, was consecrated to his office for the second time after his consecration as bishop. The practice of consecration through laying-on hands instead of just enthronement was applied to the successors of Jonas, even though they were already bishops.⁴⁵ This practice continued when the Muscovite rulers secured patriarchal status for their church in 1589. The first patriarch of Moscow, Job (1589–1605), was consecrated three times: the first time as bishop of Kolomna; the second, as metropolitan of Moscow; and the third, as patriarch of Moscow.⁴⁶

The Muscovite tsars convinced the patriarch of Constantinople to grant patriarchal status to the Russian church relatively easily. The eastern churches were economically dependent on Moscow and complied with most requests of its mighty rulers. Patriarch Jeremiah II (1572–79, 1580–84, 1587–95), when he came to Moscow to collect money, not only consecrated Job to the patriarchal office for the third time—though this was anti-canonical—but also made the following comments in his address to the tsar upon the consecration:

> Since the old Rome fell because of the Apollinarian heresy, and the Second Rome, which is Constantinople, is possessed by the godless Turks, thy great Russian Tsardom, pious Tsar . . . is the Third Rome . . . and thou alone under heaven art called the Christian Tsar in the whole world for all Christians.⁴⁷

The patriarch of Constantinople thus effectively authorized the ideology of Filofey about Moscow as the third Rome.

Remarkably, when Jeremiah came to Moscow, Boris Godunov (tsar 1598–1605) suggested he move to his domain. Jeremiah agreed at first, but when Boris offered to let him live in Vladimir instead of in Moscow, he declined the proposal. This episode confirms that, for Moscow, the elevation of its metropolitan to patriarchal status was an element of *transitio imperii*, as it had previously been also in Bulgaria and Serbia.

44. See ibid., 22–25.
45. See ibid., 49.
46. See ibid., 78–79.
47. In Wolff, "The Three Romes," 305.

In Moscow, the patriarchal office, as well as the office of tsar, received a special sacral meaning unknown in either Byzantium or the Balkans. As Uspensky remarked, "both tsar and patriarch appear to be exempt from the sphere of common canonical rules: the laws that are applicable to others do not apply to them. They seem to belong to a different and higher sphere of existence."[48]

This allows us to draw a conclusion that the autocephaly of the church of Moscow featured not only the common Balkan concept of *transitio imperii*, but became a sacred and mystical institution, which was believed to be directly connected with God. It contained a strong ideological element that actively developed within this sacrality. The new political ideology of the Muscovite tsardom grew out of the concept of the third Rome and became embedded in the autocephaly of the church of Moscow.

THE CASE OF GREECE

A new wave of autocephalies came in the first half of the nineteenth century. It was triggered by the ideas of Enlightenment and a new political identity that many peoples in Europe adopted, namely the nation.[49] The weakened and decaying Ottoman Empire provided fertile soil, from which new autocephalies sprang. Before the nineteenth century, the only political matrix that shaped the nature of autocephaly was empire. In the nineteenth century, the matrix changed and the political nature of the new states that emerged was different from the political nature of the old empires. The new states caused changes in the perception and practice of autocephaly, at least for the churches that emerged from the collapsing empires. Nationhood became the basic identity and embodiment of political sovereignty of the people. The new churches, as a result, identified themselves with nation. Autocephaly continued to be an attribute of statehood. However, because the states became national, autocephaly turned to an attribute of national sovereignty. Without having their own autocephalous churches, the national Orthodox states in the Balkans could not consider themselves sufficiently independent.

A dominant theory about autocephaly in modern scholarship is the one that identifies it with nationhood. As Alexander Schmemann put

---

48. Успенский, *Царь и патриарх*, 108.
49. See Hobsbawm, *Nations and Nationalism Since 1780*.

it, "autocephaly, if not in its origin (it was used in various senses before but always occasionally) at least in its application, is a product not of ecclesiology, but of a national phenomenon. Its fundamental historical connotation is thus neither purely ecclesiological, nor jurisdictional, but national."[50] This statement is only partially true. National awakening was one important factor in shaping the texture of the new autocephalies, but not the only one. Other values of the age of Enlightenment, such as freedom, equality, accountability, culture, literacy, and language played an important formative role as well. The struggle of the Balkan churches for their autocephaly in the nineteenth century created a momentum for their renewal. On the eve of Greek independence, Adamantios Koraïs imagined a church that would be independent from Constantinople and free of any tyranny.[51]

Like in the case of the medieval Bulgarian state, autocephaly in the nineteenth century continued featuring the issues of language. Language, as Sabrina Ramet has noted, became "a salient issue in Orthodox church politics."[52] In the age of Enlightenment, the issue of language developed to the scale of culture and identity. Language, literacy, educational system, and nationhood constituted a single complex of people's identities. Autocephaly became an intrinsic part of this complex. With any of these components missing, a nation could not pretend to be accomplished and to enjoy political independence, according to the tenets of that time.

The first autocephaly designed according to the new pattern inspired by the ideas of Enlightenment was the church of Greece.[53] It constituted an archetype for all autocephalies in the modern age, both successful and unsuccessful ones.[54] The process of establishing an independent Orthodox church in Greece began immediately after the liberation revolution of 1821. This issue was raised at the National Assemblies (*Ethnikai syneleuseis,* Ἐθνικαὶ συνελεύσεις) at Epidauros (1821), Troizena (1827), and Argos (1828). Dioceses on the territories of independent Greece lost most of their connections with the patriarchate of Constantinople. Under the

---

50. Schmemann, *Church, World, Mission*, 98.

51. Κοραῆ, *Ἀριστοτέλους Πολιτικῶν τὰ σωζόμενα*, 120.

52. Ramet, *Eastern Christianity and Politics in the Twentieth Century*, 9.

53. A study, which is regarded normative in Greece, is by Κωνσταντινίδου, *Ἡ ἀνακήρυξις τοῦ αὐτοκεφάλου τῆς ἐν Ἑλλάδι Ἐκκλησίας (1850)*. An older and yet more nuanced is the study by Frazee, *The Orthodox Church and Independent Greece, 1821–1852*.

54. See Frary, *Russia and the Making of Modern Greek Identity*, 95.

pressure of political circumstances, a gradual progress towards independence of the Greek church began. The first elected Greek governor Ioannis Kapodistrias (1827–31) tried to reverse this progress and to preserve the canonical relationship of the Greek dioceses with the patriarchate of Constantinople. He did so even in spite of the activities of the Phanar against independence of Greece.[55] However, after Kapodistrias was assassinated in 1831 and Greece adopted monarchy with the first king, Otto, invited from the Bavarian house of Wittelsbach (1815–67, reigned 1832–62), the Greek church was resolutely put onto the track of independence.

There were several political reasons for that. One was to secure the Greek independence from the High Porte. The latter often used the factor of the church to regain control over the rebel territories. Thus, only a few days after the Greek revolution began, the patriarch Gregory V was forced to anathematize those "who rise against their common protector and lawful sovereign, and against Christ."[56] The other reason was a need for consolidation of Greek society in the situation of its internal instability. The church and the state had to demonstrate unity, which was possible only if the church was independent. This meant, however, that autocephaly was envisaged not an end in itself, but as an instrument of making the church a part of the state machinery. Such was the rationale of church independence, for instance, for the member of Otto's regency, Georg Ludwig von Maurer (1790–1872), who was made responsible for arranging ecclesial matters. The third factor was Russian. Through making the church autocephalous, the Greek government wanted to weaken the Russian protectorate, which often used ecclesiastical channels to enhance itself. Needless to say, both the church of Constantinople and Russian diplomacy resisted the process of autocephalization of the Greek church, and acted in alliance with each other against it.[57]

Nevertheless, the Greek government remained firm in its intentions, and in July 1833 a *Decree about the Independence of the Greek Church* (*Diakēryxis peri tēs anexartēsias tēs Hellēnikēs Ekklēsias*, Διακήρυξις περὶ τῆς ἀνεξαρτησίας τῆς Ἑλληνικῆς Ἐκκλησίας) was proclaimed, which meant the declaration of autocephaly. The document was drafted by Ludwig von Maurer and archimandrite Theokletos Pharmakides

---

55. For instance, in 1828 the patriarch of Constantinople Agathangelos (1826–30) sent four senior hierarchs of the throne to Peloponnese and the Cyclades to agitate local population to reconcile with the sultan.

56. In Frary, *Russia and the Making of Modern Greek Identity*, 98.

57. See ibid., 94.

(1784–1860). It is noteworthy that autocephaly was proclaimed not by the church council but by the king of Greece, who enacted the Decree by his signature. The reaction of Constantinople was immediate—it broke communion with the Greek hierarchs. However, unlike in Bulgaria later on, the patriarchate avoided proceeding to anathemas and thus to a formal state of schism. Many years of negotiations between Greece and Constantinople followed, with the mediation of international diplomacy and domestic politicians, before the autocephaly of the church of Greece was eventually recognized by the patriarchate of Constantinople in 1850.

Autocephaly contributed to and reflected ideological battles in Greek society, particularly the one between "liberals" and "conservatives." The former normally supported autocephaly, while the latter struggled to preserve ties with the patriarchate in Constantinople. Thus, the protagonists of autocephaly Theokletos Pharmakides and Neophytos Vamvas (1770–1856) belonged to the "liberal" faction, while "conservative" Constantine Oikonomos (1780–1857) led the pro-patriarchal group.

Autocephaly reflected also the struggle of the Greek intellectual and political elites to invent a new Greek nation. The neo-Greek political nation was a construct inspired by the Romanticism and Neoclassicism of the early nineteenth century. It claimed its direct political descent from the Athenian democracy and built its cultural identity on the heritage of antiquity. Among many identities that the Greeks held in the Ottoman Empire, the architects of the new *Hellas* chose the minor one of "Hellen" ("Ελλην). Other identities more important for the majority of the Greek population, such as "Roman" (*Rōmios*, Ρωμιός or *Rōmaios*, Ρωμαῖος), were set aside. Modern Greece built a bridge straight to ancient Greece, bypassing Byzantium. Neoclassical admiration of the ancient Greek heritage intensified the feeling of the superiority of Greek language and culture over the Turkish "barbarianism." This feeling became a strong impetus in the struggle for the liberation of Greece from what was presented as the "Turkish yoke" and called "Turkocracy" (*Tourkokratia*, Τουρκοκρατία).

The Greek autocephaly was imposed unilaterally by the state, with the collaboration of some figures in the church. Initially, it did not have wide support in the church and society. Ordinary Greek people, clergy, and hierarchs had to be persuaded to get away from the patriarchate of Constantinople and to have their own independent church. Many of them were satisfied with the Ottoman rule. Some even believed that this rule was better than the Byzantine one. They would subscribe to the following opinion of the patriarch of Jerusalem Anthimos (1788–1808):

> See how clearly our Lord, boundless in mercy and all-wise, had undertaken to guard once more the unsullied Holy and Orthodox faith. He raised out of nothing this powerful empire of the Ottomans, in place of our Roman [Byzantine] Empire which had begun, in a certain way, to cause to deviate from the beliefs of the Orthodox faith, and he raised up the empire of the Ottomans higher than any other kingdom so as to show without doubt that it came about by divine will, and not by the power of man. . . . The all-mighty Lord, then, has placed over us this kingdom, "for there is no power but of God," so as to be to the people of the West a bridle, to us the people of the East a means of salvation. For this reason he puts into the heart of the sultan of these Ottomans an inclination to keep free the religious beliefs of our Orthodox faith and, as a work of supererogation, to protect them, even to the point of occasionally chastising Christians who deviate from their faith, that they have always before their eyes the fear of God.[58]

Hierarchs and clergy who shared these views had to be convinced that the Greek state would be better for them than Turkey or even Byzantium. This uneasy task was accomplished through what can be called "Greek civil religion." This is an instance of the larger phenomenon of civil religion studied in the sociology of religion.[59] According to Ronald Weed and John Von Heyking,

> Civil religion originally refers to the way in which a particular set of political/social arrangements come to acquire an aura of the sacred, thereby elevating their stature and enhancing their stability. It can serve as a point of reference for the shared faith of the entire state or nation, focusing on the most generalised and widely held beliefs about the history and destiny of that state or nation. It is rarely entirely spontaneous or entirely invented, and is more likely to be some combination of the two. But it plays an important role in social cohesion, providing much of the glue that binds together a society through well-established symbols, rituals, celebrations, places, and values, endowing the society with an overarching sense of spiritual unity. . . . Civil religion . . . expresses an enduring need for the divine, whether it is the

---

58. Διδασκαλία Πατερική (1798), in Ramet, "Autocephaly and National Identity," 46.
59. See Bellah and Hammond, *Varieties of Civil Religion*.

citizenry's need for the divine that provides political power for those who capitalise upon it or a religious citizenry's desire to absorb the political community at large into a wider theological destiny.[60]

The same kind of religion was developed by the activists of the Greek Enlightenment.[61] Many of them were secularists, and yet, like Jean-Jacques Rousseau, who coined the term "civil religion,"[62] they found it helpful to consolidate religious masses. The fathers of this religion have produced images and narratives, which became sacred and accepted by Greeks with truly religious enthusiasm. For instance, among the icons of Greek civil religion there was a famous picture by Nikolaos Gyzis "Hidden School" (*To krypho scholeio*, Το κρυφό σχολειό), which depicts an underground group of pupils being taught by a clergyman.[63] Metropolitan of Old Patres, Germanos (1771–1826), who blessed the flag of the Greek revolution, became a prophet of this civil religion. The day, when he supposedly did this, the 25th of March 1821, which is the Feast of Annunciation, is celebrated as the main holiday of its sacred calendar. It is not important, as many historians believe, that the "hidden school" or the consecration of flags by Germanos did not happen in reality. These national myths were powerful enough to transform the Christian *genos* of the Byzantine and Ottoman Empires, which was inclusive of many nations, to the Greek *ethnos* of the new Hellenic state. These myths enhanced the credo of Greek civil religion, which included among its articles the sacrality and superiority of the Greek nation. This religion presented it in a black and white picture, where the Greek experiences in the Ottoman Empire and the patriarchate of Constantinople were depicted in black. Thus, Greek autocephaly became a part of the civil religion, because it enabled the Greek nation to pass from slavery to freedom.

The main impetus of Greek autocephaly might have been liberation from Turkish slavery. The irony, however, is that the church, after having received independence from Constantinople, lost many of its liberties and came to be tightly controlled by the Greek state. The *Decree about the Independence of the Greek Church*, which served as the Greek church's

---

60. Weed and Von Heyking, *Civil Religion in Political Thought*, vii, 3.
61. See Δημαρά, *Νεοελληνικός Διαφωτισμός*.
62. *The Essential Rousseau*, translated by Bair, 17, 20, 107–8, 110.
63. See Κεκαυμένου, *Το κρυφό σχολειό*.

statute until 1852, granted to the civil authorities almost total control over the church. Thus, according to this document:

- The king is the leader (*archēgos*, ἀρχηγός) of the church in administrative matters (article 1).
- The church is administered by five bishops, who notably constitute the "Holy Synod of the Greek Kingdom" (*Hiera Synodos tou Basileiou tēs Hellados*, Ἱερὰ Σύνοδος τοῦ Βασιλείου τῆς Ἑλλάδος)—the synod is not of the church, but of the kingdom. The members of the synod are appointed by the government (articles 2–3).
- The members of the synod, when appointed, need to take an oath of loyalty to the king (*pistin eis ton Basilea*, πίστιν εἰς τὸν Βασιλέα).

In conclusion, the Greek autocephaly emerged as inspired by the Enlightenment. It embraced the ideas of freedom and liberation from slavery, as well as the values of culture, language, and education. It became a part of the new political and national identity of the Greek state and its people. It also created a momentum for the church to change some of its institutions, to make them more focused on people. However, this impetus sometimes led to undesired consequences. Thus, the church became integrated into the state machinery and cocooned in "civil religion." The autocephaly of the church in Greece, with all its positive and negative sides, became a prototype for other autocephalies that emerged in the Balkans soon after.

THE CASE OF BULGARIA II

The Bulgarian struggle for an independent church started soon after the church of Greece declared its autocephaly. It began with protests against abuses by the Greek metropolitans in Bulgarian towns, particularly regarding money matters. In 1838, for instance, several municipalities of the Tirnovo diocese protested against the local metropolitan, Panaretos (1838–40). They sent their petitions to both civil and ecclesial authorities in Istanbul with a request to replace Panaretos with a Bulgarian metropolitan. The petition was rejected. Such reactions on the part of Constantinople stirred further unrest among the Bulgars, who had begun demanding more freedom for themselves.

When in 1839 a new sultan, Abdülmecid I, came to power (reigned till 1861), he continued the liberal reforms of his father, sultan Mahmud II (1789–1839), and promulgated an *Imperial Edict of Reorganization* (*Tanzimât Fermânı* or *Hatt-ı Şerîf*), which enhanced the rights of the minority groups in the Ottoman Empire. This decree made the Bulgars more demanding of their own church hierarchy. Most active in this cause was the Bulgarian community in Istanbul. It united around archimandrite Neophyte Bozveli and Stojan Mihajlovski, the metropolitan-to-be Hilarion of Makarioupolis (1812–75). The two activists submitted to the High Porte a petition with the following articles:

- Bishops in the Bulgarian dioceses should be elected from the Bulgars and by the Bulgarian communities.
- Bulgars should have the right to found their own schools as well as publish books and periodicals in their own language.
- Bulgars should have their own church in Istanbul.
- In the Bulgarian settlements, judges should come from among the Bulgars and Turks.
- The Bulgarian people should have their own political representatives in Istanbul, apart from the patriarch.

This petition challenged the *millet* system by suggesting the transference of the right to judge and represent the local Orthodox community before the sultan from the patriarch of Constantinople to the community itself. Another important point of the petition advocated the Bulgarian cultural identity and education. This demand was inspired by the ideas of the Enlightenment and was similar to the demands of the Greeks in their struggle for an independent state and church. Additionally, the petition proposed to organize church life "from below," with the communities to choose their own bishops. It denounced the practice of appointing bishops "from above." This ecclesiology "from below" became a characteristic feature of the Bulgarian autocephalist movement. The proponents of the Greek autocephaly had also advocated for a return to the early church practices of electing clergy and hierarchs, as we have seen in the case of Adamantios Koraïs. However, this practice was not accepted in Greece. The petition stressed the national element in the life of the church too, but it would be incorrect to conclude that this element was promoted as the only or even as the most important one in the document.

The petition elicited negative reactions from the patriarchate and the Russian embassy in Istanbul, which at the initial stage was concerned about preserving the integrity of the church of Constantinople.[64] The Russian ambassador Vladimir Titov (1840–42) arranged for the exile of the authors of the petition to Mount Athos. The Ottoman government, however, satisfied at least one demand of the petition. In 1849, the Bulgarian community of Istanbul was allowed to have its own church in the city. They could celebrate their liturgy in Slavonic. Jurisdictionally, however, this church belonged to the patriarchate of Constantinople.

In 1856, Sultan Abdülmecid signed a decree entitled *Hatt-ı Hümayun*, in which he offered even more religious liberty and civil rights to the minorities. He also urged the *millets* to reform themselves in accordance with this decree, which applied also to the Orthodox *millet-i Rûm*. In response to the call of the sultan, the patriarchate of Constantinople gathered an assembly of the *millet-i Rûm* to discuss how to improve its life along the lines of the decree. From the forty-five delegates to the assembly, four were Bulgars. They requested that:

- the Bulgarian dioceses have Bulgarian bishops;
- the bishops be elected by people in the dioceses;
- the Slavonic language be used for liturgies;
- people control the money of the dioceses.

The assembly accepted only the first proposal. This left the Bulgarian delegates unsatisfied. Even more dissatisfied was the larger Bulgarian community of Constantinople. It divided into two parties, a radical and a moderate. The former wanted unconditional separation from the patriarchate of Constantinople. The latter remained willing to negotiate and would have been satisfied with limited independence for the Bulgarian church. Of the two parties, the former eventually gained the upper hand. On the Easter day 1850, Bishop Hilarion of Makarioupolis, during the liturgy in the Bulgarian church in Istanbul, did not commemorate the patriarch. This implied a *de facto* declaration of independence on the part of the Bulgarian church. Soon Hilarion was elected primate of this church.

The response of the Ecumenical patriarchate came after a delay of several years. Only in February 1861 did the patriarch convene a council, where he invited the former patriarchs of Constantinople, the patriarchs of Alexandria, Antioch, and Jerusalem, as well as some Bulgarian hierarchs that remained loyal to Constantinople. The council condemned the

---

64. On the background of the Russian involvement in the Bulgarian issue see Gerd, *Russian Policy in the Orthodox East*, 24–30.

Bulgarian bishops, who suspended communion with Constantinople and simultaneously satisfied some demands of the Bulgars. It was, however, too late, and the Bulgars rejected reconciliation with Constantinople.

In February 1870, Sultan Abdülaziz (reigned 1861–76) ordered the drafting of a *fermânı* that would establish an independent Bulgarian church with the status of exarchate. The sultan's document allowed the Bulgars to have their own synod. The exarch, however, would maintain accountability to the patriarch of Constantinople and would commemorate him. In addition, the exarch had to receive the holy myrrh from the patriarch. The *fermânı* was activated only in 1872. Then the Bulgarian community proceeded to electing their exarch, who was confirmed by the Ottoman government. On 11 May 1872, which is the Feast Day of St. Cyril and St. Methodius, the exarch Anthim read out an act that declared restoration of independence of the Bulgarian church.

Immediately after this, the synod of the patriarchate imposed an interdict on Anthim and all the Bulgarian church. In August 1872, the patriarch summoned a council, which was attended by the ex-patriarchs of Constantinople, the patriarchs of Alexandria and Antioch, the archbishop of Cyprus, and twenty-five other metropolitans and bishops. The patriarch of Jerusalem left the council before it took its decisions. The council issued a resolution, which defined the actions of the Bulgarian church as "phyletism," condemned them, and anathematized the entire Bulgarian church on these grounds.[65] Thus the longest schism in the modern Orthodox history began, lasting seventy-three years until the anathemas were lifted in 1945. The interdict imposed by the council in 1872 was not recognized, however, by some Orthodox churches. The churches of Jerusalem, Russia, Serbia, and Romania retained communion with the Bulgarian church.

The importance of the definition of the council of 1872 exceeded the particular situation with the Bulgarian church by far. It addressed an issue that would become common in the Orthodox world throughout the nineteenth and twentieth centuries and remains actual even now, namely phyletism. Initially this notion addressed a situation, when two

---

65. The Bulgarian church was called an "illegal gathering" (*parasynagōgē*, παρασυναγωγή). Even stronger was the wording of the preamble to the publication of the definition in the official periodical of the patriarchate of Constantinople. Here, Bulgarian phyletism was characterized as a "Bulgarian heresy" (*Boulgarikē kakodoxia*, βουλγαρικὴ κακοδοξία and *heterodoxia*, ἑτεροδοξία) and "antichristian doctrine" (*antichristianikē didaskalia*, ἀντιχριστιανικὴ διδασκαλία). Bulletin Ἐκκλησιαστικὴ ἀλήθεια 52 (1908), 553.

bishops would rule separate ethnic communities in the same city. Actually, the Bulgarian exarch stayed in Constantinople until 1913, when he moved to Sofia. At a later stage, phyletism came to mean primarily the identification of the church with nation. This meaning was implicitly encoded already in the *horos* of the council of 1872, which defined phyletism as an approach that minds the origins of peoples (*phyletikai diakriseis*, φυλετικαὶ διακρίσεις), causes controversies on the ethnic grounds (*ethnikē eris*, ἐθνικὴ ἔρις), instigates fanaticism (*zēlos*, ζῆλος), and leads to divisions (*dichostasia*, διχοστασία).[66] The conciliar condemnation did not help to heal phyletism in the Bulgarian church, though. Moreover, more churches became infected with this disease, which is now regarded as one of the most common problem in the modern Orthodox world. The Pan-Orthodox council, held in Crete in June 2016, condemned phyletism again and confirmed the ecumenical authority of the council of 1872.

In addition to the cultural and national agenda, autocephaly of the Bulgarian and other Slavic churches encompassed some social movements of that time, which can be interpreted as class struggle. "Serbs" or "Bulgars" in the nineteenth century came to mean "peasants." Ethnic Serbs and Bulgars belonging to the middle class were identified as "Greeks." In Belgrade, for example, the urban population dressed in a "Greek style." They read local newspapers that included a rubric "Grecia." It was common for the upper classes of the Serbian society to be fluent in Greek and they used it in everyday communications.[67] Consequently, through the autocephalist movement, "Slavic" classes confronted the middle and upper "Greek" classes. When the Slavic churches gained their independence, they adopted more democratic and less hierarchical patterns of governance. Lay people and priests gained more influence on the life of the church than had been possible in the Greek milieu. They had more possibilities to participate in the election of bishops and primates and generally in the matters related to church administration.

THE CASE OF UKRAINE

The autocephalies that emerged in the nineteenth century in the Balkans were liberation movements, at least in their initial phases. Some of them, particularly in Bulgaria, stood for more rights for the lower social classes

---

66. §1 in ibid., 554.
67. See Roudometof, "From Rum Millet to Greek Nation," 13.

and advocated more active participation of laity in the life of the church. They began as anti-imperial, as they developed their characteristic features in wrestling with the Ottoman and Habsburg Empires. However, as time went on the new autocephalous churches gradually and increasingly identified themselves with their respective nations and enhanced nationalist feelings among the Balkan peoples. The collapse of the Austro-Hungarian and Russian Empires after the World War I triggered a new wave of autocephalies, this time in the Eastern Europe. Autocephaly for the newly emerged churches there was also an instrument of de-imperialization. Almost all attempts at autocephaly in the twentieth century, successful or not, were anti-imperial in orientation. They gradually adopted strong national or even nationalistic elements, as well as increasingly relying on generous support from the state. Yet at their core they represent a desire to flee the empire.

Thus, the Orthodox Church of the Czech Lands and Slovakia (till 1992, the Orthodox Church in Czechoslovakia) emerged largely because of the political efforts of Czechoslovakia to shake off the burdens of the Austro-Hungarian empire.[68] Autocephaly was eventually granted to this church (in 1951 by Moscow, in 1998 by Constantinople), even though the Orthodox community of the country was tiny and not capable of sustaining itself. Similarly, Poland struggled to secure autocephaly for its Orthodox minority as a part of the process of emancipation from the Russian Empire and, later, from the Soviet Union.[69] This church received its independence first from Constantinople in 1924 and in 1948 from Moscow. Both Poland and Czechoslovakia had small Orthodox minorities among the non-Orthodox majority. Nevertheless, their governments considered it an important matter of national security to protect their sovereignty by promoting their Orthodox churches to autocephaly.

Some other countries that emerged from the Russian Empire with even smaller Orthodox groups also wanted those groups to be independent. For these countries, the Ecumenical patriarchate offered an instrument of de-imperialization as an alternative to autocephaly: *autonomy*. Autonomy implies, on the one hand, the complete independence of an autonomous church in its internal policies, and on the other hand, a formal connection with the patriarchate of Constantinople. Small Orthodox churches in the Baltic countries of Finland and Estonia chose this sort

---

68. See on this Marek and Bureha, *Pravoslavní v Ceskoslovensku v letech 1918–1953*.
69. See on this Mironowicz et al., *Autokefalie Kościoła prawosławnego w Polsce*.

of independence from Moscow. The relatively soft attitude of Constantinople to its autonomous parts, especially those that are non-Greek, as well as the non-imperialist line of the Ecumenical patriarchate during the twentieth century, made these states satisfied with the status of autonomy for their Orthodox churches.

The anti-imperial type of autocephaly can probably best be studied in the case of Ukraine. Ukraine attempted autocephaly for its church three times during the twentieth century.[70] Although each time it failed, the autocephalous movement continued to evolve. It went through different phases and adopted various features that best illustrate how the institution of autocephaly in general underwent modifications throughout the twentieth century.

The first attempt at Ukrainian autocephaly was undertaken immediately after the collapse of the Russian Empire and the creation of the Ukrainian People's Republic in 1917. The independent Ukrainian state existed until 1921. Its first socialist government was hardly interested in dealing with the church issues. The Ukrainian autocephalist movement therefore was initially spontaneous and unorganized. It emerged as a result of the national awakening.[71] When in 1918 the more conservative governments of het'man Pavlo Skoropads'ky (1873–1945) and later of the *Directoria* seized power, they offered a political support to the autocephalous movement. In 1919, a law established the Ukrainian autocephalous Orthodox church. In 1920, a synod of this church proclaimed itself autocephalous, which was confirmed in 1921 by the All-Ukrainian church council. After the Bolsheviks occupied Ukraine, in the period from 1930 to 1937, they extinguished the autocephalous movement together with the other churches.

At the first stage of its evolution, the Ukrainian autocephalist movement was emphatically national. At the same time, it featured a prominent social and even socialist agenda. It presented itself as a people's movement. It opposed itself to the Russian hierarchy in Ukraine, not only because that hierarchy was Russian, but also because it embodied the interests of the upper classes and imperial chauvinism. Ukrainian autocephalism identified itself with conciliarism (соборноправіє), which strongly emphasized ecclesiology "from below."[72] Following this

---

70. See Partykevich, *Between Kyiv and Constantinople*.

71. See Plokhy and Sysyn, *Religion and Nation in Modern Ukraine*.

72. See Власовський, *Нарис історії Української Православної Церкви*, vol. 4, 8.

ecclesiology, the autocephalous movement ran into extremities, like the consecration of the priest Vasyl' Lypkivsky (1864–1937) as metropolitan, not by bishops, but by priests (1921). This action was not recognized by other churches and seriously compromised the Ukrainian autocephalist movement.

A chance for the revival of the movement for autocephaly in Ukraine came again during the World War II. The occupation of Ukraine by the Nazis allowed the church life to re-emerge from underground, where it had been sent by the persecutions of Joseph Stalin. The German occupational administration did not enforce any consistent religious policy in Ukraine. Its policies depended on the matters of security and order and therefore varied with the situation. The Germans tended to favor the Ukrainization of the Orthodox church on the occupied territories, but this was left largely to the local German and Ukrainian authorities. They nevertheless hesitated to support, and sometimes actively opposed, the Ukrainian autocephalous church, which had been re-established in Ukraine with the assistance of the Polish Orthodox church. They preferred the "autonomous" movement, which kept loyalty to the Russian church and allowed for moderate Ukrainization.[73] The Ukrainian autocephalous movement during the World War II was anti-Soviet and anti-Communist on the one hand, and resisted the Nazis, either actively or passively, on the other. It was a part of the Ukrainian resistance movement, which opposed both the Soviets and the Germans. It was swept away, however, when Ukraine was taken back by the Soviet army. A part of it emigrated to the West, mostly to Canada and the United States.

The third phase of the autocephalous movement in Ukraine began with the collapse of the Soviet Union and the proclamation of the independent Ukrainian state in 1991. A direct descendant of the Ukrainian autocephalous church, which had been renovated during the World War II and had received canonical hierarchy from the Polish church at that time, was the Ukrainian Autocephalous Orthodox Church (UAOC). It was re-established in Ukraine in 1990 under the primacy of Mstyslav Skrypnyk (1898–1993) as a branch of the UAOC that survived after World War II in the diaspora. While in the diaspora and then in the first years after its renovation in Ukraine, the UAOC was closely connected with the dissident and anti-Soviet movements. They together shaped

---

73. See Berkhoff, "Was There a Religious Revival in Soviet Ukraine under the Nazi Regime?"

a "religio-oppositional subculture."[74] Autocephaly represented by the early UAOC essentially meant anti-Soviet dissent. In the recent years, the UAOC has lost this character and accordingly has lost its sense of direction and identity.

Its leading role in the autocephalous movement was taken over by the patriarchate of Kyiv (UOC KP), established in 1992. The person behind this jurisdiction was the metropolitan of Kyiv, Filaret (since 1966), who was eventually elected patriarch of Kyiv (1995). After Ukraine became an independent state (1991), Filaret initiated the creation of an autocephalous church, because of which he was defrocked and anathematized by the Russian church (1997).

The largest church in Ukraine remains the Ukrainian Orthodox Church (UOC). This church is a continuation of the Russian exarchate in Ukraine, which in 1990 was granted the rights of "extended autonomy." This formula, which does not exist in Orthodox canon law, is supposed to mean that the church is free in its internal governance, yet remains in unity with the Moscow patriarchate. The canonical status of the UOC, however, is formally not autonomous, though it enjoys some rights of autonomy. This church is divided over the issue of autocephaly. A part of it wants to be independent from Moscow, and the other part strongly opposes autocephaly. The latter faction has stigmatized autocephaly to the degree of presenting it a threat to the salvific capacity of the church. It effectively identifies the Moscow patriarchate with the universal church of Christ and argues that if the Ukrainian church would become autocephalous, even in a canonical way, this will cut it off the church of Christ.

The "Revolution of dignity"—as the events at the Maidan of Independence, the central square in Kyiv, during the winter 2013–14 were branded[75]—and the Russian aggression against Ukraine that followed enhanced the anti-colonial and pro-democracy character of the Ukrainian autocephalous movement. The majority of those who had been against autocephaly of the Orthodox church in Ukraine also turned against the Revolution of dignity. When the Russian troops occupied Crimea and the eastern regions of Ukraine, they collaborated with the occupants—some even participated in the conflict on the Russian side with guns. Many in Ukraine have identified the anti-autocephalist propaganda as a part of the Russian effort to keep Ukraine in its political orbit, coming in

74. See Johnston, "Religio-Nationalist Subcultures under the Communists."

75. See Hovorun, "Churches in the Ukrainian Public Square"; Hovorun, "The Church in the Bloodlands."

one package with the general anti-Ukrainian propaganda and the war. In this context, autocephaly is increasingly perceived as a vitally important instrument of liberation from the imperial past that also secures democratic development of the civil society.

THE CASE OF THE ORTHODOX CHURCH IN AMERICA

The Orthodox Church in America (OCA) features a distinct type of autocephaly. It was not inspired by the motives that led to other autocephalies like etatism, phyletism, nationalism, or even anti-imperialism. The OCA was created with the idea of building "Orthodox unity in America with full respect for, but in full independence from ethnic or political interests of the various immigrant groups."[76] American autocephaly grew in opposition to the mentality of "diaspora," which refuses to embrace fully the country of emigration as one's own, romanticizes the remote homeland, and displays strong nationalistic tendencies.

Orthodox Christianity was planted in the American soil in 1794, when the first Russian missionaries arrived in Alaska. Most prominent among them were the monk Herman (1756–1837) from the Valaam monastery in north Russia and the priest John Veniaminov, later metropolitan Innocent of Moscow (1797–1879). After Russia sold Alaska to the United States in 1867, the Russian church established a separate diocese there (1870). In the late 1860s, two Russian parishes were established in San Francisco and New York, and one Greek parish in New Orleans. In 1872, the Russian Orthodox diocese moved from Alaska to San Francisco. The Orthodox community in the United States began growing rapidly with the mass immigration of Greeks, Slavs, and Arabs. Simultaneously, a large group of the eastern-rite Catholics converted to Orthodoxy under the guidance of Alexis Toth (1853–1909). From 1898 to 1907, the diocese was supervised by bishop Tikhon Belavin, the eventual patriarch of Moscow (1918–25). He expanded the diocese to encompass the entire country and moved his see to New York. The diocese was prepared to become the basis for building a local Orthodox church in the US. This did not happen because of the Bolshevik revolution in Russia. Meletios Metaxakis (1871–1935), first in his capacity of archbishop of Athens and later as patriarch of Constantinople, also attempted to bring the diverse Orthodox immigrant groups from eastern and southern Europe into one

76. Grigorieff, "The Orthodox Church in America," 138.

ecclesiastical structure. He failed, and the American Orthodoxy divided between numerous jurisdictions and turned, as Alexander Schmemann put it, into "a blatant denial of all that learned Orthodox delegates to ecumenical gatherings were at the same time proclaiming to be the 'essence' of Orthodoxy as the True Church and the Una Sancta."[77]

The autocephaly of the Orthodox church in the United States was attempted with the ambition of coming back to the authentic "identity of the Church's 'essence' in space and time,"[78] in the words of Schmemann. The idea behind this attempt was to create an island of canonical and ecclesiological "normality" in the sea of diverse Orthodox jurisdictions. It would be a church respectful of various ethnic and cultural backgrounds, but also would unite them into one community. This autocephaly was supposed to serve as a platform to build a church that would eventually embrace all the Orthodox in America. It would also serve as a model of consolidation of the Orthodox church in other regions, primarily Western Europe.

In 1970, the patriarch of Moscow Alexiy I (1945–70), granted autocephaly to the so-called "Metropolia," a structure that developed from the old diocese of the Russian church and then lost touch with Moscow.[79] This act of the Russian church elicited strong resistance from other Orthodox jurisdictions, primarily from the patriarchate of Constantinople. Constantinople, together with some other churches, would not recognize the autocephaly of the Orthodox church in America. To this day, it is only recognized by the Russian, Bulgarian, Georgian, Polish, and Czech and Slovak churches. Thus, the Orthodox church in America has not achieved its goal so far. It did not unify Orthodox communities in the United States, but only added to their diversity.

Nevertheless, the American autocephaly constitutes a unique model of the localization of the church. It demonstrates how the church can overcome divisions along ethnic, cultural, and political lines for the sake of ecclesial unity. The example of the Orthodox church in America and its rejection by some other Orthodox churches also shows that the borderlines, which have nothing to do with the nature and purpose of the church, remain strong and capable of dividing Christians.

---

77. Schmemann, *Church, World, Mission*, 86.

78. Ibid., 95.

79. In 1947, patriarch Alexiy I imposed interdict on the "Metropolia".

Apart from its initial canonical and administrative function, through the centuries of its evolution autocephaly adopted a number of other capacities that by far exceeded its canonical rationale. It has acted among other things as a political, ideological, and cultural phenomenon. It has adopted so many noncanonical and noneccesial connotations that it appears to have become paralyzed. This paralysis was manifest in the process of preparation for the "Holy and Great Council of the Orthodox Church." The church chose not to discuss at the council the procedure for granting autocephaly, in spite of the fact that it remains one of the burning issues in inter-Orthodox relations. This is because two approaches to this issue remain irreconcilable. One is that autocephaly can be granted by the mother church. The other is that only the patriarch of Constantinople can grant autocephaly, with the consent of other churches. The Orthodox churches cannot agree on this issue and have failed to work out a solution that would be accepted at the eventual council.

When autocephaly stumbles, it has to be reinvented again, which in fact did happen many times in its history. However, the churches that will decide what autocephaly should be at the next stage of its evolution must make sure that it will not work as an instrument of fragmentation, but rather as an instrument of consolidation and harmonization of the church life.

5

Pyramids: Primacy

THE RISE OF THE administrative structures of the church raised the issue of primacy among them.[1] As structures such as canonical territories or autocephaly became more developed the issue of primacy became harder to solve. Primacy seems to be hardly compatible with the idea of sovereignty, which is embedded in the modern concept of autocephaly. For any church, to recognize the primacy of another church, implies giving up some of its sovereignty. This is the reason why it is so difficult for the Orthodox churches to reach an agreement on how to understand primacy.

Inability to arrive at a common Orthodox vision of primacy is the main obstacle in the dialogue with the Roman Catholic church. Substantial discussions on this matter during the sessions of the bilateral Orthodox-Catholic dialogue have failed to produce a common model of primacy. An essential disagreement remains regarding the nature of primacy on the universal level. For most Orthodox, this primacy is a matter of convenience and agreement between the churches. The bishop of Rome was given an honor to be *primus inter pares*, not by divine right, but only because the churches decided so. Such a position, however, is unacceptable to the Roman Catholic participants in the dialogue, who insist that the primacy of the bishop of Rome is *jus divinum*. At the same

---

1. Some theses of this chapter have appeared in Hovorun, "Does Primacy Belong to the Nature of the Church?"

time, when speaking of primacy on the "regional" level, which is the level of the autocephalous churches, both Orthodox and Roman Catholic sides agree that the primacy there is merely a matter of convention. (In fact, a few individual Orthodox theologians still disagree with this position. They insist that even on the regional level, primacy functions by divine right and is based on trinitarian and christological models.) A key to solve the problem of primacy is to decide whether primacy, thus, is a part of the nature of the church or its scaffolding, just as any other ecclesial structure.

Interpretation of primacy as a divine institution is more a characteristic feature of the western theological tradition. The initial western exegesis of the Roman primacy was based on the words of Christ: "You are Peter, and on this rock I will build my church, and the gates of hell will not prevail against it" (Matt. 16:18).[2] On the grounds of the authority of Peter, Boniface I (in office 418–22) in Late Antiquity articulated one of the earliest papal claims over the territories beyond the direct Roman influence, in eastern Illyria.[3] During the Middle Ages, the idea of the Roman primacy as an embodiment of the universal dimension of the church was re-articulated by the scholastics, who had become enamoured by the Aristotelian dialectics of particular and universal.[4] They identified the idea of universality with the particular church of Rome. The assumption that the universal is more important than particular was taken as an argument to justify the medieval Roman claims for primacy. These claims culminated in the bull promulgated by Pope Boniface VIII (in office 1294–1303), *Unam sanctam* (1302): "We declare, we proclaim, we define that it is absolutely necessary for salvation that every human creature be subject to the Roman Pontiff." The historical trajectory of papal claims from Boniface I to Boniface VIII went up by riding on the idea that papacy is a divine institution. This idea was summarized by cardinal Thomas Cajetan (1469–1534): "The authority of the pope is immediately from God and revealed in Sacred Scripture."[5]

During the twentieth century, the traditional scholastic schemata of primacy were significantly updated. In its struggle with Neoscholasticism,

---

2. See Ray, *Upon This Rock.*

3. See Dunn, "Boniface I and the Illyrian Churches on the Translation of Perigenes to Corinth."

4. See Miller, "The Divine Right of the Papacy in Recent Ecumenical Theology."

5. *De divina institutione pontifucatus Romani Pontificis* (1521), in Burns and Izbicki, *Conciliarism and Papalism*, 2.

the "new theology" (*nouvelle théologie*)⁶ refreshed the medieval interpretations of primacy, which nevertheless continued to be considered as innate to the church. For example, Hans Urs von Balthasar (1905–88), a prominent figure in the new Catholic theology, while acknowledging that the papal office should be not seen as one *above* the church, insisted that it is *innate in* the church. Papacy, to him, is the will of God, and not a simply product of the historical developments in the church:

> The office of Peter is one of several indispensable elements in the ecclesiastical structure, thus freeing it from the pyramid-like isolation to which it consented, partly involuntarily, by permitting itself to be modelled on the pattern of Imperial Rome and, partly voluntarily, in reaction to the encroachments of medieval emperors.⁷

Von Balthasar, together with other progressive Roman Catholic theologians, suggested "eucharistic ecclesiology" as a new hermeneutical instrument to reinterpret the structures of the church. Henri de Lubac (1896–1991) famously articulated the basic idea of this ecclesiology in 1953: "The Eucharist makes the church."⁸ Soon after that, the Orthodox embraced the eucharistic ecclesiology as their particular confessional identity.⁹ A protagonist of Orthodox eucharistic ecclesiology, John Zizioulas (b. 1931), has applied it to justify primacy on all levels of the church: local (communities), regional (local churches), and universal. His departure point is the level of communities, which gather around the eucharist. He derives the primacy of the bishop in a community from his presidency in the eucharist.¹⁰ Zizioulas extrapolates this primacy to the regional and universal levels of the church. For him, it is not only useful, but necessary to have a *primus* in the church on different levels.¹¹ The necessity of primacy stems from the nature of the church. Zizioulas builds his idea of primacy on the juxtaposition of one and many in the church.¹²

---

6. See Mettepenningen, *Nouvelle Théologie—New Theology*.

7. Von Balthasar, *The Office of Peter and the Structure of the Church*, 21.

8. De Lubac, *Méditation sur l'église*, 115–16; see also McPartlan, *Sacrament of Salvation*.

9. See Ware, "Sobornost and Eucharistic Ecclesiology," 227.

10. See Zizioulas, *The One and the Many*, 236–53.

11. Zizioulas, "Primacy in the Church," 125.

12. See Zizioulas, *The One and the Many*.

He turns the "one" from this conceptual pair into the "first"[13] and thus justifies primacy from the perspective of the Orthodox tradition.

In addition to eucharistic ecclesiology, Zizioulas has employed other theological foundations to substantiate primacy as an intrinsic feature of the church. He has particularly used trinitarian theology, where he emphasizes the monarchy of the Father.[14] From the unique role of the Father as the One who gives birth to the Son and sends the Holy Spirit, Zizioulas draws a conclusion about the primacy of the bishop in a community, as well as about *primus* among other primates of the local churches. In this way, he advocates the primacy of the church of Constantinople among other local Orthodox churches. In the same way, he also suggests how to accommodate the primacy of Rome in the Orthodox matrix of thinking.

John Zizioulas's theological presuppositions and conclusions regarding primacy, however, have been criticized from different perspectives. Thus, the overemphasis of the primacy of the Father in the Holy Trinity endangers the fundamental idea of the equality of the trinitarian persons. It contradicts Zizioulas's own concern not to give priority either to the nature or to the hypostases in the Holy Trinity.[15] Contrary to this intention, he certainly overstates the role of the Father. Opponents of his ecclesiology have noticed that one has a logical difficulty when seeking to pass from the assumed hierarchy in the Holy Trinity to primacy within the church. For instance, as the Father is the beginning of the other two hypostases in the Holy Trinity, so any local church that claims for itself primacy over other churches, should be parental to them.[16] This, however, does not apply to the local churches that claim primacy for themselves in real life. Only the community in Jerusalem can be regarded as a parent of all the rest of the communities. The patriarchate of Jerusalem, however, has only fourth position in the Orthodox diptycha and does not demonstrate any ambition for primacy.

13. See Shishkov, "Metropolitan John Zizioulas on Primacy in the Church."

14. See Zizioulas, *Communion and Otherness*, 113–54.

15. Zizioulas, "Primacy in the Church," 118.

16. See an observation by Andrey Shishkov: "For the principle of 'the one and the many' to be also a foundation for primacy, it has to include an additional precondition. 'The one' has to be the origin of the existence of 'the many' and source of their unity so that it may also become 'the first.' In ecclesiology however, the case is quite different. If this logic is observed in the field of ecclesiology, then there must be a local church that gives rise to the other local churches. This local church has to be 'the one' in which 'the many' find their unity." Shishkov, "Metropolitan John Zizioulas on Primacy in the Church," 214.

The problem with the interpretation of primacy as pertinent to the nature of the church seems to be even deeper. Primacy is a pinnacle of the assumed hierarchical structure of the church. If we accept that the church is hierarchical in its nature, then primacy comes as the climax of the church's hierarchy. When we assume that primacy belongs to the nature of the church, then hierarchy does too. Hierarchy here means not only bishops and priests, but any vertically ordered administrative or sacramental structure in the church.

The assumption that the church is hierarchical in its nature is widely held both in the West and East. Two early authors addressed this assumption, each in his own way. By strange coincidence, both of them chose to hide their real names: Ambrosiaster (flourished in the late 360s–mid-380s) and ps-Dionysius the Areopagite (flourished in the late fifth to the early sixth centuries). Ambrosiaster was more analytic and less metaphysical than Ps-Dionysius in explaining the church's hierarchy. He acknowledged that this hierarchy was similar to the political and social hierarchies of the Roman world in his time, particularly at the imperial court.[17] Ambrosiaster effectively projected the earthly hierarchies to the divine realities. His views surprisingly echo in the poststructuralist insight that "draws out a metaphysical background and its unquestioned role"[18] from the structures.

In contrast to Ambrosiaster and the poststructuralists, Ps-Dionysius placed the structures of the church in a metaphysical matrix and projected them from top to bottom: from God to the church. While for Ambrosiaster the social and political realities constitute a matrix for the ecclesial hierarchy, for Ps-Dionysius, it is God who is the source and cause of the orders in the church. Hierarchy, for Ambrosiaster, is conventional; it stems from the experience of human life and nature. For

---

17. Ambrosiaster used a similar language for the divine, ecclesial, social, and political hierarchies: "But Christ is the representative (*vicarius*) of the Father and the overseer (*antestes*) and therefore is also called priest (*sacerdos*). Similarly, the Holy Spirit, also sent like an overseer (*antestes*), was called priest (*sacerdos*) of the highest God, not highest priest (*summus sacerdos*) like our [bishops] take to themselves in the sacrifice, because, although Christ and the Holy Spirit are of one substance, nevertheless the rank of each one is to be preserved. And so they are called priests (*sacerdotes*) or legates, because they show forth in themselves him whose legates they are; for they are his image. And thus Christ and the Holy Spirit, having naturally the image of God, are said to be his priests (*sacerdotes*)." Questio 109. 21, in Lunn-Rockliffe, *Ambrosiaster's Political Theology*, 118; see also ibid., 44.

18. Williams, *Understanding Poststructuralism*, 29.

Pyramids: Primacy 133

Ps-Dionysius, it is sacred and descending from the heaven. This is a classical Neoplatonic outlook on the hierarchical order of the universe. It was articulated by such thinkers as Plotinus (c. 204/5–270), who wrote of radiation (*perilampsis*, περίλαμψις) of the One that goes down to the lower levels of being;[19] and Proclus (410/12–485), who developed the idea of the transmission of the "divine ray" through hierarchical structures. The Neoplatonic concept of hierarchy, in its turn, goes back to Plato and Aristotle. It is, therefore, important to understand hierarchy in Neoplatonism, Aristotle, and Plato, in order to trace the origins of the ps-Dionysian hierarchical thinking.

The Platonic model of the hierarchy of beings is the earliest one. According to Plato, things can be distinguished as existent according to participation (*metechein*, μετέχειν) or according to nature.[20] The things according to participation are inferior to the things existent *per se*. This was probably the earliest draft of the hierarchy of being, where some ways of existence were claimed to be higher than others.

Aristotle developed Plato's hierarchy of being further. In the distinction between the particular and the common, which has been explored in the chapter "Fine Pencil Lines" of this book, he ordered these categories

19. See for instance *Ennead* 5.4.2; Tollefsen, *Activity and Participation in Late Antique and Early Christian Thought*, 21.

20. See *Parmenid* 158a:
"τοῦ ἑνός. εἰ γὰρ ἕκαστον αὐτῶν μόριόν ἐστι, τό γε ἕκαστον εἶναι ἓν δήπου σημαίνει, ἀφωρισμένον μὲν τῶν ἄλλων, καθ᾽ αὑτὸ δὲ ὄν, εἴπερ ἕκαστον ἔσται.
—ὀρθῶς.
—μετέχοι δέ γε ἂν τοῦ ἑνὸς δῆλον ὅτι ἄλλο ὂν ἢ ἕν· οὐ γὰρ ἂν μετεῖχεν, ἀλλ᾽ ἦν ἂν αὐτὸ ἕν. νῦν δὲ ἑνὶ μὲν εἶναι πλὴν αὐτῷ τῷ ἑνὶ ἀδύνατόν που.
—ἀδύνατον.
—μετέχειν δέ γε τοῦ ἑνὸς ἀνάγκη τῷ τε ὅλῳ καὶ τῷ μορίῳ. τὸ μὲν γὰρ ἓν ὅλον ἔσται, οὗ μόρια τὰ μόρια· τὸ δ᾽ αὖ ἕκαστον ἓν μόριον τοῦ ὅλου, ὃ ἂν ᾖ."
English translation:
"The word 'each' implies that it is one, separated from the rest, and existing by itself; otherwise it will not be 'each.'
—True.
—But its participation in the one clearly implies that it is other than the one, for if not, it would not partake of the one, but would actually be one; but really it is impossible for anything except one itself to be one.
—Yes, it is impossible.
—And both the whole and the part must necessarily participate in the one; for the one will be a whole of which the parts are parts, and again each individual one which is a part of a whole will be a part of the whole.
—Yes."
Plato in Twelve Volumes, vol. 9, translated by Fowler, 1925.

hierarchically. The common "secondary substance," to him, is superior to the particular "primary substance," which implies a hierarchy between these categories. There is also a hierarchy within the category of the common substances, where Aristotle distinguished between species (*eidos*, εἶδος) and genus (*genos*, γένος). Genus is more general than species. Species is a subject to genus, in a similar way that the individual thing is a subject to species:

> But as the primary substances stand to the other things, so the species stands to the genus: the species is a subject for the genus (for the genera are predicated of the species but the species are not predicated reciprocally of the genera).[21]

Aristotle determined the secondary substance as a "thing *said of* a subject" (*en kath hypokeimenou*, ἐν καθ' ὑποκειμένου).[22] The hierarchy between the particular and the common categories consists in the fact that the latter can "be said of" the former. For instance, the common features of trees can be applied to any individual tree. At the same time, the particularities of an individual tree are not applicable to all trees. According to the same hierarchical order of being, genus is something that can "be said of" species, even though they both belong to the category of the common substances:

> Whenever one thing is predicated of another as of a subject, all things said of what is predicated will be said of the subject also. For example, man is predicated of the individual man, and animal of man; so animal will be predicated of the individual man also—for the individual man is both a man and an animal.[23]

---

21. Cat. 2b.17–21: "Ὡς δέ γε αἱ πρῶται οὐσίαι πρὸς τὰ ἄλλα ἔχουσιν, οὕτω καὶ τὸ εἶδος πρὸς τὸ γένος ἔχει· ὑπόκειται γὰρ τὸ εἶδος τῷ γένει· τὰ μὲν γὰρ γένη κατὰ τῶν εἰδῶν κατηγορεῖται, τὰ δὲ εἴδη κατὰ τῶν γενῶν οὐκ ἀντιστρέφει." English translation by Ackrill, *Aristotle's* Categories *and* De Interpretatione.

22. Cat. 1a.20: "Οἷον ἄνθρωπος καθ' ὑποκειμένου μὲν λέγεται τοῦ τινὸς ἀνθρώπου." English translation: "For example, man is said of a subject, the individual man." Ackrill, *Aristotle's* Categories *and* De Interpretatione.

23. Cat. 1b.10–15: "Ὅταν ἕτερον καθ' ἑτέρου κατηγορῆται ὡς καθ' ὑποκειμένου, ὅσα κατὰ τοῦ κατηγορουμένου λέγεται, πάντα καὶ κατὰ τοῦ ὑποκειμένου ῥηθήσεται· οἷον ἄνθρωπος κατὰ τοῦ τινὸς ἀνθρώπου κατηγορεῖται, τὸ δὲ ζῷον κατὰ τοῦ ἀνθρώπου· οὐκοῦν καὶ κατὰ τοῦ τινὸς ἀνθρώπου τὸ ζῷον κατηγορηθήσεται· ὁ γὰρ τὶς ἄνθρωπος καὶ ἄνθρωπός ἐστι καὶ ζῷον." English translation by Ackrill, *Aristotle's* Categories *and* De Interpretatione.

In sum, the three categories: primary substance, species, and genus, constitute a hierarchy. The primary substance is at the bottom of this hierarchy,[24] while genus is on its top. Genus is prior[25] to the category of species.[26] The category of species is closer to the primary substance than the category of genus is. In the words of Aristotle:

> Of the secondary substances the species is more a substance than the genus, since it is nearer to the primary substance. For if one is to say of the primary substance what it is, it will be more informative and apt to give the species than the genus. For example, it would be more informative to say of the individual man that he is a man than that he is an animal (since the one is more distinctive of the individual man while the other is more general); and more informative to say of the individual tree that it is a tree than that is a plant.[27]

Later Neoplatonic philosophers synthesized the Platonic hierarchy of participation with the Aristotelian hierarchy of categories, and produced their own hierarchy of being. This hierarchy is more "hierarchical," as it were, than either the Platonic or Aristotelian hierarchies. The

---

24. The secondary substances do not exist without the primary ones: "Οἷον τὸ ζῷον κατὰ τοῦ ἀνθρώπου κατηγορεῖται, οὐκοῦν καὶ κατὰ τοῦ τινὸς ἀνθρώπου, εἰ γὰρ κατὰ μηδενὸς τῶν τινῶν ἀνθρώπων, οὐδὲ κατὰ ἀνθρώπου ὅλως . . . ὥστε μὴ οὐσῶν τῶν πρώτων οὐσιῶν ἀδύνατον τῶν ἄλλων τι εἶναι" (Cat. 2a.36–2b.1, 2b.6b–2b.6c). English translation: "For example, animal is predicated of man and therefore also of the individual man; for were it predicated of none of the individual man it would not predicated of man at all. . . . So if the primary substances did not exist it would be impossible for any of the other things to exist." Ackrill, *Aristotle's* Categories *and* De Interpretatione.

25. More about the categories of priority and posteriority see Aristotle's *Metaphysics* Δ 11.

26. Cat. 15a.4–7: "Τὰ δὲ γένη τῶν εἰδῶν ἀεὶ πρότερα· οὐ γὰρ ἀντιστρέφει κατὰ τὴν τοῦ εἶναι ἀκολούθησιν· οἷον ἐνύδρου μὲν ὄντος ἔστι ζῷον, ζῴου δὲ ὄντος οὐκ ἀνάγκη ἔνυδρον εἶναι." English translation: "Genera, however, are always prior to species since they do not reciprocate as to implication of existence; e.g. if there is a fish there is an animal, but if there is an animal there is not necessary a fish." English translation by Ackrill, *Aristotle's* Categories *and* De Interpretatione.

27. Cat. 2b.7–14: "Τῶν δὲ δευτέρων οὐσιῶν μᾶλλον οὐσία τὸ εἶδος τοῦ γένους· ἔγγιον γὰρ τῆς πρώτης οὐσίας ἐστίν. ἐὰν γὰρ ἀποδιδῷ τις τὴν πρώτην οὐσίαν τί ἐστι, γνωριμώτερον καὶ οἰκειότερον ἀποδώσει τὸ εἶδος ἀποδιδοὺς ἢ τὸ γένος· οἷον τὸν τινὰ ἄνθρωπον γνωριμώτερον ἂν ἀποδοίη ἄνθρωπον ἀποδιδοὺς ἢ ζῷον, τὸ μὲν γὰρ ἴδιον μᾶλλον τοῦ τινὸς ἀνθρώπου, τὸ δὲ κοινότερον, καὶ τὸ τὶ δένδρον ἀποδιδοὺς γνωριμώτερον ἀποδώσει δένδρον ἀποδιδοὺς ἢ φυτόν." English translation by Ackrill, *Aristotle's* Categories *and* De Interpretatione.

idea of hierarchy became foundational for Neoplatonism. In the words of Ronald Hathaway, "The base ontology in Neoplatonism is a hierarchy of minds, intelligible forms, disembodied souls, embodied souls, bodies, and the underlying matter of bodies."[28] According to the Neoplatonic interpretation, hierarchy is sacred, rooted in the divine. Hence is the wording that the Neoplatonists constructed for it—"sacred principality" (*hierarchia*, ἱεραρχία).

One of the key figures in Neoplatonism, from whom Christian theology borrowed its dialectics, Porphyry of Tyre (c. 234–c. 305), particularly elaborated on the Aristotelian hierarchy of categories. He introduced a fourfold division of the categories. According to this division, all things are either substances or accidents—a distinction that reflects the earlier Platonic hierarchy of beings through participation. Therefore, they are "either universal substance or particular substance or universal accidents or particular accidents."[29] For Porphyry, "universal" (*katholou*, καθόλου) is the same as the Aristotelian "thing *said of* a subject," while the "accidents" (*symbebēkota*, συμβεβηκότα) are the same as the Aristotle's "things *in* a subject."[30] Universal can be not only a substance, but also an accident. In this case, accident applies to both species and genus.[31] Obviously, accidents are inferior to the essence, when interpreted in the terms of the hierarchy of being. This makes the hierarchy of the categories, which had been suggested by Aristotle, more complicated, and more emphatic in Neoplatonism. At the bottom of the Neoplatonic pyramid of categories, there are the accidents of the particular things, while on the top—the universal substance of genus.

---

28. Hathaway, "The Anatomy of a Neoplatonist Metaphysical Proof," 131.

29. *In Aristotelis Categorias* 4,1.71.20-24: "ἢ οὐσία καθόλου ἢ οὐσία ἐπὶ μέρους ἢ συμβεβηκότα καθόλου ἢ συμβεβηκότα ἐπὶ μέρους." English translation by Strange, *Porphyry on Aristotle Categories*, 65.

30. *In Aristotelis Categorias* 4,1.73.29-35.

31. Porphyry illustrated this by the example of knowledge as an accident of soul: "'Η γὰρ ἐπιστήμη τῇ ψυχῇ συμβεβηκυῖα ὑποκείμενον αὐτῇ ἔχει τὴν ψυχήν· ὑπόκειται γὰρ τῇ ἐπιστήμῃ ἡ ψυχή. καθολικὴ γὰρ οὖσα κατὰ τῶν μερικωτέρων ἐπιστημῶν λέγεται οἷον κατὰ τῆς γραμματικῆς· γένος γάρ ἐστιν ἡ ἐπιστήμη τῆς γραμματικῆς. ἔστι δὲ συμβεβηκὸς ἡ γραμματική, συμβεβηκὸς δὴ καὶ ἡ ἐπιστήμη." *In Aristotelis Categorias* 4,1.76.19-26. English translation: "For knowledge, which is an accident of the soul, has soul as its subject, for the soul underlies knowledge. Being universal, it is predicated of more specific forms of knowledge, for example grammatical knowledge, for knowledge is the genus of grammar. Grammar is an accident, and so is knowledge. For the species and genera of accidents are themselves accidents." Strange, *Porphyry on Aristotle Categories*, 59.

Proclus Lycaeus (412–85) went considerably further than Porphyry in developing the notion of hierarchy. Following the general Neoplatonic line of blending the Platonic and Aristotelian hierarchies of being, he added to the *ontological* hierarchies developed by Porphyry a *theological* one. He sorted out the gods of syncretic polytheism into a theological hierarchy. Proclus combined Plato's theology with the Orphic and Chaldean theogonies and interpreted them in the terms of Neoplatonic ontology. He thus produced a complex scheme with a religious "henad" as its basic element. "Henad" is a place that a god from the polytheistic pantheon occupies in the Neoplatonic structure of being. It is a "unifying goodness and has this mode of existence *qua* god; but the primal God is the Good unqualified and Unity unqualified, whilst each of those posterior to him is a particular goodness and a particular henad."[32] Proclus blended the ontological and polytheistic hierarchies into a structure, which connected the One, the upper world emanating from the One, and the perceptible world into a complex system, as Radek Chlup has illustrated in the figure below (Figure 1).

It is clear from this scheme that the big blocks of being (Being, Life, Intellect, *etc.*), according to Proclus, are ordered hierarchically. Within each block, there is an internal hierarchy of participation. What is particularly important for our argument here is that the items within these internal hierarchies correspond to similar items in other blocks. These elements are divine, and therefore the structure is *hier*archical literally, i.e., sorting out the *sacred*.

Exactly the same Proclean logic was adopted by Ps-Dionysius in describing the celestial and ecclesial hierarchies.[33] Eric Perl has epitomized the similarity and differences between them: "Proclus hymns the many modes of unity as a multiplicity of gods; Dionysius hymns God as the many modes of unity."[34] Particular coherent are their stratifications of being. Ps-Dionysius wrote in his *Divine Names* regarding this:

32. Chlup, *Proclus*, 113.
33. See Hathaway, *Hierarchy and the Definition of Order*, 37.
34. Perl, *Theophany*, 68.

Figure 1: Hierarchy and interconnectedness of beings according to Proclus.[35]

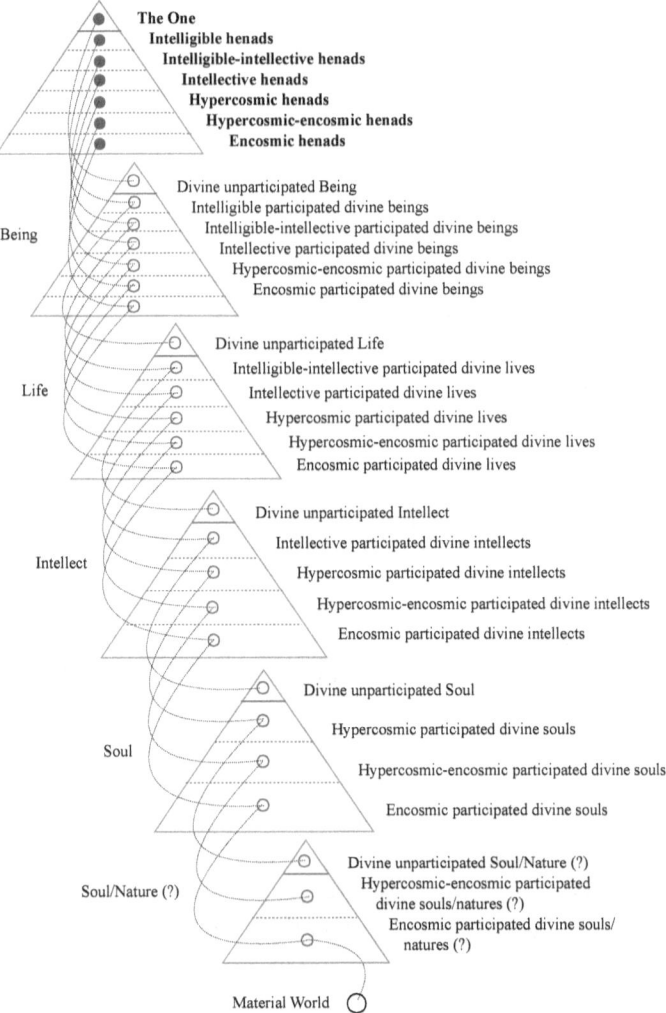

But since the divine intellects also are [in a way] above other beings, and live [in a way] above the other living things, and think and know [in a way] above sense and reason . . . they are nearer to the Good, participating in it in an eminent way, and receiving from it more and greater gifts; likewise rational beings excel sensitive ones, having more by the eminence of reason, and the

35. Based on Chlup, *Proclus*, 123.

latter [excel other living things] by sensation, and [living things excel mere beings] by life. And . . . the things which participate more in the one and infinitely-giving God are closer to him and more divine than the rest.[36]

Ps-Dionysius branded this structure of being as "hierarchy," which he defined as "a sacred order, a state of understanding and an activity approximating as closely as possible to the divine. And it is uplifted to the imitation of God in proportion to the enlightenments divinely given to it."[37] The concept of hierarchy became extremely popular and enjoyed a wide reception in the church. It influenced the church's power structures, shaped its political philosophy, and regulated church-state relations up until modernity.[38] According to Marie-Dominique Chenu, the ps-Dionysian

> "hierarchical" conception of the universe would cast over men's minds a spell comparable to that cast by the scientific mythos of evolution in the nineteenth century. The key to the understanding of the universe, and of man in the universe, was taken to be the ordered, dynamic, and progressive chain of all beings—a chain in which causality and meaning fall together, and in which each being is a "theophany," a revelation of God.[39]

Eric Perl is convincing in demonstrating how deeply and widely rooted in Neoplatonic philosophy ps-Dionysius's ontology, including his idea of hierarchy, is.[40] However, can his hierarchical concept be equally grounded in the sources of the Christian tradition? It is difficult to answer to this question affirmatively. Ps-Dionysius might have been inspired by the hierarchies in ancient Israel, both sacerdotal and political. However, these hierarchies, although definitely implied in the Torah,[41] rather mirrored the social realities around Israel, particularly the stratification and political structures in ancient Near Eastern societies.[42] Yet, more than the

36. *De divinis nominibus* V.3, PG 3, 817B. English translation by Perl, *Theophany*, 70.

37. *De coel.* 3.1, translated by Luibheid in Ivanovic, "The Ecclesiology of Dionysius the Areopagite," 29.

38. See Mousnier, *Social Hierarchies*; Denton, *Orders and Hierarchies in Late Medieval and Renaissance Europe*.

39. Chenu, *Nature, Man and Society in the Twelfth Century*, 23.

40. Perl, *Theophany*.

41. See Niditch, *The Wiley Blackwell Companion to Ancient Israel*, 307.

42. See Olyan, *Rites and Rank*, 3–5; Clements, *The World of Ancient Israel*, 130.

Torah or New Testament literature, Ps-Dionysius was influenced by later Jewish apocryphal angelology. He had access to this angelology through the Syriac Christian apocrypha, in texts such as the *Testament of Adam*.[43]

Ps-Dionysius was a pioneer of hierarchies among the fathers of the church.[44] Before him, the word "hierarchy" was scarcely used in the patristic lexicon. It occurred first under the names of Clement of Rome (c. 88–c. 97) and Hippolytus (c. 170–c. 235), but not in their genuine treatises.[45] Therefore, its use reflects views later than the time of those two men. The earliest genuine occurrence of the word is in the fourth century, when it was used by Didymus,[46] who was influenced by the Alexandrian Neoplatonic school.[47] Ps-Dionysius introduced the word into Christian theology and ecclesial practice[48] and became the most devoted user of it, with over two hundred references in total.

True, the fathers prior to Ps-Dionysius also constructed hierarchies of beings. However, in most cases they applied a different logic. They followed either the Platonic or Aristotelian models, which were not as strongly hierarchical as the Neoplatonic one.[49] Even when they relied on Neoplatonism, they were closer to Porphyry than to Proclus. This is because they preferred to build *immanent* hierarchies, which included such elements as being, life, and wisdom.[50] Although they interpreted the structures of being in terms of participation in the divine, they hesitated to produce *transcendental* hierarchies, which would have to do with the sphere of divine.[51] Therefore, their hierarchies were not quite hierarchies in the literal meaning of the word—they were not as sacred as Ps-Dionysius envisaged his own hierarchies. The most eloquent witness to this is Ambrosiaster, who, as was shown earlier in this chapter, derived hierarchy from the socio-political realities of the Roman world.[52]

43. See Arthur, *Pseudo-Dionysius as Polemicist*, 69.

44. See Muehlberger, *Angels in Late Ancient Christianity*, 21–22.

45. Ps-Clementina, *Epitome de gestis Petri praemetaphrastica* (CPG 1015(6)), 180.5; and Hippolytus's spurium *De consummatione mundi* (CPG 1910), 41.16.

46. *Fragmenta in Psalmos (e commentario altero)* (CPG 2551), fr. 461.1.

47. See O'Keefe and R. Reno, *Sanctified Vision*, 30.

48. See Louth, *Maximus the Confessor*, 30.

49. Biriukov, "Hierarchies of Beings in the Patristic Thought," 278–79.

50. See for instance *Ambiguum* 24 by Maximus the Confessor.

51. See Tollefsen, *Activity and Participation in Late Antique and Early Christian Thought*, 194.

52. *Questio* 109. 21: "Christus autem vicarius patris est et antestes ac per hoc dicitur

Moreover, the ps-Dionysian concept of hierarchy contradicts the nature of the church as it could be interpreted from the same Neoplatonic perspective, as applied to distinguish the natures in Christ. Thus, a basic assumption of classical Christology, as it was articulated in the era of Chalcedon, stems from Aristotelian-Porphyrian logic and holds that the natures of Christ and their properties are unchangeable.[53] If a property of the nature changes then the nature must change as well.[54] When applied to the nature of the church, this idea helps us identify what are its natural properties. They are the ones that never changed in the church. Otherwise their change would have altered the nature of the church. The marks of the church enlisted in the Nicene Creed: one, holy, catholic, and apostolic, can be certainly regarded as natural properties of the church. However, one cannot say the same about hierarchy. There was time when the church was not hierarchical, yet it was church. Hierarchism in the church oscillated depending on the social and political circumstances. If hierarchy belonged to the ecclesial nature, this would have made the nature of the church vulnerable to these circumstances. This is, however, unacceptable from the theological point of view. Therefore, the church is not hierarchical in its nature. The hierarchical principle is not even its natural property. It was borrowed from outside the church and remains there as its scaffolding.

In application to primacy this means that the assumption that primacy belongs to the nature of the church is not correct. This assumption

---

et sacerdos. similiter et spiritus sanctus missus quasi antestes sacerdos appellatus est excelsi dei, non summus, sicut nostri in oblatione praesumunt, quia, quamvis unius sint substantiae Christus et sanctus spiritus, unius cuiusque tamen ordo servandus est. sacerdotes igitur vel legati ideo dicuntur, quia illum in se ostendunt cuius legati sunt; sunt enim eius imago. ac per hoc Christus et sanctus spiritus naturaliter habentes dei imaginem sacerdotes eius dicuntur." In Lunn-Rockliffe, *Ambrosiaster's Political Theology*, 118.

53. The most famous text in this regard is the definition by the council of Chalcedon, which professed Christ "in two natures which undergo no confusion, no change, no division, no separation" (ἐν δύο φύσεσιν ἀσυγχύτως ἀτρέπτως ἀδιαιρέτως ἀχωρίστως γνωριζόμενον). Tanner, *Decrees of the Ecumenical Councils*, vol. 1, 86; Alberigo, *Conciliorum oecumenicorum generaliumque decreta*, 137.378-80. Unchangeability of both divinity and humanity of Christ was also emphasized by the most important theologian in the period of the christological controversies, Cyril of Alexandria: see Cyril of Alexandria, *Sermo ad Alexandrinos*, in Pusey, *Sancti patris nostri Cyrilli archiepiscopi Alexandrini in D. Joannis evangelium*, vol. 3, 539.25.

54. This was stated by the sixth ecumenical council in Constantinople (680-81): ACO2 II.2, 776.1-10.

142 Scaffolds of the Church

is rather Proclean. Indeed, quite in line with Proclus, the ontological hierarchism places the Triune God on the top of the pyramid of primacy. In the Trinity, the Father as the source of the Son and of the Holy Spirit, is the *primus inter pares*. Through the participation in the life of God, the church adopts a similar kind of primacy, which it exercises on three levels: local, regional, and universal. Each level in this scheme looks like big hierarchical blocks of the "henads" in the Proclean hierarchy of deities (see Figure 2):

Figure 2: Hierarchy of primacies.

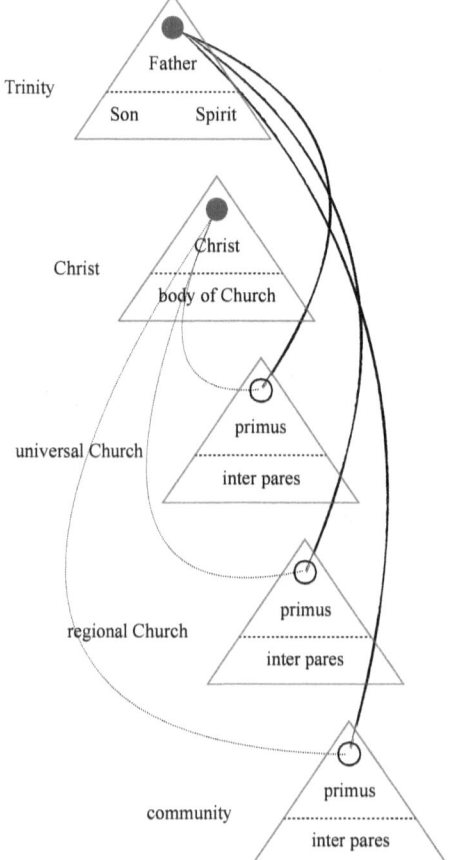

Neoplatonism and its Christian edition authored by Ps-Dionysius are the principal sources for the interpretation of primacy as intrinsic to the nature of the church. What would be, however, an alternative interpretation of primacy? Such an interpretation would consider primacy not as pertinent to the nature of the church, but as a *convenience*, which was adopted by the church during its historical journey to address various issues it faced. The canons of the church that became constituting for primacy imply such a historic convenience. The most explicit among them is the canon 28 of the council of Chalcedon:

> The fathers rightly accorded prerogatives to the see of older Rome, since that is an imperial city; and moved by the same purpose the 150 most devout bishops apportioned equal prerogatives to the most holy see of new Rome, reasonably judging that the city which is honoured by the imperial power and senate and enjoying privileges equalling older Rome, should also be elevated to her level in ecclesiastical affairs and take second place after her . . . .[55]

It is clear from this canon that primacy of the see of Rome, according to Chalcedon at least, was conditioned by the imperial status of that city. Residence of the emperor and relocation of the Roman senate to Constantinople elevated the church in this city to the second position after the church of Rome. The canon does not mention any reason for the primacy of the church of Constantinople that would transcend practical expediencies or historical circumstances. Such an interpretation of primacy became common in the eastern Roman Empire. Nilus Cabasilas (c. 1298–c. 1363), for example, in the early fourteenth century explained that the Roman primacy had developed as an administrative and not a sacred institution: "The pope has indeed two privileges: he is the bishop of Rome . . . and he is the first among the bishops. From Peter he has received the Roman episcopacy; as to the primacy, he received it much later from the blessed Fathers and the pious emperors, for it was just that ecclesiastical affairs be accomplished in order."[56]

Hierarchy *among* the churches, according to the common eastern Christian understanding, is *useful, but not sacred*. It is not really hierarchy, but an order that the church has adopted for particular historical

---

55. Tanner, *Decrees of the Ecumenical Councils*, vol. 1, 100.
56. *De primatu papae* (PG 149, 701CD).

reasons. At the same time, hierarchy *within* the churches became sacred in the Orthodox tradition. The ordering of ministries turned here to a divinely established hierarchy. This indicates inconsistency in the eastern perception of the two hierarchies: among the churches and within them. The western tradition seems to be more consistent in this regard: it takes both hierarchies as sacred. The eastern tradition, to be consistent, should consider both of them as either divine or historically conditioned.

6

Strata: Ministry

THERE WAS NO TIME when there was no ministry, and the first who came to minister the church was Jesus Christ himself (Matt 20:28). This means that ministry belongs to the nature of the church. However, the *hierarchical principle* of ministry is not a part of the church's nature. This principle emerged and developed under the pressure of historical circumstances. This hypothesis can be grounded in the early Christian writings. Ambrosiaster, who like Ps-Dionysius was a proponent of hierarchy in the church, did not derive it from any "heavenly hierarchy." He acknowledged instead its origin and evolution under the influence of the external sociopolitical factors. The early church, to him, did not have "governors" (*rectores*): "Paul writes to the church, because at that time governors were not yet appointed for individual churches."[1] It was only with its incorporation to the empire that the church adopted the hierarchical principle for its ministry.[2]

    1. Ambrosiaster, *Comm. in I Cor.*, 1:2.1: "propterea ecclesiae scribit, quia tunc (adhuc) singulis ecclesiis rectores non erant constituti." In Lunn-Rockliffe, *Ambrosiaster's Political Theology*, 107.

    2. Ambrosiaster meticulously described the early hierarchical orders as follows: "However, after churches were established and duties appointed in all places, things were arranged differently from how they had begun. For in the beginning everyone used to teach and baptize, on whatever day or at whatever time the opportunity arose. ... And so that the congregation might grow and be multiplied, at the beginning it was granted to all to evangelize, baptize, and explain the scriptures in church. But when the church had spread everywhere, small assemblies were established and rectores and

Among other factors that incurred the transformation of ministry to hierarchy, were the administrative structures of the church. Ministry itself turned to an administrative structure, with all ambivalences incurred by such a transformation. The result of this transformation was stratification of the church.[3] Strata are layers of geological formations with the same consistence located hierarchically, one above the other. The concept of geological strata was adopted in sociology, with a long list of studies exploring the stratification of society.[4] In sociology, stratification is understood as inequality in the society and its division to classes.[5] Sociological models and theories of stratification can help in explaining how lay people, deacons, priests, bishops, and primates turned into layers in the rock of the church.

The formation of geological strata is a result of centuries-long processes. The same is true with regard to church orders. They became segregated gradually with the passage of time. However, during the eruption of a volcano, hot lava that later on will form geological strata, runs in all directions blending all elements together. In the same way, the initial development of ministerial structures, whose common origin is from the flames of the Holy Spirit, was unpredictable, non-determinable, and multi-optional. This means that church orders might have been different from the threefold ones that we know now, if there were different historical circumstances. The ranks of deacons, priests, and bishops were not preset in the New Testament or established by *jus divinum*.[6]

The initial logic of ministry was non-hierarchical, with the "more important" members of the community serving the "less important"

---

other offices were appointed in the churches, so that none of the clergy who had not been ordained to the office in question (such as lectors and exorcists) would dare to take to himself an office which he knew not to be entrusted or granted to him. And so the church began by another order and Providence to be governed, because, if all had equal power, it would seem most irrational and a vulgar and cheap affair. This then is why now deacons do not preach to the people, nor do other ranks, or even laymen, baptize, nor are believers baptized on whatsoever day unless they are sick." Lunn-Rockliffe, *Ambrosiaster's Political Theology*, 107–8.

3. See Rapp, *Holy Bishops in Late Antiquity*, 7.

4. Breen and Rottman, *Class Stratification Comparative Perspectives*; Birkelund, *Class and Stratification Analysis*; Hauser et al., *The Process of Stratification*; Crompton, *Class and Stratification*; Collins, *The Credential Society*; Stopnicka Heller, *Structured Social Inequality*; Owen, *Social Stratification*; Lenski, *Power and Privilege*.

5. See Saunders, *Social Class and Stratification*.

6. See Sullivan, *From Apostles to Bishops*, 217.

ones. This logic stemmed from the ministry of Christ, who washed the feet of his disciples (John 13) and taught them: "Whoever would be great among you must be your servant, and whoever would be first among you must be your slave" (Matt 20:26-27). The initial Christian ministry was counter-cultural,[7] which meant it contrasted with the hierarchies that existed in the Jewish and Gentile worlds. John particularly stressed this distinct feature of the Christian ministry. According to Edward Schillebeeckx,

> John 21:15-19 above all contrasts service in love with hierarchical authority. . . . It is striking that in contrast to the Synoptic Gospels it does not give any list of twelve names, nor does it have any account of the calling of the Twelve. On the other hand, in II and III John there is mention of "the presbyter," a community leader who writes these letters. For some commentators this is the most important presbyter, and the community is tending towards a mono-episcopal church order, but this is difficult to reconcile with the collective witness given by these letters.[8]

The church from its very beginning right up until our days has somehow entertained the ideal of ministry as altruistic, caring, and upturning the social ranking of people in the wider world. The historical development of ministerial structures, however, often took the opposite path. The church's ministerial offices gradually became hierarchical and stratifying, i.e., creating "social distances"[9] between the ecclesial orders. Stratification began with what Max Weber (1864-1920) identified as the routinization of charisms:

> Primarily, a religious community arises in connection with a prophetic movement as a result of routinization, i.e., as a result of the process whereby either the prophet himself or his disciples secure the permanence of his preaching and the congregation's distribution of grace, hence insuring the economic existence of the enterprise and those who man it, and thereby monopolizing as well the privileges reserved for those charged with religious functions. . . . A transformation of a personal following into a permanent congregation is the normal process by which the doctrine of the prophets enters into everyday life, as the function of a permanent institution. The disciples or apostles of the

---

7. See Chadwick, *The Church in Ancient Society*, 1.
8. Schillebeeckx, *The Church with a Human Face*, 95.
9. See Bogardus, "Social Distance."

prophets thereupon become mystagogues, teachers, priests or pastors (or a combination of them all), serving an organization dedicated to exclusively religious purposes, namely a congregation of laymen.[10]

Following Weber, Joachim Wach (1898–1955) identified three stages of the routinization of charisms in religious organizations.[11] At the first stage, the immediate disciples come around a prophet and form a circle, which "is not strictly organized, but the variety of individualities and the differences in age are harbingers of future differentiation of function among the members."[12] At the second stage, the circle of disciples turns to a brotherhood. Brotherhood develops a hierarchy based on a cult, which "more than its doctrinal expression, unites and integrates the brotherhood."[13] At the third stage, the ecclesiastical body turns into a church. This requires "a differentiated organization, a passage from informal ministry to professional or formal positions of leadership. It also involves developing a public face directed to the outside world," according to Roger Haight.[14]

As the common sociological wisdom holds, social structures arise as a result of social routine.[15] The ecclesial structures, including the ministerial ones, emerged from the social routine and integration into the contemporary social structures of the Greco-Roman world. Among the structures that inspired the earliest hierarchy of the church, after it had left the cradle of Judaism and crossed the border with the Gentile world, was the Greco-Roman household. The master of the house where the Christian communities gathered received special honors and responsibilities over the community, including the one of leading the eucharist. The communities established by Paul adopted primarily the household model of organization. This model is reflected in those Pauline letters that most likely were written not by Paul himself but by his disciples.[16]

10. Weber, *The Sociology of Religion*, 61–62.
11. See Wach, *Sociology of Religion*, 130–45.
12. Ibid., 136.
13. Ibid., 140.
14. Haight, *Christian Community in History*, vol. 1, 93.
15. Borgatta and Montgomery, *Encyclopedia of Sociology*, 2822.
16. According to the estimation of Raymond E. Brown, around 90 percent of scholars believe that Paul is not an author of the pastoral epistles, 80 percent think he did not write Ephesians, and 60 percent, he did not write Colossians. Brown, *The Churches the Apostles Left Behind*, 47.

They describe structural developments in the post-Pauline communities. Thus, the Pastoral Epistles define qualifications for elders and criteria for deacons as influenced by this model.[17] Colossians 3:18–22, Ephesians 5:22–6:9, and Titus 2:4–9 impose on the Christian communities the paradigm of a Roman patriarchal family, which featured submission of all members of the house to its master. This paradigm contrasted with the original Paul's insistence that in Christ "there is neither slave nor free, there is neither male nor female" (Gal 3:28). There was an obvious shift from Paul's egalitarian approach to the pseudo-Pauline hierarchical household model, which Edward Schillebeeckx described as follows:

> The strictly hierarchical structures of the *oikos* of the time are taken over, in contrast to earlier situations in which the house communities were a free association of equals with nevertheless many kinds of authorities, on the basis of a contribution inspired by the Spirit. Now Christians had to subject themselves to the one authority.[18]

The early church experienced many charismata. Every member of the community could receive a charismatic gift and exercise it without authorization from anyone else. Paul listed a number of gifts that his communities knew: wisdom, knowledge, faith, healing, miracles, prophecy, distinguishing the spirits, leadership, speaking with tongues (1 Cor 12), and others. Members of the communities who held these gifts were identified as apostles, prophets, teachers (or catechists), miracle workers, healers, givers of support, interpreters of tongues (1 Cor 12), admonishers, benefactors, and those who show mercy (Rom 12:6–8).

After Paul, his communities displayed fewer types of charismata. The epistle to the Ephesians, which is likely post-Pauline, referred to only five of them, now associated with the following offices: apostles, prophets, evangelists, pastors, and teachers (Eph 4:11). The epistles to Timothy, which most certainly reflect the later post-Pauline situation, addressed *episkopoi* and deacons as leading offices in the communities (1 Tim 3:2, 8). A comparison of the ecclesial offices in the same communities during Paul's life and after him demonstrates the tendency to reduce the charismata and link them to offices. Charismata were gradually confined to offices. No longer could anyone hold an office, but only those who were approved by the community and its leaders. Communities were pushed

---

17. 1 Tim 3:8–13; Prusak, *The Church Unfinished*, 110.

18. Schillebeeckx, *The Church with a Human Face*, 66–67.

to associate the charismata with a limited number of offices by disorders and quarrels caused by the oft-overlapping exercise of gifts. As Schillebeeckx remarked:

> At the end of the first century we see that the conflict between authorities in the communities was decided in favour of believers who took the title of "episkopos" (presbyter) and deacon. The tendency to reserve all authority exclusively for them becomes clear. Above all, the power of the *patroni*, sponsors, of both sexes, was gradually neutralized and the phenomenon of Christian prophets, widespread within the early church and accepted and respected almost without criticism, was gradually removed. The presbyter-*episkopos* and presbyter now appropriated to themselves this prophetic authority.[19]

The concentration of various charismata in one pair of hands and their connection with established offices gave an additional impulse to the rise of the hierarchical orders in the church. Hierarchy emerges when access to the vital resources becomes limited or controlled. That is what happened when the control over the access to charismata was bestowed upon limited offices, such as presbyters.

Presbyters constituted the earliest ministerial institution in the church, according to mainstream scholarship.[20] It would be anachronistic to identify the presbyters of the first century with modern priests or bishops. At that time, the church did not yet firmly link ecclesial functions with offices, though it had started moving in that direction. It did not have a strict number of offices, either, and did not yet realize that it should. The church tried to find forms of ministry that, on the one hand, would not "extinguish the Spirit" (1 Thess 5:19) and, on the other hand, would keep the communities in order and integrity.

The office of presbyters seemed to work best for these purposes. This institution was adopted by the early Christian community from the Jewish communities and the Greek political culture. In every synagogue, there were elders (*zeqēnîm*) who had various responsibilities, including taxation, charity, and interactions with the outer world.[21] They could advice the community on how its religious service should be conducted, but they did not have any exclusive rights to perform such services.[22] The

---

19. Ibid., 66.
20. See Sullivan, *From Apostles to Bishops*, 16.
21. Brown, *The Churches the Apostles Left Behind*, 32–33.
22. Easton, *The Apostolic Tradition of Hippolytus*, 76.

Jewish presbyters were elected by the community and were ordained by laying on of hands.[23]

Although most scholars believe that the origin of the Christian presbyters is Jewish, some, like Alistair Stewart-Sykes, have argued that there is more evidence that it had Greek roots.[24] In such case, the institution of presbyters can be interpreted from a broader perspective. The term "presbyter" (*presbyteros*, πρεσβύτερος) could be then considered in connection with the ancient Greek institution of *gerousia* (γερουσία), an assembly of representatives from the leading families of the *polis*. Members of the *gerousia* had to advise rulers and to hear cases against military commanders and kings, including capital offences. They constituted a *boulē* (βουλή), which was an institution that had responsibilities for current public duties and prepared the work of the *ekklēsia*.[25] The *ekklēsia* was managed by the presbyters.

Both the Jewish synagogue and Greek *gerousia* held the office of the presbyters as collegial. So it was in the Christian church in the earliest period of its history.[26] Each community had not just one presbyter but a number of them. Presbyters in the Christian communities were equal to each other. Soon, however, one of the presbyters was commissioned to oversee the life of the community. He was thus endowed with the ministry of overseeing (*episkopē*, ἐπισκοπή). It is likely that presbyters rotated in overseeing the life of the community, and *episkopē* was a duty that passed from one presbyter to another. *Episkopos* (ἐπίσκοπος) was an adjective, not a noun. Gradually, the presbyterial ministry of overseeing turned into a distinct and permanent office. The *episkopos*, now a noun, continued to rely on the college of presbyters or *presbyterium*.

New challenges to the church, such as Gnosticism and the discipline-related schisms, together with the rapidly growing number of Christian communities, led to the further concentration of power in the hands of *episkopoi*. "As the personal symbol of the unity of a particular church, the bishop determined who was to be included in, excluded from, or re-admitted to the table of the Eucharist, and thus admitted to or excluded

23. Bohr, *The Diocesan Priest*, 16.
24. Stewart-Sykes, *The Original Bishops*, 8.
25. See Rhodes, *The Athenian Boule*.
26. This hypothesis is supported by most scholars (see Stewart-Sykes, *The Original Bishops*, 6). Stewart-Sykes, however, disagrees with this standpoint. He argues that the communities featured single leadership of *episkopoi*. In the cities with multiple communities, they constituted some form of collegiality.

from the *koinonia* or communion of the *ekklēsia*."[27] The office of *episkopos* became superior to all other church offices. The offices of presbyter and deacon were transformed to support it. The institution of *episkopos* thus made a crucial contribution to the formation of the hierarchical model of the church and eventually embodied this model, which has been characterized by scholars as "mono-episcopacy."[28]

The earliest promoter of the mono-episcopal order in the church was Ignatius of Antioch (c. 35 or 50–98 to 117). He believed that the more church authority was consolidated in one person's hands, the more it could help the church solve the new problems that it faced in the second century. Mono-episcopacy in that time was not yet a *fait accompli*; it was still just a *desideratum*. Ignatius proposed it as a solution to the problems that the church faced. Although mono-episcopacy was a post-apostolic invention and, in the terms of this book, does not belong to the nature of the church, Ignatius tried to convince his addressees to accept this solution with theological arguments:

> As, then, the Lord did nothing without the Father (either on his own or by the apostles) because he was at one with him, so you must not do anything without the bishop and presbyters. Do not, moreover, try to convince yourselves that anything done on your own is commendable. Only what you do together is right. Hence you must have one prayer, one petition, one mind, one hope, dominated by love and unsullied joy—that means you must have Jesus Christ. You cannot have anything better than that.[29]

Edward Schillebeeckx remarked about the theological arguments in favor of mono-episcopacy: "This system of authority and subjection—hierarchy—thus receives a theological and christological, ideological substructure. There is clearly a shift here, and another picture of the church emerges."[30] A century after Ignatius, the *Didascalia apostolorum*, when describing the office of *episkopos*, applied an even stronger language to endorse mono-episcopacy. This was not only a theological language, but also a political one. It spoke in the terms of the absolute power of kings:

27. Prusak, *The Church Unfinished*, 128.
28. See Haight, *Christian Community in History*, vol. 1, 101.
29. *Ad Magnes.* (CPG 1025) 7.1, in Richardson, *Early Christian Fathers*, 96.
30. Schillebeeckx, *The Church with a Human Face*, 71.

> The bishops are your high priests.... He is minister of the word and mediator, but to you a teacher, and your father after God; he begot you through the water. He is your chief and your leader, your powerful king. He rules in the place of the Almighty.[31]

The comparison of the *episkopos* to the king here became possible because of the imperial cult, which developed in the third century and penetrated into the Christian communities from the Greco-Roman world. Allen Brent, in his study of the parallels in the developments of the church hierarchy and the imperial cult in the first Christian centuries, made an interesting observation:

> The bishop as high priest now expressed in his intercommunion with other bishops the unity of the Church just as the cult of Decius Trajan, formed in the Severan ideology of the previous generation, expressed sacramentally the unity of the Empire. To be in communion with Christ you have to be in communion with a bishop who presides over a geographical territory called a diocese. In order to be in communion with other Christians outside your diocese, your bishop has to be in communion with their bishop and so on.... Participation in the Imperial Cult, superintended by the Emperor as Pontifex Maximus, would lead to incorporation into the body of the Empire through the unifying light of ὁ Κακάκαλλος κοσμοκράτωρ. Participation in the Christian Cult, superintended by bishops in an intercommunion focused on the bishop of Rome, would lead to incorporation into the Church as the Body of Christ.[32]

As Ignatius had expected, the concentration of authority in one pair of hands indeed helped the church to solve many of its problems. It consolidated communities and brought more peace and order to their life. It also allowed communities to better communicate with each other and strengthened the inter-communal links. The office of *episkopos* gave a solution to the problem of representing communities on the regional and universal levels. It made possible the church councils, where *episkopoi* represented their people. At the same time, mono-episcopacy had unintended side effects. It contributed to a further routinization of the charisms, and their reduction. This, in turn, provoked movements like Montanism, which sought more charismatic offices in the church.

---

31. *Didascalia apostolorum* (CPG 1738) 9.3–4 in Johnson, *Worship in the Early Church*, 229.

32. Brent, *The Imperial Cult and the Development of Church Order*, 2–4.

Montanism and similar movements were conservative and nostalgic about the church as it had been before the rise of mono-episcopacy; they opposed mono-episcopacy as novelty. Various opinions and "divisions" (1 Cor 11:19) within one community, which had been tolerated earlier by default, now survived depending on the open-mindedness of the *episkopos* there. Those who disagreed with the *episkopos* on the matters of discipline and doctrine, either justifiably or unjustifiably, were more likely to separate themselves from the community, instead of staying in and keeping their opinions. This was the cause of the schisms like Novatianism.[33]

The rise of the office of *episkopos* also led to an increasing division between clergy and laity.[34] A link that traditionally connected the community with its ministers was the process of the election of clergy.[35] By the third century, this tradition ceased to be kept ubiquitously. Initially, the ordination of clergy had three principal elements: election, reception by community, and the laying-on of hands. The former was believed to be even more important than the latter. After the third century, however, the laying-on of hands became more important than the voice of the community in choosing and receiving candidates for ministry.[36]

An early witness to the change was Hippolytus of Rome (c. 170–c. 235). In his *Apostolic Traditions*, he criticized as modernism the way, in which Zephyrinus (c. 199–c. 217) and Calixtus (c. 217–c. 222) became bishops of Rome. Because they were not elected by the people of the city, Hippolytus refused to recognize them.[37] He insisted that, in order to be faithful to the apostolic tradition, the procedure of installing a new bishop must include choosing by the entire congregation:

> Let the bishop be ordained (being in all things without fault), chosen by all the people. And when he has been proposed and

---

33. Novatianism was a rigorist movement that affected mostly the western church. It was branded after Novatian, a Roman presbyter and theologian, who was disappointed by the election of Cornelius as bishop of Rome in 251. Novatian and his followers deprecated concessions to the fallen. The movement survived into the fifth century. See Papandrea, *Novatian of Rome and the Culmination of Pre-Nicene Orthodoxy*; Papandrea, *The Trinitarian Theology of Novatian of Rome*.

34. See Brown, *The Body and Society*, 142.

35. See Norton, *Episcopal Elections*; Christophe, *L'élection des évêques dans l'église latine au premier millénaire*; Thier, *Hierarchie und Autonomie*.

36. See Schillebeeckx, *The Church with a Human Face*, 138–39.

37. See ibid., 133.

found acceptable to all, the people being assembled on the Lord's day together with the presbytery and such bishops as may attend, let [the choice] be generally approved. Let the bishops lay hands on him and the presbytery stand by in silence. And all shall keep silence, praying in their heart for the descent of the Spirit. After this one of the bishops present, at the request of all, laying his hand on him [who is ordained bishop], shall pray thus . . . .[38]

At approximately the same time in the East, Origen (c. 185–c. 254) insisted that the appointment of presbyters for local congregations must have the consent of the congregation. At ordinations, he wrote, "the presence of the people is required, so that they may all know and be certain that the man elected to the priesthood stands out from all the people in learning, holiness, and eminence in every kind of virtue."[39]

Lack of people's participation in choosing leaders for their communities, which in the third century was considered an exception, in the fourth century became a common practice.[40] Alternative factors began to play an increasing role, such as: bishops who themselves either nominated their successors or in their capacity of metropolitans appointed bishops of lower ranks, and civil authorities.[41] The shift in the tradition of the ordination of clergy occurred at a different rate in the East and in the West, being slower in the West. Pope Leo as late as in the fifth century wrote: "He who must preside over all must be chosen by all."[42] In the West, congregations continued to participate in the elections of their clergy until the eleventh century.[43] In the East, however, the changes happened sooner. Already in the fourth century, the council of Laodicea in Phrygia (363–64) ordered that the "crowd" (ochlos, ὄχλος) was not to decide about the election of new community leaders: "The election of those who are to be appointed to the priesthood is not to be committed to the multitude."[44]

---

38. *Traditio apostolica* (CPG 1737) 1.2 in Jay, *The Church*, 56.

39. *In Levit.* (CPG 1416) 6.3 in Jay, *The Church*, 61.

40. While speaking about common practice, we should keep in mind a wide diversity of practices in the minor local churches, as this has been indicated in the collected volume Leemans et al., *Episcopal Elections in Late Antiquity*.

41. See Schillebeeckx, *The Church with a Human Face*, 148.

42. *Ad Anast.* (CPL 1656: PL 54, 634).

43. See Prusak, *The Church Unfinished*, 158.

44. Canon 13: "μὴ τοῖς ὄχλοις ἐπιτρέπειν τὰς ἐκλογὰς ποιεῖσθαι τῶν μελλόντων

The exclusion of lay people from the election process had some good reasons. Sometimes their participation in the election of clergy, especially of bishops in the big cities, was accompanied by the outbursts of violence.[45] This prompted civil authorities to take the process of election into their own hands, for the purpose of public safety. A more important reason, however, was the adaptation of Christianity to the political culture of the Roman Empire. The incorporation of the bishops to the imperial bureaucracy transformed the patterns of promotion to the hierarchical ranks. The administrative positions in the state were filled not democratically by elections, but by appointment from superior authorities. Therefore, the more the bishops became like the state clerks, the less the people participated in their promotion.

Another reason for changes in episcopal elections was the Roman institute of patronage. As Peter Norton has remarked, in Roman society "patronage, influence and personal recommendation were crucial to advancement in all walks of life, and the support of the local aristocracy would have been desirable and often, one suspects, decisive, especially if they were able to direct their *clientelae* or tenants to lobby or take part in the election."[46] This culture of patronage deeply affected the church and contributed to the shifts in its structures.[47] The role of privileged lay people in episcopal elections increased dramatically, while the general lay participation was reduced. The church took this as a problem. It promulgated a number of canons that protected the ordination of clergy from political interferences. Thus, apostolic canon 30 confronted the situation that had become common in the fourth century: "If any bishop shall have obtained his church through secular rulers, let him, and all who communicate with him, be deposed and excommunicated."[48]

In facing this problem, the church had one of two ways to follow: either to guarantee that all, and not just a few VIPs, would decide who would get to be a bishop or to transfer this right of selection to the

καθίστασθαι εἰς ἱερατεῖον." Fulton, *Index Canonum*, 254–55.

45. See Norton, *Episcopal Elections*, 71.

46. Ibid., 53.

47. The contributors to Cooper and Hillner, *Religion, Dynasty, and Patronage in Early Christian Rome*, for instance, argue that the Roman patronage was crucial in the formation of papacy.

48. "Εἴ τις ἐπίσκοπος κοσμικῆς ἄρχουσι χρησάμενος, δι' αὐτῶν ἐγκρατὴς ἐκκλησίας γένηται, καθαιρείσθω καὶ ἀφοριζέσθω, καὶ οἱ κοινωνοῦντες αὐτῷ ἅπαντες." Fulton, *Index Canonum*, 88–89.

bishops alone. It chose the latter way: to make the corporation of bishops responsible for its own replenishment, which was easier tactically, but not strategically. In the long run, this made the bishops a caste relying on itself and thereby increased stratification in the church. The life of the church, nevertheless, turned out to be more complicated than the adopted strategies had promised. As Peter Norton has demonstrated, the choice of the people in electing the church leadership did not disappear altogether. Even when the masses were deprived of direct participation in the elections, they continued exercising the right of approval or veto.[49]

The decisive role of the VIPs in the elections of bishops did not disappear either, despite the threats of severe punishments. The church had to warn the trespassers repeatedly, without however achieving the desired result. Thus, the seventh ecumenical council (787) repeated the threats of the earlier councils: "Any election of a bishop, priest, or deacon brought about by the rulers is to be null and void."[50] This threat did not work either, so the council of Constantinople (869–70) a century later had to come back to the practice, which had been already widespread in the East, that bishops should be elected by other bishops. The council also explicitly indicated why it insisted on this practice, namely because of the recidivous interference of influential lay figures:

> This holy and universal synod declares and decrees, in agreement with earlier councils, that the promotion and consecration of bishops should be done by means of an election and decision of the college of bishops. So it promulgates as law that no lay authority or ruler may intervene in the election or promotion of a patriarch, a metropolitan, or any bishop, lest there be any irregularity leading to improper confusion or quarrelling, especially since it is wrong for any ruler or other lay person to have any influence in such matters. Rather he should be silent and mind his own business until the election of the future bishop has been completed with due process by the ecclesiastical assembly ....[51]

The integration of the church into the imperial structures after Constantine accelerated the process of transformation of the ministries to hierarchical strata.[52] These strata were adjusted to the social grid of Late

---

49. Norton, *Episcopal Elections*, 71.
50. Canon 3, in Tanner, *Decrees of the Ecumenical Councils*, vol. 1, 140.
51. Canon 22, in ibid., 182–83.
52. See Schillebeeckx, *The Church with a Human Face*, 132; Drake, *Constantine*

Antiquity. Thus, for instance, the curial class, which constituted the urban elites, provided most candidates for bishops.[53] The bishops gradually assumed some important civil duties, such as presiding over state courts.[54] Under the emperor Theodosius (reigned 379–95), the ecclesial order was legally structured on the basis of civil bureaucracy.[55] It became a separate and privileged class,[56] and adopted a strict internal hierarchy. By analogy with the civil administrative hierarchy, bishops turned into church officers of the first rank, while presbyters became officers of the second rank. To reach the higher ranks, one had to pass through the lower first.[57] Clergy as whole, as an *ordo clericorum*, became distinct from the rest of the church. They received numerous state privileges, including a salary from public funds and exemption from taxes.

The new privileged classes replaced the class of the Gentile priests, and appropriated some features of the latter. Among the duties of the college of pagan priests had been that of protecting the integrity and welfare of the empire, *salus populi*. Now this duty was transferred to the corpus of the Christian clergy.[58] The leaders of the Christian communities, following the logic of the imperial religion, became servants of the Christian cultus—*sacerdotes*. This changed their identity from community leaders (elders: *presbyteroi*, πρεσβύτεροι) to priests (*hiereis*, ἱερεῖς) of

---

and the Bishops; Stephens, Canon Law and Episcopal Authority.

53. Leemans et al., *Episcopal Elections in Late Antiquity*, 7.

54. See Lamoreaux, "Episcopal Courts in Late Antiquity."

55. See Schillebeeckx, *The Church with a Human Face*, 141.

56. As Peter Norton remarks, "Although the clergy never wore the *cingulum*, the official's belt of office in the secular world, it is not unrealistic to claim that in episcopal elections, we are looking at the choice of important functionaries within the secular state. . . . Compared to the precarious alternative employment open to such men as, say, a private tutor or a municipal orator, a bishopric, which was after all a post held for life, must have seemed an attractive career option. From the time of Constantine, membership of the clergy conferred on its lucky holders immunity from the crippling civic duties that fell on the shoulders of the *curiales*, and the more astute might even try to use their clerical status as a tax shelter. There were also other advantages—a letter from Basil of Caesarea expresses annoyance that the lower ranks of the Cappadocian clergy were being swollen by those wishing to escape conscription into the army." Norton, *Episcopal Elections*, 4.

57. See Prusak, *The Church Unfinished*, 157. Ambrosiaster, for instance, maintained that bishops and presbyters belonged to the same order, although they were of different ranks. *Questio* 101.2 in Prusak, *The Church Unfinished*, 159.

58. Schillebeeckx, *The Church with a Human Face*, 142.

the sacraments. "Sacerdotalization"[59] of the Christian ministry led to its fixation on the sacraments and to a further loosening of its connection with the community. The sacraments as such also became disconnected from the community. Their focus shifted to the good of the entire *populus Romanus* and its state. The celebration of the eucharist became an exclusive prerogative of the clergy as ministers of the public cult. The increasing gap between clergy and lay people created a distance between the community and eucharist.[60]

After the conversion of the empire, the dramatically growing Christianity spread from the cities in the countryside. From being members of the bishop's entourage, presbyters became bishops' delegates in the villages. There, their ministry concentrated on the eucharist even more. This enhanced the transformation of the formerly communal office of presbyter to the sacerdotal office of priest, who performed hierourgy in the name of his bishop.[61] These developments contributed to dramatic changes in the perception of the eucharist. From the "common action" (*leitourgia*, λειτουργία) of the community, the eucharist turned into a sacred ceremony (*sacramentum* or *mystērion*, μυστήριον) performed by a priest.[62] From a communal event, the eucharist gradually developed to a venerated relic,[63] as remote from the community as the holy from the profane. What Nicholas Denysenko has called "liturgiolatry"[64] substituted liturgy proper. In result, as Bernard Prusak remarks:

> By the fifth century, a professional clerical ladder had been erected in the midst of the laity, and even its bottom rung was considered a step above lay men and lay women. Laicization was the worst possible punishment for clerics, who became visibly distinguished by their tonsure in the sixth century. The "clericalization" so characteristic of later centuries had begun.[65]

Exactly in this period, the stratification of the church became grounded theologically: clerical strata turned to ecclesial *onta*. As it has been demonstrated in the chapter "Pyramids: Primacy," Ps-Dionysius

---

59. Ibid., 144–46.
60. See ibid., 143.
61. See ibid., 140–41.
62. See Prusak, *The Church Unfinished*, 184–5.
63. See ibid., 195.
64. Denysenko, *Liturgical Reform After Vatican II*.
65. Prusak, *The Church Unfinished*, 157.

should be credited for introducing to the Christian theology the Neoplatonic idea of hierarchy as pertinent to the sphere of divine. By analogy with the "heavenly hierarchy," he consecrated also the ministerial orders and made them divine. In tune with the contemporary tendency towards sacramentalization of the church, Ps-Dionysius constructed his ecclesial hierarchy around the mysteries. Even the structure of the mysteries as such is hierarchical to him. The eucharist holds the central place in this hierarchy. It is "the sacrament of sacraments."[66] Ps-Dionysius ordered the ecclesial hierarchy in accordance, on the one hand, with their proximity to God, and on the other hand, with their role in the eucharist:

> The holy sacraments bring about purification, illumination, and perfection. The deacons form the order which purifies. The priests constitute the order which gives illumination. And the hierarchs, living in conformity with God, make up the order which perfects. As for those who are being purified, so long as they are still at this stage of purification they do not partake of the sacred vision or communion. The sacred people is the contemplative order. The order of those made perfect is that of the monks who live a single-minded life. Thus, our own hierarchy is blessedly and harmoniously divided into orders in accordance with divine revelation and therefore deploys the same sequence as the hierarchies of heaven. It carefully preserves in its own human way the characteristics which enable it to be like God and conform to him.[67]

Ps-Dionysius reserved the highest rank in the ecclesial hierarchy for the bishops. He was the first in Christian literature who called them "hierarchs." They thus became the highest "ecclesial things" (*onta*, ὄντα) in the church. At the bottom of Ps-Dionysius's hierarchy are lay people. They are divided into three categories: those being purified, the communicants, and the monks. Those being purified constitute three groups: the catechumens, the possessed, and the penitents. The group of the communicants includes those who are purified and need to be illuminated. Priests are in charge of them. The monks have passed both purification and illumination. They enjoy the most complete perfection accessible for the lay order.[68] Half a millennium after Ps-Dionysius, the Byzantine

---

66. *De eccl.* (CPG 6601) 3.1 in Ivanovic, "The Ecclesiology of Dionysius the Areopagite," 31.

67. *De eccl.* (CPG 6601) 6.3.5 in ibid., 35.

68. *De eccl.* (CPG 6601) 6.1 in ibid., 34.

monk Niketas Stethatos (c. 1005–c. 1090) from the Stoudion monastery adjusted the original Areopagitic hierarchy to the hierarchical structures in the church of his time. Thus, in his interpretation, the angelic "thrones," "cherubim," and "seraphim" correspond to the offices of patriarchs, metropolitans, and archbishops; the "lordships," "powers," and "authorities" are related to bishops, priests, and deacons; sub-deacons, readers, and monks represented to him the ranks of "principalities," "archangels," and "angels."[69]

From these theoretical constructs, the practice of the church accepted the idea of the ecclesial hierarchy and its structuring around the role of each order in the sacraments. The criterion of holiness and perceptibility of the divine light was dropped as unimplementable. The way in which ps-Dionysian Neoplatonic thought was received in the church, created—both in the East and West—a powerful momentum toward a further separation of clergy and laity. At the same time, it facilitated an assimilation between the civil and ecclesial strata that appeared to be on the same level of the hierarchical ladder. Offices in the church hierarchy became much like the corresponding offices in the political system. In other words, the strata within the church became more remote from each other, while the corresponding classes in the church and society came closer to one another, up to the point of assimilation. Bernard Prusak describes this situation as follows:

> The prevailing political structure of the medieval world was monarchical. Secular or temporal power and authority flowed downward from emperors and kings, princes and lords, nobles and knights; it was exercised over peasants and serfs who worked the land and wielded no power, and over the merchant class that later emerged in cities and towns. The pattern prevalent in secular society would be mirrored in the conception of the medieval Church as a papal monarchy, in which spiritual power and authority descended from the pope—down through archbishops, bishops, abbots, archdeacons, canons, and ordinary priests—and was exercised over the faithful. Although primarily supposed to be spiritual leaders within the Church, bishops would also be drawn into the temporal political power structure. As bishops within the Church, they were to lead their people to union with God; but, as lords within a feudal society,

69. See Louth, *Greek East and Latin West*, 333–34.

they also ruled their domains and worked with the king in ruling the kingdom.[70]

During the Middle Ages, the hierarchical structures, both in the eastern and western churches, reached their apotheosis. They were highly sophisticated, theologically conceptualized, and effective in securing authority for both the church and civil leaders. The church leadership identified itself with the church proper, in the same way as political elites identified themselves with the state. They both became perceived as an intrinsic part of the divine order. The fine line of the demarcation between the community and its ministers that had existed in the early Christian centuries turned into a high wall between lay people and hierarchs. Hierarchs found themselves behind the same side of the wall with the political leadership and the nobility.

---

70. Prusak, *The Church Unfinished*, 178.

7

Frontiers:
The Boundaries of the Church

AN INTERNALLY STRATIFIED CHURCH with developed administrative structures has a tendency to be centripetal and autarkic. It often considers itself in parallel to, not in the world, where it is called to go and preach. The divisions and separations inside the church often serve as a model for building the church's relations with the world outside. The mentality of sharp-cut borderlines extrapolate itself from within the church to its borderlines that separate it from the world. An alternative to the mentality of sharp-cut borderlines is the open mentality of frontiers. Frontiers are a key image to understanding what the church is in its nature and how it is related to the world.

Arguably, it is not a coincidence that the early church, whose internal structures were not yet ossified, was more eager to expand. It was also rather silent about its external borderlines and of what lay beyond them. Indeed, even the crises of Arianism, "Nestorianism," and "monophysitism," when, judging by modern criteria, masses of Christians found themselves on the opposite sides of the church divide, did not trigger any significant theological reflection on the issue of whether salvation is possible on that side of the divide and, if so, why and to what extent. The furthest point that the early theologians went to in dealing with the issue of the external borders of the church and salvation outside those borders was the canonical criteria of acceptance into the church of people *coming from* heresies and schisms. Only pastoral urgency forced theologians to touch on this issue. As regarded the theological understanding of the church boundaries and the space beyond them, they preferred to leave the matter undisturbed by enquiries.

Theologians in North Africa were the only exception in this conspiracy of silence. They developed a number of theological points concerning the borders of the church in dealing with the Novatianist and Donatist schisms. Although these schisms were of a significantly lesser extent than the eastern divisions had been, they produced more theological reflection, as can be found in the writings of Cyprian of Carthage (c. 200–258), Optatus of Milevis (flourished in the fourth century), Augustine of Hippo (354–430), and Fulgentius of Ruspe (c. 462–527 or c. 467–532). The most radical in the group was Cyprian. He coined the famous formula *salus extra ecclesiam non est*—outside the church there is no salvation.[1] Augustine[2] and Fulgentius[3] repeated this thesis, though they were not as radical as Cyprian in their attitude to the sacraments outside the church. While Cyprian categorically rejected any possibility of valid sacraments *extra ecclesiam*, Augustine recognized their validity for those who come to reconcile with the church:

> All things [i.e., the sacraments] were indeed theirs before, but profited them nothing, because they had no charity. For what truth is there in the profession of Christian charity by him who does not embrace Christian unity? When, therefore, they come to the Catholic Church, they gain thereby not what they already possessed, but something which they had not before—namely that those things which they possessed begin then to be profitable to them. For in the Catholic Church they obtain the root of charity in the bond of peace and in the fellowship of unity.[4]

The theological claim that *salus extra ecclesiam non est* did not travel far beyond North Africa until the Middle Ages.[5] The rise of the papacy and the related criteria of belonging to the church gave new life to Cyprian's statement. Now it was connected with the papal office. Subjection to the Roman pontiff as a criterion of belonging to the church delineated

1. *Ep.* (CPL 50) 73.21.2.
2. *De baptismo* (CPL 332) 4.17.24; *De unico baptismo* (CPL 336) 6.8.9.
3. *De fide ad Petrum* (CPL 826) 79.
4. *Ep.* 61.2 (CPL 262) in Jay, *The Church*, 86–87.
5. See Thomas Aquinas, *Summa theologiae* 4.73.3: "Dictum est autem quod res sacramenti est unitas corporis mystici, sine qua non potest esse salus, nulli enim patet aditus salutis extra Ecclesiam."

new ecclesial borders and thus redefined the perimeter of salvation. Salvation of individuals now depended on his or her unity with the bishop of Rome, as this was expressed in the aforementioned bull *Unam sanctam* (1302).[6] This concept of the church's borders reached a new level in the polemics between Rome and the Reformation,[7] particularly concerning the visible and invisible church. The issue of the church borders turned out to be denominational. It became used as a weapon to impose or reject authority and to gain more theological trophies in the denominational wars.

Although this war was mostly between the Roman Catholic church and the churches of Reformation, the eastern churches also joined in it. The easterners employed the arguments of the western churches and used them to work out their own criteria of acceptance for converts to Orthodoxy. Until the fall of Constantinople (1453), the eastern church did not have any common rule for receiving Catholic converts to Orthodoxy. Practices varied from a confession of errors to (re)baptism. Cardinal Humbert (1015–61), for instance, protested in 1054 that the Greeks "rebaptize those who have been baptized in the name of the Holy Trinity, and primarily the Latins."[8] The Lateran council IV (1215) accused the easterners of the same. At the same time, Theodore Balsamon suggested around 1190 that Latins should be received into Orthodoxy only by confessing faith.[9] In the fifteenth century, the Orthodox received the westerners by anointing them with holy myrrh,[10] a practice that was confirmed by the council of Constantinople in 1484.[11] In the seventeenth century, the Greeks began baptizing Latin converts again.[12] The Moscow council of 1620 made this practice obligatory within the territory of Muscovy. The church of Kyiv under Constantinople at the same time received

---

6. Denzinger and Hünermann, *Enchiridion symbolorum*, 494.875.

7. See the works of Lorenzo da Brindisi (1559–1619): "Et paulo ante, ostendens quod extra Ecclesiam nulla sit salus." *Lutheranismi hypotyposis*: p. I: *Hypotyposis Martini Lutheri* 5.13.5; "O qualia haec sunt divinae bonitatis quam magna beneficia! Magnum beneficium est, magnum utique et ineffabile, remissio peccatorum et salus animarum; extra Ecclesiam vero non est salus neque peccatorum remissio, sicut nec vera fides aut Dei cognitio." *Quadragesima* 4.1.5.

8. *Commemoratio* (PL 143, 1003B).

9. *Interrogationes canonicae* (PG 138, 968B).

10. See Καρμήρη, Τὰ δογματικὰ καὶ συμβολικὰ μνημεία τῆς Ὀρθοδόξου καθολικῆς ἐκκλησίας, vol. 1, 425.

11. See ibid., vol. 2, 987–89.

12. See Ware, *Eustratios Argenti*, 67.

Latins by confession only. In 1755, the patriarch of Constantinople, Cyril V (in office 1748–51; 1752–57), issued a *horos* that demanded the baptism of all Latin converts.[13] Members of his synod, however, opposed the move of the patriarch and dethroned him. Nevertheless, the *horos* of 1755 remains a valid synodic decision on the issue and has not been replaced by any other official decision. As for Protestants, the patriarch of Constantinople Parthenios II (in office 1644–43; 1648–51) issued a directive that requested their (re)baptism. A council of the church of Jerusalem, however, decided in 1672 that baptism for Protestants is not necessary. In Russia, when Tsar Peter I (reigned 1682–1725) in 1718 asked Patriarch Jeremiah III (in office 1716–26; 1732–33) about receiving Protestants, the answer was in favor of only anointing them with myrrh.

These oscillations of practice and the absence of a firm, common Orthodox attitude toward the baptisms of Roman Catholics and Protestants imply that the easterners did not have a clear idea about where they would draw the borders of the church. Their attitude to baptism in other denominations reflected the varying historical circumstances rather than a firm theological position. At the same time, the Orthodox church clearly identified itself with the *Una sancta ecclesia*. So did the Roman church, which also called itself *Sancta Catholica Apostolica Romana Ecclesia*.[14] Until the ecumenical era, both believed that they offered the exclusive possibility of salvation, which is therefore impossible in other churches.

The Orthodox and the Roman Catholic churches commonly developed two approaches to the questions that they faced through their participation in the ecumenical movement that started at the beginning of the twentieth century. One is exclusivist and the other inclusive. Each of these two attitudes is in effect a range of opinions, overlapping at certain points. The exclusivist approach ranges from, at one end of the spectrum, the strict identification of the canonical and soteriological borders of the church to, at the other end, allowing some undefined churchly space outside the confessional borders. The inclusive attitude starts with the same idea of an undefined churchly space outside the confessional borders and can reach the extreme of the rejection of any borders. The difference between the two approaches in their extreme versions is clear: no space

---

13. Mansi, vol. 38, coll. 617–21.

14. *Constitutio dogmatica de fide catholica*, adopted by Vatican I. Tanner, *Decrees of the Ecumenical Councils*, vol. 2, 805.32.

granted between the canonical and soteriological borders of the church *versus* no soteriological borders of the church whatsoever.

More nuanced is the difference between the two approaches in their moderate range where they agree that there is a space of salvation outside the canonical borders of the church. The difference between the two approaches at this point is that the exclusive approach finds excuses to narrow this space, while the inclusive approach struggles to make it as wide as possible. The difference between the two, therefore, is in the dynamics: narrowing *versus* widening the space of "limited" grace. The two approaches have not been reconciled despite many theological attempts to do so. Both the Orthodox and the Roman Catholic churches have failed to produce a synthesis of the two attitudes and thus to come closer to a "universal theory" of the borders of the church.

The emergence of pluralistic and open societies was in many senses a painful experience for the churches that held strongly to an exclusivist ecclesiology and considered themselves to be vessels outside of which salvation would be impossible. The dramatically increased mobility of the population in the modern era forced the traditional denominations into immediate personal interactions that revealed Christian virtue in others and challenged many of the old theological stereotypes that fed the exclusivist ecclesiologies. This enhanced an inclusive attitude toward the limits of the church in both East and West. The Orthodox exclusivism was not as strong as the Roman Catholic version, so inclusivism manifested itself in the East earlier than in the West.[15]

As early as in the mid-nineteenth century, metropolitan Filaret of Moscow (1782–1867) claimed, for instance, "I will dare not to call as false any Church which believes that Jesus is Christ. . . . My justified respect for the teaching of the eastern Church," he continues, "does not mean that I judge or accuse western Christians and the western Church."[16] Filaret would not say that there is no salvific grace outside the Orthodox church. At the end of his life, he wrote, "An Orthodox Christian is supposed, in the spirit of love, joyfully to find a preserved grace outside of the Orthodox Church."[17] Another prominent hierarch of that time, Metropolitan Platon Gorodetsky of Kyiv (1803–91), in the same vein uttered his famous sentence, "Our earthly walls do not reach the sky." He said this

---

15. Some theses of this chapter have appeared in Cyril Hovorun, "Borders of Salvation: Reading Fathers with Russian Theologians."

16. Дроздов, *Собрание мнений и отзывов Филарета*, 29, 35.

17. Ibid., 29, 35.

when he visited a Catholic congregation in the town of Korostyshev in Ukraine in 1884. He also called the Orthodox and the Catholic churches "cousins."

This line was continued and brought to an extreme in the writings of Archpriest Pavel Svetlov (1861–1945), who was a professor of theology at the university of Kyiv. He did not find any meaningful reason why all Christian churches should stay separated from each other. Divisions between all Christians, he believed, were caused by historical misunderstandings and survived because of confessional arrogance. In reality, however, all churches in both East and West constitute the one universal church of Christ. Each of them has unlawfully appropriated for itself Christian universality.[18]

Svetlov's ideas corresponded to those of the "branch theory," which had emerged from the Oxford Movement.[19] This theory became popular among some Russian theologians, especially those in the diaspora. One of its supporters was Anton Kartashev (1875–1960), the last tsar's official who was responsible for the church (*ober-procuror* of the Holy Synod), later a minister of confessions in the temporary government of Russia after the first revolution in February 1917, and finally a refugee and a professor of church history in Paris. The universal church, according to Kartashev, is invisible. All particular churches that have preserved apostolic succession and feed their faithful with the Word of God constitute parts and manifestations of the true church of Christ.[20] Nicholas Zernov (1898–1980), who was an activist in Orthodox-Anglican dialogue, believed the same. For him, it was impossible to define or find the borders of the universal church.[21]

Nicholas Berdiaev (1874–1948), a prominent philosopher and religious thinker, did not even try to do that much. Not only did he find the existing divisions between the churches meaningless; he also believed that even all the churches put together did not constitute the universal church. For Berdiaev, the universal church is an eschatological category that exists "much deeper and much higher" than the empirical churches.[22]

---

18. Светлов, *Христианское вероучение в апологетическом изложении*, vol. 1, 209.

19. See Brown and Nockles, *The Oxford Movement*, 225–26.

20. Карташев, "Соединение Церквей в свете истории," 107.

21. Зернов, "Православие и англиканство," 58.

22. Бердяев, "Вселенскость и конфессионализм," 69–70.

More cautious was Sergey Bulgakov (1871–1944). On the one hand, he was a supporter of the idea of an invisible universal church that reaches far beyond its visible borders. For him, the church

> in some sense considers everything within the borders of baptism as belonging to itself, even if that is separated from it.... Therefore, there is a certain external zone of the Church, which goes beyond its borders; there are ecclesial connections, which do not coincide with unity of the Church organization. The body of Church does not exactly coincide with its visible borders. It also has a peripheral zone. The visible Church also includes a Church, which is invisible not only beyond this world, but also in this world. It is always correlated with this hidden and potential ecclesiality in one or another way. Hence the conclusion that there is an *ecclesia extra ecclesiam*, or better to say, *extra muros*.[23]

On the other hand, Bulgakov did not relativize the confessional borders. For him, the hidden ecclesiality was not undefined but clearly Orthodox. Any heterodoxy that belongs to the *ecclesia extra ecclesiam* is *potentially* Orthodox. Any non-Orthodox church is capable of offering the sacraments and salvation to its faithful insofar as it is potentially Orthodox and makes its Orthodoxy manifested.[24]

In Greece,[25] Ioannis Karmires (1904–93), Professor of Systematic Theology at the University of Athens, believed that the principle that "there is no salvation outside the church" was not based on the Scripture. Therefore, it should not be applied in any strict sense. Salvation is possible outside the one catholic church, which for him was identical with the Orthodox church. Salvation is possible, according to Karmires, not only for other Christians, but also for people from other religions who live a righteous life.[26] In the same vein, Metropolitan Damaskinos Papandreou (1936–2011) urged the Orthodox and the Catholics to recognize other Christian communities as the church in the full sense of the word.[27]

The protagonists of the inclusive ecclesiology in the Roman Catholic church were chiefly the theologians of the *nouvelle théologie*.[28] In 1937,

---

23. Булгаков, "Очерки учения о Церкви," 10.
24. Ibid., 21–22.
25. See Clapsis, "The Boundaries of the Church: An Orthodox Debate."
26. Καρμήρη, "'Η παγκοσμιότης τῆς ἐν Χριστῷ σωτηρίας."
27. Παπανδρέου, *Τὸ θέλημα τοῦ Θεοῦ*, 17.
28. See Mettepenningen, *Nouvelle Théologie—New Theology*.

Yves Congar (1904–95) in his work *Chrétiens désunis*[29] addressed the issue of ecclesiality beyond the boundaries of the Roman Catholic church. He wrote:

> The disunion of Christians is verily a rending of Christ and a continuance of His passion. But it also testifies, with the multitude of the saved to some of whom He is not even a name, that He is a saving Victim, and that He came into the world to save it rather than to dominate it. This is the reason, as it seems to us, why His saving work reaches beyond the visible ark of salvation, the Catholic Church, and why the reality of His mercy as Savior surpasses the visible realm of His Kingship; why the Church, too, saves to a greater extent than she rules, and secretly incorporates more members than she can claim as subjects.[30]

Congar's early position concerning this issue was grounded on the belief that there is one church of Jesus Christ, which is identical with the Roman Catholic church. Only within it is salvation possible. Non-Catholics can be considered members of the Catholic church in an invisible and impoverished manner. They belong to the church not effectively and visibly (*re*), but imperfectly and invisibly (*voto*).[31] Congar called for considering them not "heretics" but "separated brothers." Christian communities that are not in union with Rome maintain some elements of the church.[32] At that early stage, Congar ascribed some ecclesiality to non-Catholic Christians individually, but not to their communities.[33] Later, he gave more weight to the Protestant communities as agents of salvation and "potential parts" of the one church,[34] though he preferred to call them "ecclesial communities" rather than "churches."[35]

Gregory Baum (b. 1923) is less hesitant about the ecclesial status of the Protestant churches. He has advocated applying the term "church" to the Protestant churches, though with reservations and unofficially.[36] He has also considered the restoration of church unity not in the terms

---

29. Congar, *Chrétiens désunis*; English translation: Congar, *Divided Christendom*.
30. Congar, *Divided Christendom*, 223–24.
31. See Koskela, "Yves Congar's Vision of Ecclesiality," 44.
32. See ibid., 42.
33. Congar, *Divided Christendom*, 242.
34. See Koskela, "Yves Congar's Vision of Ecclesiality," 52–53.
35. Congar, "Le développement de l'évaluation ecclésiologique des églises non catholiques," 219, 240–41.
36. See Koskela, "Yves Congar's Vision of Ecclesiality," 57–58.

of conversion and reunion with Rome but as a journey shared by all churches:

> The time will come, and is already coming, when all who are faithful to the gracious will of God shall transcend the divisions and enter into one community. We believe that this community of saints, established in glory on the last day, will be in continuity with the Catholic Church.... But this reunion will not be like the victory of one group over another; it will be the fulfillment of the hopes of all of us.[37]

Baum wrote this on the eve of the Vatican II, which was to be the apogee of the Catholic inclusiveness in regard to other Christian churches. The council's constitution *Lumen gentium* in particular stated that the one

> church, set up and organised in this world as a society, subsists in the catholic church, governed by the successor of Peter and the bishops in communion with him, although outside its structure many elements of sanctification and of truth are to be found which, as proper gifts to the church of Christ, impel towards catholic unity.[38]

This constitution identified both the visible and the invisible aspects of the church as comprising one church, which "subsists" in the Roman church under the leadership of the pope. "Subsists" here replaced the more categorical "is" from the earlier drafts of the constitution. At the same time, it recognized elements of the church of Christ outside the Roman church. More explicit on this particular issue was Vatican's II decree on ecumenism, *Unitatis redintegratio*. This document demonstrated an open and inclusive approach to the "Churches and ecclesial communities separated from the Roman apostolic see." It made a distinction in its treatment of the eastern churches and the churches of the Reformation. Concerning the latter, it stated:

> Though the ecclesial communities which are separated from us lack the fullness of unity with us flowing from baptism, and though we believe they have not retained the proper reality of the eucharistic mystery in its fullness, especially because the sacrament of orders is lacking, nevertheless when they commemorate his death and resurrection in the Lord's supper, they

---

37. Baum, *The Catholic Quest for Christian Unity*, 70–71.
38. §8, Tanner, *Decrees of the Ecumenical Councils*, vol. 2, 854.

profess that it signifies life in communion with Christ and look forward to his coming in glory. For these reasons dialogue should include among its subjects the Lord's Supper and other sacraments, worship, and the church's ministry.[39]

The decree was even more positive about the eastern churches, recognizing all their sacraments:

These churches, though separated from us, yet possess true sacraments, above all, by apostolic succession, the priesthood and the Eucharist, whereby they are still linked with us in closest intimacy. Therefore some worship in common, given suitable circumstances and the approval of church authority, is not merely possible but to be encouraged.[40]

Karl Rahner (1904–84), who influenced the ecclesiology of Vatican II, developed the original concept of "anonymous Christianity":[41]

I see thousands around me—I see whole cultures, whole epochs of history around me, before and after me—who are not explicitly Christian. I see the approach of times in which Christianity will no longer be a matter of course in Europe and in the whole world. I know all that, but ultimately it cannot trouble me. Why not? Because everywhere I see a *nameless Christianity*, and because I do not see my own explicit Christianity as one option among others which contradict it. I see nothing other in my Christianity than the explicit recognition and home-coming of everything in the way of truth and love which exists or could exist anywhere else.[42]

For Rahner, "anonymous Christians" include even those who do not believe in Christ but who in their way of life are close to the Christian teaching. For Rahner, the idea of anonymous Christianity was "a way of

---

39. § 22, ibid., 919–20.

40. § 15, ibid., 917.

41. See Moore, "Karl Rahner's Notion of the Anonymous Christian"; Hebblethwaite, "The Status of 'Anonymous Christians'"; Kanyike, "The Anonymous Christian and the Mission of the Church"; Costa, "Karl Rahner's Anonymous Christian"; Martini, "Anonymous Christians, Anonymous Faith in Karl Rahner's Theological Thought"; Wong, "Anonymous Christians: Karl Rahner's Pneuma-Christocentrism and an East-West Dialogue."

42. In the essay "On the Possibility of Christian Faith Today," in Rahner, *Theological Investigations*, vol. 5, 9.

stating the relationship of Christianity to the 'world.'"[43] It was his answer to the challenges of modernity and globality that Christianity faced. Not everyone agreed with this answer. Henri de Lubac would accept that there are "anonymous Christians," but not "anonymous Christianity." Hans Urs von Balthasar (1905–88) and Hans Küng (b. 1928) considered Rahner's concept to be dangerous and misleading.[44] Yet, this concept remains one of the most inclusive in Catholic ecclesiology.

The inclusivism of Vatican II also provoked negative reactions, though not explicit. These reactions are believed to be connected with the activities of the Congregation for the Doctrine of the Faith, especially when Pope Emeritus Benedict XVI held office there. Joseph Ratzinger, in his early works, was as open in his attitude toward the non-Catholic churches as Congar, Baum, or Rahner. For him, the category of heresy was no longer applicable to faithful Protestants. He was even ready to recognize some ecclesiality within the Protestant communities:

> Something that was once rightly condemned as heresy cannot later simply become true, but it can gradually develop its own positive ecclesial nature which the individual is presented with as his church, and in which he lives as a believer, not a heretic.[45]

He called these other churches "sisters": "We can ask at least that the two communities—Catholic and Protestant—regard each other as 'sisters in the Lord.'"[46]

When Ratzinger switched to more conservative positions, however, he preferred either not to speak on this issue at all or spoke through official statements. One such statement was the declaration *Dominus Iesus* promulgated by the Congregation for the Doctrine of the Faith in 2000. This document explored the relation of Christianity with other religions and the world. It also addressed some ecclesiological issues and in particular, the Roman Catholic attitude toward other Christian churches.[47] In §17, the declaration stated clearly that "the ecclesial communities which have not preserved the valid Episcopate and the genuine and integral substance of the Eucharistic mystery, are not Churches in

---

43. In Hebblethwaite, "The Status of 'Anonymous Christians,'" 49.
44. See ibid., 47.
45. Ratzinger, *The Open Circle*, 125.
46. Ibid., 128.
47. *De Iesu Christi atque Ecclesiae unicitate et universalitate salvifica*, in Lora, *Enchiridion Vaticanum*, 656–709.

the proper sense."⁴⁸ At the same time, baptism is regarded as a link with the church of Christ, even though imperfect: "Those who are baptized in these communities are, by Baptism, incorporated in Christ and thus are in a certain communion, albeit imperfect, with the Church."⁴⁹

As for the eastern churches, their ecclesial character and the validity of their eucharist was confirmed. However, the declaration stressed that Vatican II understood them to be "true particular Churches." This means that, from the Roman perspective, they do not constitute one church but a multiplicity of local churches that, "while not existing in perfect communion with the Catholic Church, remain united *to* her by means of the closest bonds." This is no longer a relationship between the sisters. The wording of the declaration implies a subjection of the eastern "particular churches" to the bishop of Rome who "has and exercises [primacy] over the entire Church."⁵⁰ The idea of universal primacy was indirectly confirmed when in 2005 Pope Benedict XVI gave up one of his titles, "Patriarch of the West."

Similar exclusivist tendencies are also common in the Christian East. Alexey Khomiakov, who often accused Rome of exclusivism, actually spoke a similar language. He stated that "only those communities can consider themselves quite Christian which preserve unity with the Eastern Patriarchates or enter this unity."⁵¹ As a result, only those sacraments are valid which are performed "inside the Orthodox Church."⁵² Those sacraments that have been performed outside the Orthodox church, primarily the eucharist, are "incomplete." They receive the "fullness and completeness of the Orthodox mystery" only through reconnection with the Orthodox church. According to Khomiakov, the act of conversion to the Orthodox church is itself a "repeating" of the sacraments from outside the church.⁵³ In this point, he apparently followed Augustine. Khomiakov confessed his agnosticism regarding the possibilities of salvation for those who do not belong to the Orthodox church. They can, however, be connected to it by invisible ties. These ties will be revealed on the Day

---

48. English translation available on the website of the Holy See: http://goo.gl/xj22xd [accessed October 21, 2015].

49. Ibid.

50. Ibid.

51. Хомяков, *Учение о Церкви*, 73.

52. Хомяков, *Письмо к редактору "L'union chrétienne,"* 267.

53. Ibid., 267.

of Judgment. Khomiakov also recognized that "the earthly and visible Church is not yet the fullness and completeness of the entire Church."[54]

Khomiakov's approach was continued in an even stricter sense at the beginning of the twentieth century by two conservative Russian hierarchs, Metropolitan Anthony Khrapovitsky (1863–1936) and Archbishop Hilarion Troitsky (1886–1929). They further developed the positions of Khomiakov as a theory of *oikonomia*. This theory goes back to the Greek theologians Nicodeme the Hagiorite (1749–1809) and Athanasios of Paros (c. 1721–1813), who in the late eighteenth century dealt with the problem of receiving converts from the Roman Catholic church. They insisted that the normative practice of the church is to receive everyone through "rebaptism." They called this normative practice *akribeia* (ἀκρίβεια). It reflects what the church truly believes about itself, its sacraments, and salvation. The church nevertheless allows some concession to those who want to join it. This concession is called *oikonomia* (οἰκονομία). As Nicodeme put it, "it is not possible to consider *oikonomia*, which sometimes was used by some of the Fathers, either as a law or as a pattern to follow."[55]

Metropolitan Anthony explained *oikonomia* as a means of removing psychological obstacles to the true church in the way of the heterodox and schismatics so that they do not feel embarrassed to be treated the same as pagans or Jews. When they join the church, the forms of the mysteries that they had received outside of it immediately "get filled" with grace.[56] Archbishop Hilarion articulated this idea more clearly:

> The truth of the unity of the Church excludes the possibility of grace for sacramental practices in societies outside the Church. ...[57] The Church is one, and only it can possess all the fullness of the gracious gifts of the Holy Spirit. Whoever, in whatever way, has stepped out of the Church, either due to heresy or to schism or to a self-ordered gathering, loses communion with the grace of God. That is why the mysteries that are accomplished outside the Church cannot bestow grace. Only for the benefit of the Church, in order to facilitate joining it, the rite of baptism is allowed to be not repeated, if it has been performed in a correct

54. Хомяков, *Учение о Церкви*, 56.
55. Ἀγαπίου καὶ Νικοδήμου, *Πηδάλιον*, 371.
56. Храповицкий, "Ответ на третье письмо секретаря Всемирной Конференции Епископальной Церкви в Америке," 887–88.
57. Троицкий, *Очерки из истории догмата о Церкви*, 70.

way outside the Church. This is not because this rite had already been a gracious mystery, but in hope that the gift of grace will be received through reconciliation with the body of the Church.[58]

This approach of Metropolitan Anthony's was fully incarnated in the ecclesiology of the Russian Orthodox Church Outside Russia (ROCOR), which he cofounded after the Bolshevik revolution. This church gradually came to reject all varieties of ecumenism. It went so far as to accuse other Orthodox churches of not being Orthodox because of their participation in the ecumenical movement and it broke relations with them for this reason. For some time, this church even practiced the rebaptism of those who joined it from other local Orthodox churches, particularly from the Moscow patriarchate. In effect, the ROCOR believed at that time that salvation was impossible outside the boundaries of its own jurisdiction, which is as such an interesting illustration of the correlation between the idea of jurisdiction and external borders of the church.

Some modern Greek theologians and canonists even now apply the binary of *akribeia-oikonomia* in addressing the problem of the borders of the church, though not in the same extreme sense. Vlasios Pheidas (b. 1936), for instance, reasons in the following way:

> The Orthodox Church moves, according to the specific circumstances, between canonical "acribeia" and ecclesial economy, recognising by economy the validity (κῦρος) of the sacraments of those ecclesiastical bodies. Yet, such a practice of "economy" does not overthrow the canonical "acribeia," which also remains in force and expresses the exclusive character of Orthodox ecclesiology.
>
> This observation is really important, because it reveals that the canonical recognition (ἀναγνώρισις) of the validity of sacraments performed outside the Orthodox Church: a) is done by economy, b) covers only specific cases in certain given instances, and c) refers to the validity of the sacraments only of those who join the Orthodox Church, and not of the ecclesiastical bodies to which belong those who join the Orthodox Church.[59]

Georges Florovsky (1893–1979), in contrast, criticized the *oikonomia* theory. He directed his critique mostly at Metropolitan Anthony Khrapovitsky. He argued that it is highly hypocritical to accept those who come from the "graceless space" outside the church, as the followers of

---

58. Ibid., 83.
59. Phidas, "The Limits of the Church in an Orthodox Perspective," 527.

that theory believed, by leading them to understand that grace is to be found there. Those who support the idea that the space around the church is graceless should not apply *oikonomia*, but must strongly warn that grace can be received only in the church.[60] Trying to draw up an alternative theory, Florovsky started by reaffirming Cyprian: "Whatever Cyprian said about the unity of the Church and mystery can be and should be accepted. However, one should not draw the line of the Church body only through the dots of canon law."[61] "Through its practice, the Church witnesses that beyond its canonical threshold there is a continuation of its mystical territory, and the 'external world' does not begin immediately."[62]

Florovsky tried to follow two lines of reasoning concerning the issue of the church borders.[63] On the one hand, he firmly held to the idea of the one church as identical with the Orthodox church. He rejected the theories of branches and the invisible church. On the other hand, he was reasonably ecumenical[64] and allowed for some undefined ecclesiality and possibility of salvation outside the Orthodox church. Florovsky tried to reconcile these two points, without, however, much success. He eventually had to recognize that he has more questions than solutions to offer to the issue of the church borders.[65] His ecclesiological agnosticism became an Orthodox theological mainstream.

Following this line, patriarch of Moscow Sergiy Stragorodsky (1867–1944) carefully avoided two extremes: the theory of *oikonomia* and the theory of branches. He stated that, on the one hand, the Orthodox church is one, holy, catholic, and apostolic. All other churches have separated from it.[66] On the other hand, those who fell out of the church still "retained some connection with it. Together with this connection, they retained some possibility (which may be invisible and incomprehensible for us) of using the gracious and life-giving juice that fills the Church."[67]

60. Флоровский, "О границах Церкви," 18–19.

61. Ibid., 17.

62. Ibid., 16.

63. See Gavrilyuk, *Georges Florovsky and the Russian Religious Renaissance*, 226.

64. Florovsky was an active participant in the *Faith and Order Commission* and published a number of works on ecumenism: Florovsky, *The Collected Works of Georges Florovsky*, vol 13.

65. Флоровский, "О границах Церкви," 26.

66. Страгородский, "К вопросу о том, что нас разделяет со старокатоликами," 1249.

67. Страгородский, "Об отношении Церкви Христовой к отделившимся от

It should be remarked here that Stragorodsky wrote an important book called *The Orthodox Teaching on Salvation*,[68] which marked a shift from the juridical to a more organic understanding of salvation as dependent on grace, love, and the deeper engagement of human personality into the salvific process. Stragorodsky applied his understanding of salvation to the reasoning about the borders of the church.

After the Russian church reemerged from the Stalin's persecutions and joined the ecumenical movement, it began again reflecting on the issues of the borders of the church and salvation. Again, it followed the paradigm of balances, on the one hand confirming the identity of the Orthodox with the universal church, and on the other hand recognizing some ecclesiality outside the church. This paradigm has been fully embodied in the statement "Basic principles of the attitude of the Russian Orthodox Church to heterodoxy."[69] This document was received by the council of bishops of the Russian church in 2000. It states that the Orthodox church and the one church of Christ are fully identical (1.1). Other Christian communities should be considered to have fallen away (1.4). At the same time, as the document continues, "communities that have fallen away were never considered completely deprived of the grace of God. A break in church communion inevitably leads to damages in the life of grace, but not to its complete disappearance" (1.15).

The balanced ecclesiology proved to be effective in reconciling various groups within the church that hold opposite opinions about the participation of the church in the ecumenical movement. On the one hand, it makes promises to those who stand firm for their church as the only church of Jesus Christ. On the other hand, it flirts with its ecumenically minded members. However, this eclectic ecclesiology fails to give a consistent solution to the issue of the church boundaries. Georges Florovsky, as we have seen, felt the insufficiency of the method of balances and tried to find different approaches. Even more critical of any existing method of solving the problem was another prominent Russian ecclesiologist of the twentieth century, Nikolay Afanasiev (1893–1986). He recognized that all previous attempts to produce a synthesis of the doctrine of the church

---

нее обществам," 4–5.

68. Страгородский, Православное учение о спасении, 1895.

69. Available on the official website of the Moscow patriarchate: http://goo.gl/zP-b3jn [accessed October 21, 2015].

giving a reasonable solution to the problem of sacraments and salvation outside of the church had failed.[70]

Probably, this problem has no solution at all, until we get rid of the conventional image of a borderline between the church and non-church as sharp-cut edge. We assume that this image goes back to Cyprian of Carthage. However, what was the borderline in the time of Cyprian? The Roman Empire at that time did not have borders; it had *frontiers* that constantly moved. The frontiers were supposed to expand as far as possible and had to include as much land and as many peoples as possible. The frontiers were not lines but territories, sometimes vast, fill with numerous peoples. The political and civil status of those lands was different from both the Roman dominion and the *barbarikon* (τὸ βαρβαρικόν): the *Pax Romana* did not fully cover those people with its protection, so they were exposed to risks of various sorts.

This image of frontiers would be probably closer to the early church's understanding of its borders and could better serve in dealing with the dilemmas of the church boundaries. When Cyprian referred to the impossibility of salvation outside the church, he might have had in mind a picture of the fertile and well-protected core Roman territory surrounded by frontiers of uncertain status. Those frontiers extended far away and vanished somewhere in the waterless and windy barbarian wilderness of "Libya" and "Phazania" inhabited by uncivilized and helpless *Gaetuli*, *Garamantes* and *Nasamones* (Map 3).

Such a vision is not dualistic but realistic. It is a vision of the church that does not look for excuses to lock its gates and build strong walls around it. This church rather looks for opportunities to open them up as widely as possible. This church tries to reach the most remote places and peoples and make them its own territory and citizens. This church works hard to irrigate desert lands and make them fertile. It struggles to change the mind of the inhabitants of these lands from hostility to favor, and then to make them its own people.

---

70. Афанасьев, *Вступление в Церковь*, 139.

180   Scaffolds of the Church

Map 3: Roman frontiers in North Africa in time of Cyprian of Carthage.[71]

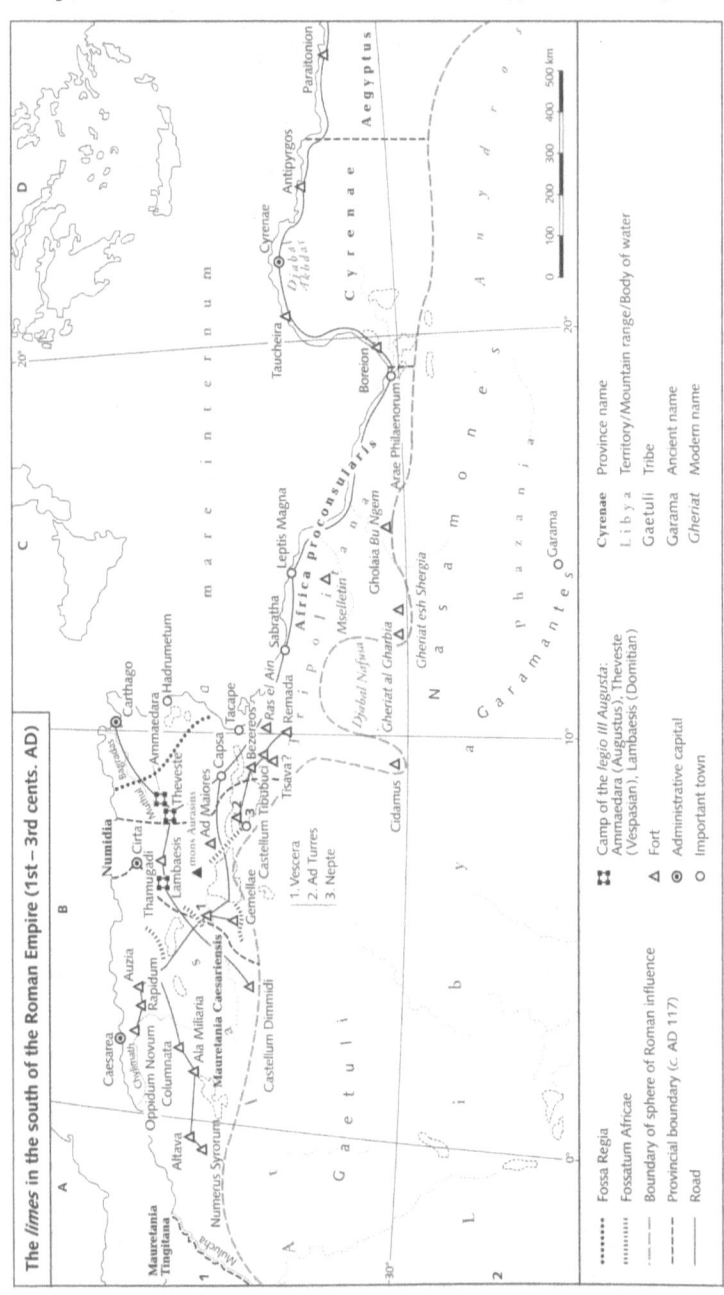

71. Source: Wittke et al., *Historical Atlas of the Ancient World*, 212.

Conclusions:
From Structuralism to Poststructuralism and Beyond

THERE ARE TWO BASIC approaches to the structures of the church. According to one, the structures constitute an intrinsic part of the church's nature, having been implanted in the ecclesial body from the beginning. Doubts about their infallibility are next to blasphemy. This approach can be characterized as "ontological" because it regards the structures as inseparable parts (*onta*, ὄντα) of the church.[1] Without them, the church ceases to be the church. Theologians who follow this line try to anchor ecclesial institutions in the Trinity and the Incarnation, and draw parallels between the heavenly and ecclesial hierarchies.

This book has taken a different approach, which I would call "conventional," i.e., based on what is accepted or agreed upon by the churches for their convenience. My purpose has been to demonstrate that the ecclesial structures emerged in the course of history, as instruments to facilitate the church's pursuit of particular goals. From time to time, these instruments can break down or turn against the church, and must therefore be repaired or possibly even discarded—precisely to further the same ends for which they were originally designed. Because they grow complex and self-sufficient, they need to be deconstructed, to recover their original rationale. This book's work of deconstruction does not seek to destroy the structures, but rather to keep them open, so they can be readjusted to their original meaning. It makes them consistent with themselves.

---

1. It is tempting but incorrect to identify this approach as "onto-theology." However, this Kantian term had different meaning in the writings of the Prussian philosopher and those who borrowed the term from him, including Martin Heidegger and Jacques Derrida.

Keeping a distance between the nature of the church and its structures helps avoid two equally disturbing interpretations of church history. One presents this history to be smooth and consistent from the apostolic age to our days. This book, through the examples of supra-communal administration and ministry in the church, has demonstrated that such a perception of history cannot stand up to the evidence. It concurs with the critique by Michael Foucault, who regarded continuous history as "the indispensable correlative of the founding function of the subject: the guarantee that everything that has eluded him [the historian] may be restored to him; the certainty that time will disperse nothing without restoring it in a reconstituted unity."[2] In other words, the assumed continuity of the ecclesial structures is secured by the observer who believes in their continuity by believing in the continuity of the church proper—a view that this book considers problematic. On the other hand, the Foucauldian interpretation of the structures as a sequence of radical disruptions would imply disruptions in the church proper if the structures were identified with the church's nature.[3] This is something that cannot be accepted from the Christian theological standpoint. This book's argument saves the continuity of the church by distinguishing its structures, with their undeniable disruptions, from its nature.

This does not mean, however, that the nature of the church is not vulnerable to sin and corruption. Because the church is both human and divine, the sins of its members offend its nature. However, they are like the sins of Zacchaeus (Luke 19:1–10) and Mary Magdalene (Mark 8:2). The sins of the structures are different: they are the sins of the Pharisees and the teachers of the law (Matt 5:20). When the institutions that are supposed to restrain the sins of its faithful themselves fall into sin, this is more severe than the sins of the ordinary members of the church.

The lexeme "the nature of the church" has been derived from the language of the Aristotelian-Porphyrian dialectics. In this language, the core of the church can be presented as its "nature" (*physis*, φύσις). The ecclesial structures do not belong to this *physis*. Neither should they be regarded as natural properties (*idiotētes*, ἰδιότητες) of the church. They are adjacent to the church, like scaffolding to an edifice. The basic assumption of Aristotelian dialectics holds: whatever commonly belongs to all individuals sharing in the same nature and does not change is

---

2. Foucault, *The Archaeology of Knowledge and the Discourse on Language*, 12.
3. See Poster, "Foucault and History," 117.

pertinent to this nature. When certain features apply only to some individuals, or when they disappear and reappear, they are not part of the common nature. In the case of the church, this means that only what was always observable in the entire church belongs to its nature.

Communities have always been part of the church. We cannot imagine or point historically to the church without communities in which Christ is present and the gifts of the Spirit are distributed among the faithful. The same holds for baptism, the eucharist, and ministry: every community has always had them without any disruption. Communities, sacraments, and their ministering therefore belong to the nature of the church. Their liturgical forms and their theological interpretation might change from century to century, but they themselves are a constant across the church's existence. Sacramental, pastoral, and administrative leadership also belongs to the nature of the church, as long as it is exercised *within* the community. This leadership adopted various historical forms and incarnated in the offices of apostles, presbyters, bishops, and priests acting in the name of bishop.

On the supra-communal level, however, the ministry of leadership does not belong to the nature of the church, because there was time when there was no supra-communal level. On this level, the role of the bishops is administrative and as such constitutes a part of the ecclesial structures. Other administrative supra-communal structures of the church, such as canonical territory, autocephaly, *etc.*, do not belong to its nature either, because there was a time when they were not. If they belonged to the ecclesial nature, this nature would be administrative. This does not mean they are not important. Their importance is in securing the full participation of the communities in the common nature of the church. Indeed, communities can be considered hypostases of the church only if they fully share in the common nature through confessing the same faith, performing the same sacraments, and preserving communion with each other. If they fail in at least one of these criteria, they cease partaking in the common ecclesial nature and become schismatic or heretical. The structures of the church were designed to ensure that this does not happen to the communities. If they serve communities and facilitate their partaking in the nature of the church, they accord to this nature (*kata physin*, κατὰ φύσιν, to use the phrase of Maximus the Confessor). If they fail to fulfill this mission or begin to serve themselves, they harm the church and go against its nature (*para physin*, παρὰ φύσιν).[4]

4. *Opuscula theologica et polemica* 20 (CPG 7697: PG 91, 236 A–B).

Another language into which the structures of the church can be translated is that of structuralism and poststructuralism. The fundamental premise of structuralism is that social structures influence the ideas and behaviors of the individuals and groups that embrace them. This assumption comes close to the hypothesis of this book that the ecclesial structures built on the basis of ecclesiological beliefs in turn modified ideas about the church and influenced its members' models of behavior. The behavioral implications of the structures have proven stronger, in some cases, than even the words of the Gospels.

This justifies the critique of the ecclesial structures that has been proposed in this book. The critique is congruent with the methods of social analysis employed in modern critical theory. To illustrate how this theory can work in ecclesiology, let us take for example the ideas of the prominent social theorist Michael Walzer. He has identified three models of social criticism: discovery, invention, and interpretation.[5] All three, in my judgment, are applicable to the structures of the church. Moreover, to frame the ecclesial institutions critically, these models should ideally be applied together. The first model, that of discovery, is revelational and religious: "Someone must climb the mountain, go into desert, seek out the God-who-reveals, and bring back his word."[6] Without this kind of discovery of the church's nature, its structures would be either confused with the latter or rejected as irrelevant to it. As for the second model, the church often invented the structures it needed or reinvented them when their older iterations became useless. Finally, all of the structures need critical re-interpretation in order to be readjusted to their initial rationale and to the nature of the church. Axel Honneth, building on the critical taxonomy of Walzer, articulated it in an alternative way: he presented invention and interpretation as construction and reconstruction, and added to them "genealogy."[7] In tune with Honneth's taxonomy, the critique exercised in this book helped us *construct* the concept of the nature of the church. However, this construction work would be incomplete without *reconstruction* of the structures that serve the nature. Finally, *genealogical* critique, for Honneth, aims to show how the norms of the social order "serve to legitimate a disciplinary or repressive practice."[8] This translates into my argument that vulnerability has been embedded in the ecclesial

---

5. Walzer, *Interpretation and Social Criticism*.
6. Ibid., 4–5.
7. Honneth, *Pathologies of Reason*, 72–76.
8. Ibid., 76.

structures from their beginning. Addressing the deviations of the structures, therefore, does not mean getting rid of the structures altogether—another important conclusion of the book.

Structuralism holds that there are social structures that remain invariable across time and space. This tenet seems to cohere with the "ontological" approach which regards the structures of the church to be universal, unchangeable, and established by God. In this point, my book and structuralism diverge. I have argued that the structures of the church are not universal, do change, and are not established by God. In this, the book comes closer to poststructuralism. The poststructuralists assume that even basic social structures change over time. In coherence with this standpoint, the book demonstrates the changeability of the ecclesial structures in both form and meaning. It proves what the poststructuralist Gilles Deleuze (1925–95) believed about structures: that they are the cause of the evolution of what they represent.[9] Thus, for instance, when autocephaly was instrumentalized by political rulers during the Middle Ages, it departed radically from what it had held in the Late Antiquity an opposition to the structural changes incurred by political expediencies. Although the name of this structure remained the same for centuries, its underlying tenet changed. The same pattern of change can be discerned in the evolution of the clerical orders and the laity. Priestly ministry is embedded in the church, but the manner in which particular ministries serve the church is subject to change. These changes, in turn, change how ministry is perceived.

At some stage, ministry became perceived as hierarchy. Hierarchy is, in some sense, a superstructure that encompasses most of the ecclesial structures. The notion of hierarchy was adopted by the church under the influence of Neoplatonism and as a result of the church's coalescence with the Roman world. It gradually conquered most domains of the church, and primarily its ministry. The three ranks of clerical orders replaced a wider variety of ministerial offices and charisms in the earliest Christian community. After the three-fold order became accepted and institutionalized, it gradually modified the idea of ministry. Thus, it induced a shift from non-hierarchical *diakonia* to hierarchical privilege. This, in turn, created and widened the gap between clergy and laity. As a concept and *stratum* within the church, the "laity" has arisen as a consequence

---

9. See Williams, *Understanding Poststructuralism*, 54.

of hierarchization. There was time when there was no "laity"—which, therefore, cannot be regarded a concept encoded in the original idea of the church.

According to the theory of social stratifications, class divisions in society are sustained by "the valued resource that is seen to be the *most* important in people's life."[10] Applied to the church, this principle would mean that when the most highly valued resource becomes access (primarily through priesthood) to the divine—rather than common Christian identity—a "social distance" is created between the orders in the church, particularly between priests and lay people. Such distances are undoubtedly contrary to the intention of the early Christians to eliminate any kind of social gaps that separated people from each other in the world outside the church. The famous words of Paul to the Galatians—"There is neither Jew nor Greek, there is neither slave nor free, there is neither male nor female, for all of you are one in Christ Jesus" (3:28)—had been directed precisely against such social distances.

The words of Paul should not necessarily be taken as a directive to dismantle the established ministerial orders. They should nevertheless underscore the need for the already existing stratification to be transformed from alienating to relational and communicational. In the terminology of Maximus the Confessor, the church orders as such should not change, but *how* they interact with each other should change. When the church appears to its members not as a structure but as a relationship, the hierarchical orders do not divide the ecclesial body.[11] According to Pierre Bourdieu, social strata come closer to each other when they realize their belonging to the same cultural space.[12] The same can be said about the church. The "social distance" between its hierarchical orders diminishes when their members do not forget that all of them—lay people, priests, bishops, and patriarchs—belong to the *same* space of grace and salvation. When their identities as lay people, priests, bishops, and primates prevail over their common Christian identity, stratification is exacerbated.

10. Bottero, *Stratification*, 6.

11. This would be in the same vein as the attitude to the social strata developed by the *Cambridge Social Interaction and Stratification* group, which is focused on the relational patterns of stratification. Its method is based on the idea "that differential association is an essential feature of social stratification arrangements. . . . Differential association can be seen as a way of defining proximity within a social space and that this social space can be reconstructed from the distances between groups." See the website of the group: www.camsis.stir.ac.uk [accessed September 11, 2015].

12. See Bourdieu, *Distinction*.

Stratification is a result of a dichotomization between "us" and "them."[13] This dichotomy is often at work in the church: lay people counterpose themselves to priests, bishops to lay people, and so forth. The "us versus them" pattern also sharpens the perception of the edges of the church, its members' understanding of themselves as "us" and those outside the church as "them." This dichotomy creates a vicious circle of alienation both inside and outside the church, when polarization between "us" and "them" *in* the church increases polarization between the church and the world and vice versa.

Hierarchization and stratification in the church are enhanced by dualism. When there is a sharp divide between the holy and unholy, the hierarchical priesthood is needed as an isthmus from the secular to the divine. The narrower the bottleneck to the holy, the more developed the hierarchy of those who provide access to it. At the same time, when access to the holy is unlimited, there is no need for a hierarchy of mediators. Christ as the great high priest (Heb 4:14) made the holy accessible for everyone in his church. Therefore, the task of the Christian "priests" is different from the task of the priests of the Jewish temple or in the polytheistic cults. The priesthood in the Christian communities does not exist to exploit the restrictions of access to the holy, but to help the members of the community to use as fully as possible the abundance of grace granted by Christ to everyone without measure (John 3:34). Such an idea of the Christian priesthood, however, has been blurred by the sharp, dualistic perception of the church as an island of the holy in the sea of the unholy. The same dualistic perception modified the idea of the church's boundaries, which evolved from an undefined frontier to a clear-cut demarcation line that separates the church from the non-church.

Although hierarchy and dualism have had a major impact on the ecclesial structures, they are imagined and not real features of the church. Valerie Ahl and T. F. H. Allen in their study of the theory of hierarchy have noticed that any perception of complex systems tend to be hierarchical, even when these systems are not hierarchical *per se*.[14] This important observation is applicable to the ecclesial hierarchy: as the structures of the church grew more complex, the *self-perception* of the church became more hierarchical. It is not a coincidence, therefore, that both processes—those of complication and hierarchization—accelerated

---

13. Cannadine, *Class in Britain*, 19–20.
14. See Ahl and Allen *Hierarchy Theory*, 191.

simultaneously in the third century.[15] The metropolitan system and the office of *episkopos* came to prominence, culminating in the fifth century, when Justinian legalized the complexity of the ecclesial structures and Ps-Dionysius laid down the metaphysical foundations for the church hierarchy. The theory of Ahl and Allen substantiates my suggestion that it is not the church *per se* which has become hierarchical, but its self-perception and structures.[16]

In this light, I agree with the poststructuralist Roland Barthes that the hierarchical order is not natural, but cultural. When this order is taken for natural, it easily slides into ideology.[17] This ideology, in its manifestation in the church, can be called hierarchism. Hierarchism projects the malfunctions of the structures onto the nature of the church and thereby compromises the latter. Alternatively, the malfunctions of the structures are justified as if they were the church proper. As a result, corruption and despotism turn "holy." They flourish in the church to an extent that would be unacceptable in secular institutions. Paradoxically, secular institutions, despite their lack of religious ethics, can handle such issues as corruption and despotism more easily. This is because they do not regard themselves to be metaphysical. An exception might be the dictators who exercise their power as metaphysical. In their case, all sorts of corruption and despotism become easily accepted as attached to the metaphysics of dictatorial power. The church's metaphysics is different: it is embedded in its very nature, because the church is not only social, but also a divine reality. When the structures of the church are not properly distinguished from its human-divine nature, their malfunctions, because of the metaphysical dimension of the church, can be easily accepted as sacrosanct. They cease to be ethically inappropriate and are instead seen as tolerable or even holy—something similar to the sacred prostitution in antiquity. This tendency exacerbates the vices of the structures.

No structure of the church is immune to deviations and abuses. Even when an abuse is corrected, the remedy can become abusive as well.[18] For example, many nowadays consider the election of bishops by people to be a panacea against bishops' authoritarianism. In contrast to this belief, a number of early authors, including Origen and Gregory of

15. See Stewart-Sykes, *The Original Bishops*, 5.

16. See Hovorun, *Meta-Ecclesiology*, 37–68.

17. Barthes, *Mythologies*, translated by Annette Lavers, 155–56.

18. Poststructuralists would say in this regard that deconstruction cannot be reduced to a formula or algorithm. See Williams, *Understanding Poststructuralism*, 30.

Nazianzus, complained about lay participation in the election of bishops. They criticized in particular the populism of the candidates, the application of secular criteria by the electors, and the frequent practice of the former bribing the latter.[19] When the participation of lay was minimized or excluded, however, this soon came to be regarded as a problem, for instance by John Chrysostom. Thus, two opposite practices, which were supposed to correct each other, turned abusive. They demonstrate that there is no "once and forever" solution to any of the church's problems. To provide at least temporary solutions, however, all structures should be periodically adjusted in accordance with the church's needs and the structures' *raison d'être*.

Sometimes, the reasons for existence of the structures are speculative. Yet they are capable of causing dramatic changes in the empirical reality of the church. This is the case with the distinction between universal and particular in the church. The eastern church developed most of its structures on the basis of particularity, including the patriarchates, canonical territory, and autocephaly. In contrast to the East, the western church favored the idea of universality, which supported the institution of the papacy. The lack of balance between universality and particularity caused abuses of both concepts and eventually led to the schism between East and West. The western idea of the universal church and the eastern idea of local churches contributed to the disconnection of both churches from community. They shifted the "hypostatic weight" of ecclesiality from community to primacy and territory, respectively. In the case of Rome, the pope with his curia became the center of ecclesial gravity. In the case of the eastern churches, it was the patriarch (or archbishop or metropolitan in some cases) with his administration. As the West over-focused on the idea of the global authority of the pope, so the East became obsessed with local jurisdictions.

The western and eastern ecclesiological traditions can come to terms with each other only insofar as they restore the balance between universality and particularity. Communities, which suffer from the misbalances most, are also a key to the restoration of balance. No one particular community can identify itself with the universal church, nor can any supra-communal structure. When the territorial and administrative structures of the church substitute for communities and claim for themselves the right to express either ecclesial universality or particularity, both the universality and particularity of the church become ephemeral,

---

19. See Norton, *Episcopal Elections*, 178.

not grounded in the reality of the church life. Only by focusing on a community are structures of the church made tangible and meaningful. *Community* is the foundation of the church's universality and particularity. It holds the Petrine keys to the issue of primacy, on both universal and regional levels. That kind of primacy is legitimate which serves the well-being of communities.

Dioceses, metropolises, and patriarchates, to function properly, should refocus on communities as well. Without communities in focus, they tend to identify themselves with the church. Then the structures cease to preserve the integrity of the church and become church-dividing structures, harming the communities and themselves. These structures have been presented in the book as partition walls, initially designed to reduce quarrels in God's house but instead often causing more quarrels. When the members of a family quarrel and stop talking to each other, they lock the doors to their rooms from inside. Then the partition walls divide the family: instead of making the life of the members of a household comfortable, they isolate them from each other. This often happens to the inter-church relations, when supra-communal structures, be they dioceses or patriarchates, isolate themselves from others. Such dysfunction in inter-communal relationship has been explored in the book as jurisdictionism.

Jurisdictionism occurs when local churches become obsessed with their corporate interests. Such interests often clash with one another. As a result, local Orthodox churches, while declaring a need to have a common voice and a single position in witnessing to the modern world, in effect wage hot or cold jurisdictional wars over canonical territories and other corporate rights. Their primates cease commemorating each other in the liturgy; their representatives avoid concelebrating liturgies; they may also threaten one another with schisms or excommunications when their interests are not met; they refuse to come to a Pan-Orthodox Council to celebrate their unity. These jurisdictional wars overshadow their understanding of belonging to one universal church, which often remains a figure of speech or a vague concept to which only lip-service is paid.

Hierarchism and jurisdictionism are instances of structure-centrism, which takes hold when the ecclesial structures cease to serve the mission of the church and become an ends in themselves.[20] Then the church becomes subject to its own structures, which reproduce and

---

20. See Schillebeeckx, *The Church with a Human Face*, 209.

sustain themselves instead of serving the people of God. So it often happens that, instead of safeguarding the unity of the church, the church's structures provoke divisions within it; instead of preserving order, they cause disorder. When the structures dominate the church and become ends in themselves, they knock it out of its way. Eric Gritsch called this "the heresy of structure."[21] Avery Dulles characterized this "heresy" as "institutionalism":

> By institutionalism we mean a system in which the institutional element is treated as primary. . . . Institutionalism is a deformation of the true nature of the Church—a deformation that has unfortunately affected the Church at certain periods of its history, and one that remains in every age a real danger to the institutional Church.[22]

Institutionalism diminishes what the church is: the church then shrinks to the narrow confines of its hierarchal orders and its jurisdictions. It betrays its universal call and replaces it with the particular interests of its parts. It turns into a "simulacrum," to use a poststructuralist term. For Gilles Deleuze, simulacrum is a system that has lost its "prior identity."[23] The church that identifies itself with its structures does exactly this: it loses its focus on the kingdom of God as its original destination and identity. The first and best way for the church to get rid of simulacra is to refocus on what belongs to its nature and to reframe its structures in accord with their original meaning.

Institutionalism forces the church into a difficult dilemma: should "the interests of the church" be identified with the corporate interests of the ecclesial hierarchy, or with the interests of the people of God? Not infrequently these two interests come into conflict. For instance, it often happens that the hierarchy collaborates with corrupt and inhumane regimes, which act against the interest of the people. Such co-operation is then justified as being in the "interests of the church." However, such justification expresses only the interests of one or a few groups in the church, and is contrary to the interests of the majority of church members. The church can avoid sinister collaboration when it is not reduced to its hierarchy or administrative structures but is understood as a living body comprising the entire people of God.

21. Gritsch, "The Church as Institution," 454.
22. Dulles, *Models of the Church*, 40.
23. Deleuze, *Difference and Repetition*, 299; see Somers-Hall, *Deleuze's Difference and Repetition*, 193.

All abuses of the ecclesial structures are encapsulated in ecclesiocentrism. This arch-abuse happens when the church is perceived as possessing a self-sufficient value and autonomy with its own purpose, which is not always compatible with the life of God, the breath of the Spirit, and *diakonia* to the community and wider society. The ecclesiocentric separation of the church from God leads to its separation from the life of its own people and vice versa. The church then impedes relations between the faithful and God and among the people, instead of facilitating them. An ecclesiocentric church—a church literally "turned in on itself"—loses its relational character and becomes an island isolated from both people and God. This island may be considered holy, yet its holiness turns out on closer examination to be bare, meaningless, and profane. It is like the island of Delos nowadays: not inhabited, with only tourists exploring its scattered ruins. The church can only be freed from ecclesiocentrism when it is not preoccupied with itself, but gives itself fully to God, to God's people, and to God's world. The church is faithful to its nature and purpose when it is kenotic, self-emptying. The church is true to itself when it strives to serve and is not content to be served.

Dysfunctions of the ecclesial structures, like diseases in the organism, are interrelated. Ecclesiological sins have a certain order, similar to the one that Evagrius Ponticus (345–99) proposed for individual sins.[24] The images employed in this book are supposed to establish the causality between various structural shortcomings. Thus, the partition walls of supra-communal structures turn to jurisdictional strongholds surrounded by ditches. Together, they enhance hierarchical pyramids and stratification in the body of the church. This causality is loop-like: hierarchy and *strata*, in turn, make the walls of the jurisdictions inside them higher (Figure 3).

It is an illusion to suppose that our struggle with the abuses of the ecclesial structures will eventually lead to their complete correction. The abuses will come back again and again, in different forms. Even if one generation has found the best solution to a problem, the next generation should seek for new solutions, because the old ones will not work for long. This does not mean, however, that battling with ecclesial sins is meaningless. From the poststructuralist point of view, the failures of church structures can be beneficial to the church. Indeed, they can make every generation of church members rethink the church's true purpose

---

24. *Practicus* (CPG 2430), 6; see Corrigan, *Evagrius and Gregory*, 44.

and nature, in order to find the wisest ways of dealing with its institutional deviations. The church's persistent problems urge its members to learn better how they personally relate to it. As Raymond Brown has put it, "The greatest peril facing a well-ordered institutional church is not the peril of new ideas but the peril of no ideas."[25] Every generation of Christians should make sense of the structures of the church anew. This implies rediscovery of the initial rationales that gave birth to the ecclesial structures.

Figure 3: Causality of the "ecclesiological sins."

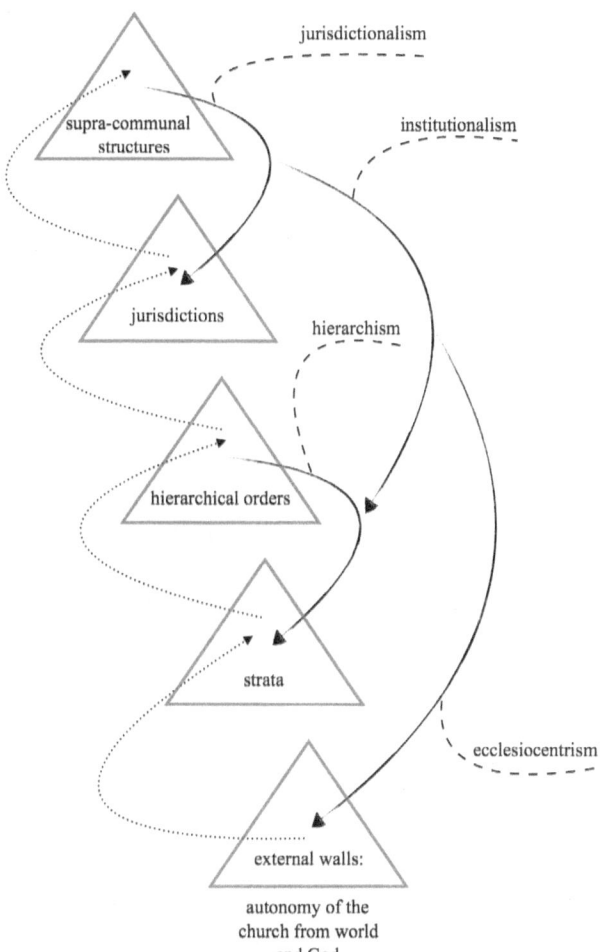

---

25. Brown, *The Churches the Apostles Left Behind*, 40.

Modernity has become particularly helpful in this process. Having detached itself from the church, modernized society has become a mirror in which the church has been able to see many of its ecclesiological sins. Sometimes the church has voluntarily accepted the image in the mirror. In most cases, however, it has refused to recognize its faults. Often it has had to change by force as a result. The Eastern church was a pioneer in this regard. As early as the fifteenth century, the Ottomans, who destroyed the political and social mechanisms that had led to multiple abuses of the structures of the church, effectively liberated it from many of them. In the West, the liberation of the church from the ossification of its structures came with some delay. Part of the western church radically emancipated from many of its *-isms* during the Reformation (however, soon it would embark on new *-isms*). Another part, which refused to change and instead strengthened its structures, waited until Vatican II, which inaugurated the emancipatory processes in the Roman Catholic church.

The dismantling of secular hierarchies in western societies during the second half of the twentieth century forced the churches there to accept similar processes for themselves. As in the third century, when the hierarchical sociopolitical patterns of the Roman Empire encouraged the church to adopt contemporary territorial and administrative structures, so the rise of egalitarianism and the democratization of the modern society helped the churches to reconsider and sometimes restructure their institutions in accordance with new cultural patterns. However, these patterns are not completely new for the church. Some of them can be traced back to the early Christian traditions. The dialogue with modernity thus helped the church rediscover its original ethos. This dialogue made the church realize, as Roger Haight puts it, that "juridical authority alone cannot hold churches together; only denser and subtler bonds of faith and love manifested in respect can keep different churches in communion with each other."[26]

In the wake of new social paradigms and a refreshed perception of what constitutes the church, the twentieth century boomed with various theological projects of emancipation, both in the East and in the West. In the Roman Catholic church, such projects were carried out by theologians including Yves Congar, Edward Schillebeeckx, Hans Küng, and Paul Lakeland. They particularly targeted the structures of the church.

---

26. Mannion and Mudge, *The Routledge Companion to the Christian Church*, 388.

Among their concerns was to re-establish the connections between hierarchical orders and communities. Küng has summarized this concern as follows:

> Congregations and offices are mutually dependent. Neither congregations without offices nor offices without congregations constitute the Church. Neither should the office be raised above the congregations in a self-glorifying, autonomous way (this would be the absolutism of ecclesiastical office and the dissolution of the one Church)—nor should the office be overwhelmed by the congregations (that would be a radical sectarian democracy and likewise a dissolution of the one Church). Rather, the office under the Lord in the congregation must serve it in the proclamation of the Word, the administration of the Sacraments, and the direction of the Church. Thus the congregation and the offices serving in it together constitute the great ecumenical council of the Church.[27]

Orthodox theologians have developed their own emancipatory projects, which also deal with the issues of the ecclesial structures and their relationship with the communities. Nikolay Afanasiev (1893–1966), John Romanides (1927–2001), Alexander Schmemann (1921–83), and their followers chose the eucharist as a lever to move the church forward and to reestablish healthy connections between the ecclesial structures and communities. This is a paradoxical approach, since the medieval fixation on the eucharist had led the church to various abuses of its structures and marginalization of the communities. Nevertheless, in the interpretation of the modern theologians who follow the line of eucharistic ecclesiology, the eucharist reconnects a priest or a bishop with the community. Eucharistic ecclesiology is still an ambivalent instrument of emancipation for communities. It can be used for both deconstruction and reconstruction of the walls inside and outside the church. The theology of John Zizioulas (b. 1931) illustrates this ambiguity. His own emancipatory project is based on the category of personhood. The personalist approach indeed softens the sharp lines of separation between the ecclesial strata. At the same time, it does not eliminate altogether the polarization between them, a point Miroslav Volf observed in the eucharistic ecclesiology of Zizioulas:

> The task of the *ordo* of the laity in saying the liturgical "amen," and the corresponding task of the *ordo* of bishops to act in *persona Christi*, make the Eucharistic gathering into a strictly

27. Küng, *Structures of the Church*, 195.

bipolar event. Neither do the various tasks of the presbyters and deacons interrupt this bipolarity. The presbyters and deacons surround the bishop and stand opposite the people; together with the bishop, they constitute the one pole, while the laity represents the other pole.[28]

A Swedish Orthodox theologian Michael Hjälm (b. 1968) develops an original emancipatory project that goes beyond eucharistic ecclesiology, through the theory of communicative action proposed by Jürgen Habermas (b. 1929).[29] Hjälm has synthesized a concept of "ritual action" that is

> intended to reveal the identity of the Ecclesia. Without identity, we are left with a never-ending debate and a continuous atomization where every answer exponentially provokes more questions. Communicative action is intended for the reaching of mutual understanding, making subjects accountable and responsible. Without communicative action we are bound on a long walk into the never-ending sea of being. Ritual action and communicative action are therefore co-dependent, but in a dialectical relation. If they are confused there is a risk that being-in-the-world becomes a negation of true Being. . . . The missionary imperative in the Ecclesia is dependent on the co-existence of ritual action and communicative action. Without the former the Church loses its particularity and identity and does not reveal itself in the world as a subject, and without the latter the message becomes a negation, stating what the Church is not, but without any positive outcomes.[30]

The emancipatory intention behind this book has been coherent with what Nick Crossley has branded as "relational sociology."[31] It reveals the relational character of the social systems. I have argued in my earlier book that the church is not a thing but a relationship.[32] Applied to the subject of this book, this would mean that the ecclesial structures should be perceived not as ontological but *relational*. They accomplish their mission only when they serve the relations of church members with each other and with God.

28. Volf, *After Our Likeness*, 116.
29. See Hjälm, *Liberation of the Ecclesia*.
30. Ibid., 312–13.
31. Crossley, *Towards Relational Sociology*, 4.
32. See Hovorun, *Meta-Ecclesiology*, 152.

Speaking about the relational character of the social systems, Crossley has identified a dichotomy between the volitional agency of human individuals and the social structures to which they belong. This dichotomy is similar to the dilemma of the church structures: how does it deal with freedom and personality?[33] There are two basic approaches to this dilemma in the theories of social structures: one emphasizes the structures and the other human agency. The former holds that structures are pertinent to the social systems and in this capacity limit freedom of individual agents. The structures stem from within the human psyché. The latter approach is more affirmative of human agency. Even though it does not deny the framing capacities of the social structures, it places them outside the human soul. The former approach is closer to structuralism, while the latter overcomes it as poststructuralist.[34]

This book, in dealing with the dilemma of ecclesial structures vis-à-vis the human agency of church members, confirms on the one hand the importance of the structures. They have a capacity to enforce human agency and make it more productive. They also safeguard the agency from sliding into abuses. Although they do not eliminate the potentiality of such abuses altogether, they significantly restrict it. On the other hand, the book places the ecclesial structures outside the nature of the church, which is intrinsically relational and accommodating of human freedom. The structures should likewise also accommodate human freedom. If they do not, they wound the church and damage the human beings in it. They thus dehumanize the church. When they do this in the name of the divine authority, with the self-awareness of divinely established institutions, they in effect *desecrate* the church.

This constitutes one more reason why the structures of the church should not be considered sacrosanct. That they serve holy ends does not mean they have divine origins. They emerged and were developed by the church as *instruments of convenience* and *outcomes of conventions*. All structures have from time to time deviated from their initial purpose and rationale. Some of them have perished as a result. Others have been renewed over time, such as, for example, the clerical orders of bishops, presbyters, and deacons. In other cases, completely new structures have emerged under old names, as has occurred with autocephaly. It has always been up to the church to decide which structures to forget and

33. See Parsons, *Social Structure and Personality*.
34. See Parker, *Structuration*.

which to reinterpret or remake. This means that the church can create new structures when it deems necessary.

I would like to conclude this book with an extensive quote from the French poststructuralist Roland Barthes. His essay "Plastic" revolves around a metaphor that epitomizes what I intended to say about the ecclesial structures and their relationship to the nature of the church:

> More than a substance, plastic is the very idea of its infinite transformation;... it is less a thing than the trace of a movement. ... The quick-change artistry of plastic is absolute: it can become buckets as well as jewels. Hence a perpetual amazement, the reverie of man at the sight of the proliferating forms of matter, and the connections he detects between the singular of the origin and the plural of the effects. ... The scope of the transformations gives man the measure of his power, and since the very itinerary of plastic gives him the euphoria of a prestigious free-wheeling through Nature. ... The price to be paid for this success is that plastic, sublimated as movement, hardly exists as substance. Its reality is a negative one: neither hard nor deep, it must be content with a "substantial" attribute.... It is a "shaped" substance: whatever its final state, plastic keeps a flocculent appearance, something opaque, creamy and curdled, something powerless ever to achieve the triumphant smoothness of Nature ....[35]

---

35. Barthes, *Mythologies*, translated by Lavers, 97–99.

Appendix 1: The Structure of the Roman Empire in the Fourth Century[1]

I Praefectura oriens (capital: Constantinople)
    I 1 Dioecesis oriens (Antioch)
        1 Libya superior
        2 Libya inferior
        3 Thebais
        4 Aegyptus Iovia
        5 Aegyptus Herculia
        6 Arabia
        7 Arabia nova
        8 Augusta Libanensis
        9 Palaestina
        10 Phoenice
        11 Syria Coele
        12 Augusta Euphratensis
        13 Cilicia
        14 Isauria
        15 Cyprus
        16 Mesopotamia
        17 Osrhoëna
    I 2 Dioecesis Pontica (Nicomedia)
        1 Bithynia
        2 Cappadocia
        3 Galatia
        4 Paphlagonia
        5 Diospontus
        6 Pontus Polemoniacus

1 Based on Wittke et al., *Historical Atlas of the Ancient World*, 224.

        7 Armenia minor
  I 3 Dioecesis Asiana (Ephesus)
        1 Lycia et Pamphylia
        2 Phrygia prima
        3 Phrygia secunda
        4 Asia
        5 Lydia
        6 Caria
        7 Pisidia
        8 Hellespontus
        9 Insulae
  I 4 Dioecesis Thraciae (Philippopolis)
        1 Europa
        2 Rhodope
        3 Thracia
        4 Haemimontus
        5 Scythia
        6 Moesia inferior

II Praefectura Illyricum (Thessalonica)
  II 1 Dioecesis Moesiae (Thessalonica)
        1 Dacia mediterranea
        2 Dacia ripensis
        3 Moesia superior / Margensis
        4 Dardania
        5 Macedonia
        6 Thessalia
        7 Achaea
        8 Praevalitana
        9 Epirus nova
        10 Epirus vetus
        11 Creta

III Praefectura Italia (Mediolanum)
  III 1 Dioecesis Pannoniae (Aquincum)
        1 Pannonia inferior
        2 Savensis/Savia
        3 Dalmatia
        4 Valeria

5 Pannonia superior
6 Noricum ripense
7 Noricum mediterraneum
III 2.1 Dioecesis Italia annonaria (Mediolanum)
    1 Venetia et Histria
    2 Aemilia et Liguria
    3 Flaminia et Picenum
    4 Tuscia et Umbria
    5 Alpes Cottiae
    6 Raetia
III 2.2 Dioecesis Italia suburbicaria (Roma)
    1 Campania
    2 Apulia et Calabria
    3 Lucania et Brutii
    4 Samnium
    5 Sicilia
    6 Sardinia
    7 Corsica
III 3 Dioecesis Africa (Carthago)
    1 Africa proconsularis
    2 Byzacena
    3 Numidia Cirtensis
    4 Numidia militiana
    5 Mauretania Caesariensis
    6 Mauretania Sitifensis
    7 Tripolitana

IV Praefectura Galliae (Augusta Treverorum)
IV 1 Dioecesis Britanniae (Londinium)
    1 Britannia prima
    2 Britannia secunda
    3 Maxima Caesariensis
    4 Flavia Caesariensis
IV 2 Dioecesis Galliae (Augusta Treverorum)
    1 Belgica prima
    2 Belgica secunda
    3 Germania prima
    4 Germania secunda
    5 Sequania

       6 Lugdunensis prima
       7 Lugdunensis secunda
       8 Alpes Graiae et Poeninae
IV 3 Dioecesis Viennensis (Vienna/Constantina)
       1 Viennensis
       2 Narbonensis prima
       3 Narbonensis secunda
       4 Novempopulana
       5 Aquitania prima
       6 Aquitania secunda
       7 Alpes maritimae
IV 4 Dioecesis Hispaniae (Augusta Emerita)
       1 Baetica
       2 Lusitania
       3 Carthaginiensis
       4 Gallaecia
       5 Tarraconensis
       6 Mauretania Tingitana
       7 Baleares

Appendix 2: Rulers[1]

Roman emperors	
Constantine I	324–37
Constantius II	337–61
Julian	361–63
Jovian	363–64
Valens	364–78
Theodosios I	379–95
Arkadios	395–408
Theodosios II	408–50
Marcian	450–57
Leo I	457–74
Leo II	474
Zeno	474–75
Basiliskos	475–76
Zeno (restored)	476–91
Anastasios I	491–518
Justin I	518–27
Justinian I	527–65
Justin II	565–78
Tiberios II Constantine	578–82
Maurice	582–602
Phokas	602–10
Herakleios	610–41
Constantine III and Heraklonas	641

1 Based on Jeffreys et al., *The Oxford Handbook of Byzantine Studies*, 962–71.

Appendix 2: Rulers

Constans II	641–68
Constantine IV	668–85
Justinian II	685–95
Leontios	695–98
Tiberios III	698–705
Justinian II (restored)	705–11
Philippikos Bardanes	711–13
Anastasios II	713–15
Theodosios III	715–17
Leo III	717–41
Constantine V	741–75
Artabasdos	741–42
Leo IV	775–80
Constantine VI	780–97
Eirene	797–802
Nikephoros I	802–11
Staurakios	811
Michael I	811–13
Leo V	813–20
Michael II	820–29
Theophilos	829–42
Michael III	842–67
Basil I	867–86
Leo VI	886–912
Alexander	912–13
Constantine VII	913–59
Romanos I Lekapenos (as senior emperor)	920–44
Romanos II	959–63
Nikephoros II Phokas	963–69
John I Tzimiskes	969–76
Basil II	976–1025
Constantine VIII	1025–28
Romanos III Argyros	1028–34

Michael IV the Paphlagonian	1034–41
Michael V Kalaphates	1041–42
Zoe and Theodora	1042
Constantine IX Monomachos	1042–55
Theodora (again)	1055–56
Michael VI Stratiotikos	1056–57
Isaac I Komnenos	1057–59
Constantine X Doukas	1059–67
Eudokia	1067
Romanos IV Diogenes	1068–71
Eudokia (again)	1071
Michael VII Doukas	1071–78
Nikephoros III Botaneiates	1078–81
Alexios I Komnenos	1081–1118
John II Komnenos	1118–43
Manuel I Komnenos	1143–80
Alexios II Komnenos	1180–83
Andronikos I Komnenos	1183–85
Isaac II Angelos	1185–95
Alexios III Angelos	1195–1203
Isaac II (restored) and Alexios IV Angelos	1203–4
Alexios V Mourtzouphlos	1204
Constantine (XI) Laskaris	1204 (Nicea)
Theodore I Laskaris	1204–22 (Nicea)
John III Doukas Vatatzes	1222–54 (Nicea)
Theodore II Laskaris	1254–58 (Nicea)
John IV Laskaris	1258–61 (Nicea)
Michael VIII Palaiologos	1259–82
Andronikos II Palaiologos	1282–1328
Michael IX Palaiologos	1294–1320
Andronikos III Palaiologos	1328–41
John V Palaiologos	1341–91
John VI Kantakouzenos	1341–54

Appendix 2: Rulers

Andronikos IV Palaiologos	1376–79
John VII Palaiologos	1390
Manuel II Palaiologos	1391–1425
John VIII Palaiologos	1425–48
Constantine XI (XII) Palaiologos	1448–53
Empire of Nicea	
Constantine (XI) Laskaris	1204
Theodore I Laskaris	1204–22
John III Doukas Vatatzes	1222–54
Theodore II Laskaris	1254–58
John IV Laskaris	1258–61
Michael VIII Palaiologos	1259–82 (from 1261 at Constantinople)
Despotate of Epiros	
Michael I	1204–15
Theodore	1215–30 (emperor from 1224 in Thessalonica)
Thessalonica	
Manuel	1230–37
John	1237–44
Demetrios	1244–46 (defeated by John Vatatzes in 1246)
Thessaly	
John I	1271–96
Constantine	1296–1303
John II	1303–18
Epiros	
Michael II	c. 1231–71

Nikephoros I	1271–96
Thomas	1296–1318
Nicholas Orsini	1318–25
John Orsini	1325–35
Nikephoros II	1335–40
Empire of Trebizond	
Alexios I	1204–22
Andronikos I	1222–35
John I	1235–38
Manuel I	1238–63
Andronikos II	1263–66
George	1266–80
John II	1280–97
Alexios II	1297–1330
Andronikos III	1330–32
Manuel II	1332
Basil	1332–40
Eirene	1340–41
Anna	1341
Michael	1341
Anna (again)	1341–42
John III	1342–44
Michael (again)	1344–49
Alexios III	1349–90
Manuel III	1390–1416
Alexios IV	1416–29
John IV	1429–59
David	1459–61
Despotate of the Morea	
Manuel Kantakouzenos	1348–80
Matthew Kantakouzenos	1380–83
Demetrios Kantakouzenos	1383

Theodore I Palaiologos	1383–1407
Theodore II Palaiologos	1407–43
Constantine and Thomas Palaiologos	1443–49
Thomas and Demetrios Palaiologos	1449–60
Latin rulers at Constantinople	
Baldwin I of Flanders	1204–5
Henry of Flanders	1206–16
Peter of Courtenay	1217
Yolande	1217–19
Robert of Courtenay	1221–28
Baldwin II (1231–1237 John of Brienne)	1228–61
Bulgar rulers	
First Bulgarian empire 681–971	
Asparuch	681–702
Tervel	702–18
Anonymous	718–25
Sevar	725–39
Kormisoš	739–56
Vinech	756–62
Teletz	762–5
Sabin	765–67
Umar	767
Toktu	767–72
Pagan	772
Telerig	c. 772–77
Kardam	777–c. 803
Krum	c. 803–14
Dukum, Dicevg	814
Omurtag	814–31
Malamir	831–36
Presiam	836–52

Boris I Michael	852–89
Vladimir	889–93
Symeon	893–927
Peter	927–69
Boris II	969–71
The Bulgars' "Macedonian" empire 976–1018	
Samuel	976–1014
Gabriel Radomir	1014–15
John Vladislav	1015–18
The second Bulgarian empire 1186–1396	
Asen I	1186–96
Peter	1196–97
Kalojan	1197–1207
Boril	1207–18
Ivan Asen II	1218–41
Kaloman Asen	1241–46
Michael Asen	1246–56
Constantine Tikh	1257–77
Ivailo	1278–79
Ivan Asen III	1279–80
George I Terter	1280–92
Smiletz	1292–98
Čaka	1299
Theodore Svetoslav	1300–1322
George II Terter	1322–23
Michael Šišman	1323–30
Ivan Stephen	1330–31
Ivan Alexander	1331–71
Ivan Šišman	1371–93 (at Tirnovo)
Ivan Stracimir	1360–96 (at Vidin)

Grand Župans	
Štefan Nemanja	c. 1168–96
Štefan I	1196–1217
Štefan Radoslav	1217–27/28
Štefan Vladislav	1227/28–34
Štefan Uroš I	1234–76
Štefan Dragutin	1276–82
Štefan Uroš II	1282–1321
Štefan Uroš III	1321–31
Štefan Uroš IV Dušan	1331–55 (emperor from 1345)
Štefan Uroš V	1355–71
Islamic rulers	
Caliphs	
The four "rightly-guided" Caliphs, direct descendants of Muhammad	
Abu Bakr	632–34
Umar I	634–44
Uthman	644–56
Ali	656–61
Umayyad dynasty	
Mu'awiyya I	661–80
Yazid I	680–83
Mu'awiyya II	683–84
Marwan I	684–85
Abd al-Malik	685–705
Walid I	705–15
Suleiman	715–17
Umar II	715–20
Yazid II	720–24

Hisham	724–43
Walid II	743–44
Yazid III	744
Ibrahim	744
Marwan II	744–50
Abbasid dynasty	
as-Saffah	750–54
al-Mansur	754–75
al-Mahdi	775–85
al-Hadi	785–86
Harun ar-Rashid	786–809
al-Amin	809–13
al-Ma'mun	813–33
al-Mu'tasim	833–42
al-Wathiq	842–47
al-Mutawwakil	847–61
al-Muntasir	861–62
al-Musta'in	862
al-Mu'tazz	862–66
al-Muhtadi	866–69
al-Mu'tamid	869–92
al-Mu'tadid	892–902
al-Muqtafi	902–8
al-Muqtadir	908–32
al-Qahir	932–34
al-Radi	934–40
al-Muttaqi	940–43
al-Mustakfi	943–46
al-Muti	946–74
at-Ta'i	974–91
al-Qadir	991–1031
al-Qaim	1031–75
al-Muqtadi	1075–94

al-Mustazhir	1094–1118
al-Mustarshid	1118–35
ar-Rashid	1135–36
al-Muqtafi	1136–60
al-Mustanjid	1160–70
al-Mustadi	1170–80
an-Nasir	1180–1225
az-Zahir	1225–26
al-Mustansir	1226–58
al-Musta'sim	1258
Seljuk Sultans of Rum	
Suleiman I	1077–86
Kilij Arslan I	1092–1107
Malik Shah	1107–16
Masud I	1116–56
Kilij Arslan II	1156–92
Kaikhusraw I	1192–96
Suleiman II	1196–1204
Kilij Arslan III	1204
Kaikhusraw I (again)	1204–10
Kaikawus I	1210–20
Kaikubad I	1220–37
Kaikhusraw II	1237–45
Kaikawus II	1246–57
Kilij Arslan IV	1248–65
Kaikubad II	1249–57
Kaikhusraw III	1265–82
Masud II	1282–1304
Kaikubad III	1304–7
Masud III	1307–8

Ottoman Sultans	
Osman	1288–1326
Orhan	1326–62
Murad I	1362–89
Bayezid I	1389–1402
Mehmet I	1402–21
Suleiman	1402–10
Musa	1411–13
Mehmet I	1413–21
Murad II	1421–44
Mehmet II Fatih "the Conqueror"	1444–6
Murad II (again)	1446–51
Mehmet II Fatih "the Conqueror" (again)	1451–81
Bayezid II	1481–1512
Selim I	1512–20
Suleiman I	1520–66
Selim II	1566–74
Murad III	1574–95
Mehmed III	1595–1603
Ahmed I	1603–17
Mustafa I	1617–18
Osman II	1618–22
Mustafa I (again)	1622–23
Murad IV	1623–40
Ibrahim	1640–48
Mehmed IV	1648–87
Suleiman II	1687–91
Ahmed II	1691–95
Mustafa II	1695–1703
Ahmed III	1703–30
Mahmud I	1730–54
Osman III	1754–57

Mustafa III	1757–74
Abdülhamid I	1774–89
Selim III	1789–1807
Mustafa IV	1807–8
Mahmud II	1808–39
Abdülmecid I	1839–61
Abdülaziz I	1861–76
Mehmed Murad V	1876
Abdülhamid II	1876–1909
Mehmed V	1909–18
Mehmed VI	1918–22

Appendix 3: Bishops of Constantinople[1]

Alexander	314–37
Paul I	337–39, 341–42, 346–51
Eusebios	339–42
Makedonios I	342–46, 351–60
Eudoxios	360–70
Demophilos	370–79
Gregory I of Nazianzos	379–81
Nectarios	381–97
John I Chrysostom	398–404
Arsakios	404–5
Attikos	406–25
Sisinnios	426–27
Nestorios	428–31
Maximianos	431–34
Proklos	434–46
Flavianos	446–49
Anatolios	449–58
Gennadios I	458–71
Akakios	472–89
Fravitas	489–90
Euphemios	490–96

1 The bishops of Byzantion before the transfer there of the capital, some of them legendary, are not counted here, as this see was of no particular significance before the transfer of the capital. Based on Jeffreys et al., *The Oxford Handbook of Byzantine Studies*, 972–73; Cobham, *The Patriarchs of Constantinople*, 89–96.

Appendix 3: Bishops of Constantinople

Makedonios II	496–511
Timothy I	511–18
John II the Cappadocian	518–20
Epiphanios	520–35
Anthimos I	535–36
Menas	536–52
Eutychios	552–65, 577–82
John III Scholastikos	565–77
John IV the Faster	582–95
Kyriakos	595–606
Thomas I	607–10
Sergios I	610–38
Pyrrhos	638–41, 654
Paul II	641–53
Peter	654–66
Thomas II	667–9
John V	669–75
Constantine I	675–77
Theodore I	677–79, 686–87
George I	679–86
Paul III	688–94
Kallinikos I	694–706
Kyros	706–12
John VI	712–15
Germanos I	715–30
Anastasios	730–54
Constantine II	754–66
Niketas I	766–80
Paul IV	780–84
Tarasios	784–806
Nikephoros I	806–15
Theodotos	815–21
Anthony I	821–37
John VII Grammatikos	837–43

Appendix 3: Bishops of Constantinople

Methodios I	843–47
Ignatios	847–58, 867–77
Photios I	858–67, 877–86
Stephen I	886–93
Anthony II	893–901
Nicholas I Mystikos	901–7, 912–25
Euthymios I	907–12
Stephen II	925–27
Tryphon	927–31
Theophylaktos	933–56
Polyeuktos	956–70
Basil I	970–74
Anthony III	974–79
Nicholas II	979–91
Sisinnios II	996–98
Sergios II	1001–19
Eustathios	1019–25
Alexios	1025–43
Michael I Keroularios	1043–58
Constantine III	1059–63
John VIII Xiphilinos	1064–75
Kosmas I	1075–81
Eustratios	1081–84
Nicholas III	1084–1111
John IX	1111–34
Leo	1134–43
Michael II	1143–46
Kosmas II	1146–47
Nicholas IV Mouzalon	1147–51
Theodotos I	1151–53
Neophytos I	1153–54
Constantine IV	1154–57
Loukas	1157–70
Michael III	1170–78

Chariton	1178–79
Theodosios	1179–83
Basil II	1183–86
Niketas II	1186–89
Dositheos	1189, 1189–91
Leontios	1189
George II	1191–98
John X	1198–1206
Michael IV	1208–14
Theodore II	1214–16
Maximos II	1216
Manuel I	1217–22
Germanos II	1222–40
Methodios II	1240
Manuel II	1244–54
Arsenios	1255–59, 1261–64
Nikephoros II	1260
Germanos III	1265–66
Joseph I	1266–75, 1282–83
John XI Bekkos	1275–82
Gregory III	1283–89
Athanasios I	1289–93, 1303–9
John XII	1294–1303
Niphon I	1310–14
John XIII Glykys	1315–19
Gerasimos I	1320–21
Isaias	1323–32
John XIV Kalekas	1334–47
Isidoros I	1347–50
Kallistos I	1350–53, 1355–63
Philotheos Kokkinos	1353–54, 1364–76
Makarios	1376–79, 1390–91
Neilos	1379–88
Anthony IV	1389–90, 1391–97

Appendix 3: Bishops of Constantinople

Kallistos II Xanthopoulos	1397
Matthew I	1397–1410
Euthymios II	1410–16
Joseph II	1416–39
Metrophanes II	1440–43
Gregory III	1443–50
Gennadios II Scholarios	1454–56, 1462, 1464
Isidore II	1456–62
Sophronios I	1463–64
Joasaph I	1465–66
Mark II	1466
Symeon I (1st time)	1466
Dionysios I	1467–71
Symeon I (2nd time)	1471–75
Raphael I	1475–76
Maximos III	1476–81
Symeon I (3rd time)	1482–86
Nifon II (1st time)	1486–88
Dionysios I (2nd time)	1488–90
Maximos IV	1491–7
Nifon II (2nd time)	1497–98
Joachim I (1st time)	1498–1502
Nifon II (3rd time)	1502
Pachomios I (1st time)	1503–4
Joachim I (2nd time)	1504
Pachomios I (2nd time)	1504–13
Theoliptos I	1513–22
Jeremias I	1522–45
Joannikios I	1526
Dionysios II	1546–56
Joasaph II	1556–65
Metrophanes III (1st time)	1565–72
Jeremias II (1st time)	1572–79
Metrophanes III (2nd time)	1579–80

Jeremias II (2nd time)	1580–84
Pachomius II	1584–85
Theoleptos II	1585–86
Jeremias II (3rd time)	1587–95
Matthew II (1st time)	1596
Gabriel I	1596
Theophanes I	1597
Meletios I Pigas (overseer)	1597–98
Matthew II (2nd time)	1598–1602
Neophytos II (1st time)	1602–3
Matthew II (3rd time)	1603
Raphael II	1603–7
Neophytos II (2nd time)	1607–12
Cyril I Lucaris (overseer)	1612
Timothy II	1613–20
Cyril I (2nd time)	1620–23
Gregory IV	1623
Anthimos II	1623
Cyril I (3rd time)	1623–33
Cyril II (1st time)	1633
Cyril I (4th time)	1633–34
Athanasios III (1st time)	1634
Cyril I (5th time)	1634–35
Cyril II (2nd time)	1635–36
Neophytos III	1636–7
Cyril I (6th time)	1637–38
Cyril II (3rd time)	1638–39
Parthenios I	1639–44
Parthenios II (1st time)	1644–46
Joannikios II (1st time)	1646–48
Parthenios II (2nd time)	1648–51
Joannikios II (2nd time)	1651–52
Cyril III (1st time)	1652
Athanasios III (2nd time)	1652

Appendix 3: Bishops of Constantinople

Paisios I (1st time)	1652–53
Joannikios II (3rd time)	1653–54
Cyril III (2nd time)	1654
Paisios I (2nd time)	1654–55
Joannikios II (4th time)	1655–56
Parthenios III [24 Mar.]	1656–57
Gabriel II	1657
Parthenios IV (1st time)	1657–62
Dionysios III	1662–65
Parthenios IV (2nd time)	1665–67
Clement	1667
Methodios III	1668–71
Parthenios IV (3rd time)	1671–73
Dionysios IV (1st time)	1671–73
Gerasimos II	1673–74
Parthenios IV (4th time)	1675–76
Dionysios IV (2nd time)	1676–79
Athanasios IV	1679
James (1st time)	1679–82
Dionysios IV (3rd time)	1682–4
Parthenios IV (5th time)	1684–85
James (2nd time)	1685–86
Dionysios IV (4th time)	1686–87
James (3rd time)	1687–88
Kallinikos II (1st time)	1688
Neophytos IV	1688–9
Kallinikos II (2nd time)	1689–93
Dionysios IV (5th time)	1693–94
Kallinikos II (3rd time)	1694–1702
Gabriel III	1702–7
Neophytos V	1707
Cyprian I (1st time)	1707–9
Athanasios V	1709–11
Cyril IV	1711–13

Cyprian I (2nd time)	1713–14
Kosmas III	1714–16
Jeremias III (1st time)	1716–26
Paisios II (1st time)	1726–32
Jeremias III (2nd time)	1732–33
Seraphim I	1733–34
Neophytos VI (1st time)	1734–40
Paisios II (2nd time)	1740–43
Neophytos VI (2nd time)	1743–44
Paisios II (3rd time)	1744–48
Cyril V (1st time)	1748–51
Paisios II (4th time)	1751–52
Cyril V (2nd time)	1752–57
Kallinikos III	1757
Seraphim II	1757–61
Joannikios III	1761–63
Samuel I (1st time)	1763–68
Meletios II	1768–69
Theodosios II	1769–73
Samuel I (2nd time)	1773–74
Sophronios II	1774–80
Gabriel IV	1780–5
Prokopios	1785–89
Neophytos VII (1st time)	1789–94
Gerasimos III	1794–97
Gregory V (1st time)	1797–98
Neophytos VII (2nd time)	1798–1801
Kallinikos IV (1st time)	1801–6
Gregory V (2nd time)	1806–8
Kallinikos IV (2nd time)	1808–9
Jeremias IV	1809–13
Cyril VI	1813–18
Gregory V (3rd time)	1818–21
Eugenios II	1821–22

Appendix 3: Bishops of Constantinople

Anthimos III	1822–24
Chrysanthos	1824–26
Agathangelos	1826–30
Constantios I	1830–34
Constantios II	1834–35
Gregory VI (1st time)	1835–40
Anthimos IV (1st time)	1840–41
Anthimos V	1841–42
Germanos IV (1st time)	1842–45
Meletios III	1845
Anthimos VI (1st time)	1845–48
Anthimos IV (2nd time)	1848–52
Germanos IV (2nd time)	1852–53
Anthimos VI (2nd time)	1853–55
Cyril VII	1855–60
Joachim II (1st time)	1860–63
Sophronios III	1863–66
Gregory VI (2nd time)	1867–71
Anthimos VI (3rd time)	1871–73
Joachim II (2nd time)	1873–78
Joachim III (1st time)	1878–84
Joachim IV	1884–86
Dionysios V	1887–91
Neophytos VIII	1891–94
Anthimos VII	1895–97
Constantine V	1897–1901
Joachim III (2nd time)	1901–12
Germanos V	1913–18
Meletios IV	1921–23
Gregory VII	1923–24
Constantine VI	1924–25
Basil III	1925–29
Photios II	1929–35
Benjamin	1936–46

Maximos V	1946–48
Athenagoras	1948–72
Dimitrios	1972–91
Bartholomew	1991–

Appendix 4: Bishops of Rome[1]

Linus	c. 67–c. 76
Cletus or Anacletus	c. 76–c. 88
Clement I	c. 88–c. 97
Euaristus	c. 97–c. 105
Alexander I	c. 105–c. 115
Sixtus I	c. 115–c. 125
Telesphorus	c. 125–c. 136
Hyginus	c. 136–c. 140
Pius I	c. 140–c. 155
Anicetus	c. 155–c. 166
Soter	c. 166–c. 175
Eleutherius	c. 175–c. 189
Victor I	c. 189–c. 199
Zephyrinus	c. 199–c. 217
Calixtus I	c. 217–c. 222
Hippolytus (antipope)	217–35
Urban I	222–30
Pontian	230–35
Anterus	235–6
Fabian	236–50
Cornelius	251–53
Novatian (antipope)	251
Lucius I	253–54

1 Based on *Annuario pontificio per l'anno 2014*, 7–20; *The Columbia Electronic Encyclopedia*, 6th ed.: http://goo.gl/OI7Gmp [accessed October 21, 2015]; *New Catholic Encyclopedia*, v. 11, 574–76.

Stephen I	254–57
Sixtus II	257–58
Dionysius	259–68
Felix I	269–74
Eutychian	275–83
Caius	283–96
Marcellinus	296–304
Marcellus I	c. 308–9
Eusebius	309–c. 310
Miltiades or Melchiades	311–14
Sylvester I	314–35
Marcus	336
Julius I	337–52
Liberius	352–66
Felix II (antipope)	355–65
Damasus I	366–84
Ursinus (antipope)	366–67
Siricius	384–99
Anastasius I	399–401
Innocent I	401–17
Zosimus	417–18
Boniface I	418–22
Eulalius (antipope)	418–19
Celestine I	422–32
Sixtus III	432–40
Leo I	440–61
Hilarius	461–68
Simplicius	468–83
Felix III (or II)	483–92
Gelasius I	492–96
Anastasius II	496–98
Symmachus	498–514
Lawrence (antipope)	498–505
Hormisdas	514–23

Appendix 4: Bishops of Rome

John I	523–6
Felix IV (or III)	526–30
Boniface II	530–32
Dioscurus (antipope)	530
John II	532, 533–35
Agapetus I	535–36
Silverius	536–37
Vigilius	537–55
Pelagius I	556–61
John III	561–74
Benedict I	575–79
Pelagius II	579–90
Gregory I	590–604
Sabinian	604–6
Boniface III	607
Boniface IV	608–15
Deusdedit, or Adeodatus I	615–18
Boniface V	619–25
Honorius I	625–38
Severinus	638, 640
John IV	640–42
Theodore I	642–49
Martin I	649–55
Eugene I	654–57
Vitalian	657–72
Adeodatus II	672–76
Donus	676–78
Agatho	678–81
Leo II	682–83
Benedict II	684–85
John V	685–86
Conon	686–87
Theodore (antipope)	687
Paschal (antipope)	687

Appendix 4: Bishops of Rome

Sergius I	687–701
John VI	701–5
John VII	705–7
Sisinnius	708
Constantine	708–15
Gregory II	715–31
Gregory III	731–41
Zacharias	741–52
Stephen II	752
Stephen II (or III)	752–57
Paul I	757–67
Constantine (antipope)	767–69
Philip (antipope)	768
Stephen III (or IV)	768–72
Adrian I	772–95
Leo III	795–816
Stephen IV (or V)	816–17
Paschal I	817–24
Eugene II	824–27
Valentine	827
Gregory IV	827–44
John (antipope)	844
Sergius II	844–47
Leo IV	847–55
Benedict III	855–58
Anastasius (antipope)	855
Nicholas I	858–67
Adrian II	867–72
John VIII	872–82
Marinus I	882–84
Adrian III	884–85
Stephen V (or VI)	885–91
Formosus	891–96
Boniface VI	896

Appendix 4: Bishops of Rome

Stephen VI (or VII)	896–97
Romanus	897
Theodore II	897
John IX	898–900
Benedict IV	900–903
Leo V	903
Christopher (antipope)	903–4
Sergius III	904–11
Anastasius III	911–13
Lando	913–14
John X	914–28
Leo VI	928
Stephen VII (or VIII)	928–31
John XI	931–35
Leo VII	936–39
Stephen VIII (or IX)	939–42
Marinus II	942–46
Agapetus II	946–55
John XII	955–64
Leo VIII	963–65
Benedict V	964–66
John XIII	965–72
Benedict VI	973–74
Boniface VII (antipope)	974, 984–85
Benedict VII	974–83
John XIV	983–84
John XV	985–96
Gregory V	996–99
John XVI (antipope)	997–98
Sylvester II	999–1003
John XVII	1003
John XVIII	1004–9
Sergius IV	1009–12
Benedict VIII	1012–24

Gregory (antipope)	1012
John XIX	1024–32
Benedict IX	1032–44
Sylvester III	1045
Benedict IX	1045
Gregory VI	1045–46
Clement II	1046–47
Benedict IX	1047–48
Damasus II	1048
Leo IX	1049–54
Victor II	1055–57
Stephen IX (or X)	1057–58
Benedict X (antipope)	1058–59
Nicholas II	1058–61
Alexander II	1061–73
Honorius II (antipope)	1061–64
Gregory VII	1073–85
Clement III (antipope)	1080, 1084–1100
Victor III	1086–87
Urban II	1088–99
Paschal II	1099–1118
Theodoric (antipope)	1100
Albert (antipope)	1102
Sylvester IV (antipope)	1105–11
Gelasius II	1118–19
Gregory VIII (antipope)	1118–21
Calixtus II	1119–24
Honorius II	1124–30
Celestine II (antipope)	1124
Innocent II	1130–43
Anacletus II (antipope)	1130–38
Victor IV (antipope)	1138
Celestine II	1143–44
Lucius II	1144–45

Eugene III	1145–53
Anastasius IV	1153–54
Adrian IV	1154–59
Alexander III	1159–81
Victor IV (antipope)	1159–64
Paschal III (antipope)	1164–68
Calixtus III (antipope)	1168–78
Innocent III (antipope)	1179–80
Lucius III	1181–85
Urban III	1185–87
Gregory VIII	1187
Clement III	1187–91
Celestine III	1191–98
Innocent III	1198–1216
Honorius III	1216–27
Gregory IX	1227–41
Celestine IV	1241
Innocent IV	1243–54
Alexander IV	1254–61
Urban IV	1261–64
Clement IV	1265–68
Gregory X	1271–76
Innocent V	1276
Adrian V	1276
John XXI	1276–77
Nicholas III	1277–80
Martin IV	1281–85
Honorius IV	1285–87
Nicholas IV	1288–92
Celestine V	1294
Boniface VIII	1294–1303
Benedict XI	1303–4
Clement V	1305–14
John XXII	1316–34

Nicholas V (antipope)	1328–30
Benedict XII	1334–42
Clement VI	1342–52
Innocent VI	1352–62
Urban V	1362–70
Gregory XI	1370–78
The schism (1378–1417)	
Roman Line	
Urban VI	1378–89
Boniface IX	1389–1404
Innocent VII	1404–6
Gregory XII	1406–15
Avignon Line	
Clement VII (antipope)	1378–94
Benedict XIII (antipope)	1394–1423
Clement VII (antipope)	1423–29
Benedict XIV (antipope)	1425–30
Pisan Line	
Alexander V (antipope)	1409–10
John XXIII (antipope)	1410–15
Martin V	1417–31
Eugene IV	1431–47
Felix V (antipope)	1439–49
Nicholas V	1447–55
Calixtus III	1455–58
Pius II	1458–64
Paul II	1464–71
Sixtus IV	1471–84
Innocent VIII	1484–92
Alexander VI	1492–1503
Pius III	1503
Julius II	1503–13
Leo X	1513–21

Adrian VI	1522–23
Clement VII	1523–34
Paul III	1534–49
Julius III	1550–55
Marcellus II	1555
Paul IV	1555–59
Pius IV	1559–65
Pius V	1566–72
Gregory XIII	1572–85
Sixtus V	1585–90
Urban VII	1590
Gregory XIV	1590–91
Innocent IX	1591
Clement VIII	1592–1605
Leo XI	1605
Paul V	1605–21
Gregory XV	1621–23
Urban VIII	1623–44
Innocent X	1644–55
Alexander VII	1655–67
Clement IX	1667–69
Clement X	1670–76
Innocent XI	1676–89
Alexander VIII	1689–91
Innocent XII	1691–1700
Clement XI	1700–1721
Innocent XIII	1721–24
Benedict XIII	1724–30
Clement XII	1730–40
Benedict XIV	1740–58
Clement XIII	1758–69
Clement XIV	1769–74
Pius VI	1775–99
Pius VII	1800–1823

Leo XII	1823–29
Pius VIII	1829–30
Gregory XVI	1831–46
Pius IX	1846–78
Leo XIII	1878–1903
Pius X	1903–14
Benedict XV	1914–22
Pius XI	1922–39
Pius XII	1939–58
John XXIII	1958–63
Paul VI	1963–78
John Paul I	1978
John Paul II	1978–2005
Benedict XVI	2005–13
Francis	2013–

Bibliography

Ahl, Valerie, and T. F. H. Allen. *Hierarchy Theory: A Vision, Vocabulary, and Epistemology*. New York: Columbia University Press, 1996.
Alberigo, Guiseppe, ed. *Conciliorum oecumenicorum generaliumque decreta: editio critica*. Turnhout: Brepols, 2006.
Ando, Clifford. "The Administration of the Provinces." In *A Companion to the Roman Empire*, edited by David S. Potter, 175–92, Malden, MA: Blackwell, 2006.
Arthur, Rosemary A. *Pseudo-Dionysius as Polemicist: The Development and Purpose of the Angelic Hierarchy in Sixth-Century Syria*. Aldershot, UK: Ashgate, 2008.
Augustine. *The City of God*. Translated by Marcus Dods. New York: Modern Library, 1993.
Bailey, Leon. *Critical Theory and the Sociology of Knowledge: A Comparative Study in the Theory of Ideology*. New York: Lang, 1994.
Balthasar, Hans Urs von. *The Office of Peter and the Structure of the Church*. San Francisco: Ignatius, 1986.
Barnes, Jonathan. *Porphyry. Introduction*. Oxford: Oxford University Press, 2003.
Barth, Karl. *Church Dogmatics*. Edinburgh: T. & T. Clark, 1956.
Barthes, Roland. *Mythologies*. Translated by Annette Lavers. New York: Noonday, 1972.
Baum, Gregory. *The Catholic Quest for Christian Unity*. Glen Rock, NJ: Paulist, 1962.
Bellah, Robert, and Phillip Hammond. *Varieties of Civil Religion*. San Francisco: Harper & Row, 1980.
Berkhoff, Karel C. "Was There a Religious Revival in Soviet Ukraine under the Nazi Regime?" *The Slavonic and East European Review* 78/3 (2000) 536–67.
Bernhardt, Rudolf, and Peter Macalister-Smith. *Encyclopedia of Public International Law*. Amsterdam: North-Holland, 1992.
Biriukov, Dmitry. "Hierarchies of Beings in the Patristic Thought: Maximus the Confessor, John of Damascus, and the Palamites." *Scrinium* 10 (2001) 275–300.
Birkelund, Gunn Elisabeth, ed. *Class and Stratification Analysis*. Bingley, UK: Emerald, 2013.
Bodel, John P., and Saul M. Olyan. *Household and Family Religion in Antiquity*. Oxford: Blackwell, 2008.
Bogardus, Emory. *Social Distance*, Los Angeles: University of Southern California, 1959.
Bogatyrev, Sergei. "Reinventing the Russian Monarchy in the 1550s: Ivan the Terrible, the Dynasty, and the Church." *The Slavonic and East European Review* 85/2 (2007) 271–93.
Bohr, David. *The Diocesan Priest: Consecrated and Sent*. Collegeville, MN: Liturgical, 2009.

Borgatta, Edgar F., and Rhonda J. V. Montgomery, eds. *Encyclopedia of Sociology*. 2nd ed. Vol. 4. New York: Macmillan Reference USA, 2000.

Bottero, Wendy. *Stratification: Social Division and Inequality*. London: Routledge, 2005.

Bourdieu, Pierre. *Distinction: A Social Critique of the Judgement of Taste*. Cambridge: Harvard University Press, 1984.

Bowersock, G. W. *Empires in Collision in Late Antiquity*. Waltham, MA: Brandeis University Press, 2012.

Breen, Richard, and David B. Rottman. *Class Stratification Comparative Perspectives*. London: Routledge, 2014.

Brent, Allen. *The Imperial Cult and the Development of Church Order: Concepts and Images of Authority in Paganism and Early Christianity before the Age of Cyprian*. Leiden: Brill, 1999.

Brown, Peter. *The Body and Society: Men, Women, and Sexual Renunciation in Early Christianity*. New York: Columbia University Press, 1988.

Brown, Raymond Edward. *The Churches the Apostles Left Behind*. New York: Paulist, 1984.

Brown, Stewart J., and Peter Benedict Nockles. *The Oxford Movement: Europe and the Wider World 1830–1930*. Cambridge: Cambridge University Press, 2012.

Brubaker, Leslie, and John F. Haldon. *Byzantium in the Iconoclast Era (c.680–850): A History*. Cambridge: Cambridge University Press, 2011.

Burns, J. H., and Thomas M. Izbicki. *Conciliarism and Papalism*. Cambridge: Cambridge University Press, 1997.

Burtchaell, James Tunstead. *From Synagogue to Church: Public Services and Offices in the Earliest Christian Communities*. Cambridge: Cambridge University Press, 1992.

Butler, Rex D. *The New Prophecy & "New Visions": Evidence of Montanism in the Passion of Perpetua and Felicitas*. Washington, DC: Catholic University of America Press, 2006.

Calvin, Jean. *Letters of John Calvin*. Edited by Jules Bonnet. New York: Franklin, 1973.

Cameron, Averil. *The Mediterranean World in Late Antiquity, AD 395–600*. London: Routledge, 1993.

Cameron, Ron, and Merrill P. Miller. *Redescribing Christian Origins*. Atlanta: Society of Biblical Literature, 2004.

Cannadine, David. *Class in Britain*. New Haven: Yale University Press, 1998.

Caseau, Béatrice. "Sacred Landscapes." In *Interpreting Late Antiquity: Essays on the Postclassical World*, edited by G. W. Bowersock, Peter Brown, and Oleg Grabar, 21–59. Cambridge: Harvard University Press, 2001.

Chadwick, Henry. *The Church in Ancient Society*. Oxford: Oxford University Press, 2003.

Chandler, Alfred D. *Strategy and Structure: Chapters in the History of the Industrial Enterprise*. Cambridge: MIT Press, 1962.

Chlup, Radek. *Proclus: an Introduction*, Cambridge: Cambridge University Press, 2012.

Christophe, Paul. *L'élection des évêques dans l'église latine au premier millénaire*. Paris: Cerf, 2009.

Clapsis, Emmanuel. "The Boundaries of the Church: An Orthodox Debate." *Greek Orthodox Theological Review* 35/2 (1990) 113–27.

Clements, R. E., ed. *The World of Ancient Israel: Sociological, Anthropological, and Political Perspectives*. Cambridge: Cambridge University Press, 1989.

Cobham, Claude Delaval. *The Patriarchs of Constantinople*. Cambridge: Cambridge University Press, 1911.
Colebrook, Claire, ed. *Jacques Derrida: Key Concepts*. London: Routledge, 2014.
Collins, Randall. *The Credential Society: An Historical Sociology of Education and Stratification*. New York: Academic Press, 1979.
Congar, Yves. *Chrétiens désunis, principes d'un "oecuménisme" catholique*. Paris: Cerf, 1937.
———. "Le développement de l'évaluation ecclésiologique des églises non catholiques." *Revue de droit canonique* 25 (1975) 168–98.
———. *Divided Christendom: A Catholic Study of the Problem of Reunion*. London: Bles, 1939.
Cooley, Alexander. *Logics of Hierarchy: The Organization of Empires, States, and Military Occupations*. Ithaca, NY: Cornell University Press, 2005.
Cooper, Kate, and Julia Hillner. *Religion, Dynasty, and Patronage in Early Christian Rome, 300–900*. Cambridge: Cambridge University Press, 2007.
Corrigan, Kevin. *Evagrius and Gregory: Mind, Soul, and Body in the 4th Century*. Farnham, UK: Ashgate, 2009.
Costa, Gavin D. "Karl Rahner's Anonymous Christian: A Reappraisal." *Modern Theology* 1/2 (1985) 131–48.
Crompton, Rosemary. *Class and Stratification: An Introduction to Current Debates*. Cambridge: Polity, 1993.
Crossley, Nick. *Towards Relational Sociology*. London: Routledge, 2011.
Dadeshkeliani, Ilamaz. *The Autocephaly of the Orthodox Church of Georgia*. Paris: Schneider, 1922.
Darrouzès, Jean. *Notitiae episcopatuum ecclesiae Constantinopolitanae*. Paris: Institut français d'études byzantines, 1981.
Deleuze, Gilles. *Difference and Repetition*. Translated by Paul Patton. New York: Columbia University Press, 1994.
Demacopoulos, George, and Aristotle Papanikolaou, eds. *Orthodox Constructions of the West*. New York: Fordham University Press, 2013.
Denton, Jeffrey Howard. *Orders and Hierarchies in Late Medieval and Renaissance Europe*. Toronto: University of Toronto Press, 1999.
Denysenko, Nicholas E. *Liturgical Reform After Vatican II: The Impact on Eastern Orthodoxy*. Minneapolis: Fortress, 2015.
Denzinger, Heinrich, and Peter Hünermann. *Enchiridion symbolorum definitionum et declarationum de rebus fidei et morum*. Bologna: EDB, 1995.
DeVille, Adam. "Sovereignty, Politics, and the Church: Joseph de Maistre's Legacy for Catholic and Orthodox Ecclesiology." *Pro Ecclesia* 24 (2015) 366–89.
Dignas, Beate, and Engelbert Winter. *Rome and Persia in Late Antiquity*. Cambridge: Cambridge University Press, 2007.
Drake, H. A. *Constantine and the Bishops: The Politics of Intolerance*. Baltimore, MD: Johns Hopkins University Press, 2000.
Dulles, Avery. "The Church, the Churches, and the Catholic Church." *Theological Studies* 33/2 (1972) 199–234.
———. *Models of the Church*. New York: Doubleday, 1991.
Dunn, Geoffrey D. "Boniface I and the Illyrian Churches on the Translation of Perigenes to Corinth: The Evidence and Problems of Beatus Apostolus (JK 350)." *Sacris Erudiri* 53/1 (2014) 131–46.

———. "The Church of Rome as a Court of Appeal in the Early Fifth Century: The Evidence of Innocent I and the Illyrian Churches." *The Journal of Ecclesiastical History* 64/4 (2013) 679–99.

Durkheim, Émile. *The Elementary Forms of the Religious Life*. 1915. Reprint. London: Allen and Unwin, 1976.

———. *Les formes élémentaires de la vie religieuse: le système totémique en Australie*. Paris: Alcan, 1912.

Easton, Burton Scott. *The Apostolic Tradition of Hippolytus*. Cambridge: Cambridge University Press, 2014.

Eckstein, Arthur M. *Rome Enters the Greek East: From Anarchy to Hierarchy in the Hellenistic Mediterranean, 230–170 BC*. Oxford: Blackwell, 2008.

École française d'Athènes. *Exploration archeologique de Delos*. Paris: Fontemoing, 1909.

Elder-Vass, Dave. *The Causal Power of Social Structures*. Cambridge: Cambridge University Press, 2010.

Eliade, Mircea. *The Sacred and the Profane: The Nature of Religion*. New York: Harcourt, Brace and World, 1957.

Evangeliou, Christos. *Aristotle's Categories and Porphyry*. Leiden: Brill, 1988.

Evans, J. A. S. *The Age of Justinian: the Circumstances of Imperial Power*. London: Routledge, 1996.

Filo, Julius, ed. *Christian World Community and the Cold War*. Bratislava: Vaško, 2012.

Fisher, Greg. *Arabs and Empires Before Islam*. Oxford: Oxford University Press, 2015.

Florovsky, Georges. *The Collected Works of Georges Florovsky. Vol 13: Ecumenism*. Vaduz: Büchervertriebsanst, 1989.

Frary, Lucien J. *Russia and the Making of Modern Greek Identity, 1821–1844*, Oxford: Oxford University Press, 2015.

Frazee, Charles A. *The Orthodox Church and Independent Greece, 1821–1852*, Cambridge: Cambridge University Press, 1969.

Fulton, John. *Index Canonum: The Greek Text, an English Translation, and a Complete Digest of the Entire Code of Canon Law of the Undivided Primitive Church*. London: Wells Gardner, Darton & Co., 1883.

Gavrilyuk, Paul. *Georges Florovsky and the Russian Religious Renaissance*. Oxford: Oxford University Press, 2014.

Gerd, Lora. *Russian Policy in the Orthodox East*. Berlin: De Gruyter, 2014.

Godfrey, John. *The Church in Anglo-Saxon England*. Cambridge: Cambridge University Press, 1962.

Granfield, Patrick. "The Church as *Societas Perfecta* in the *Schemata* of Vatican I." *Church History* 48/4 (1979) 431–46.

Grigorieff, Dmitry. "The Orthodox Church in America: An Historical Survey." *Russian Review* 31/2 (1972) 138–52.

Gritsch, Eric W. "The Church as Institution: From Doctrinal Pluriformity to Magisterial Mutuality." *Journal of Ecumenical Studies* 16 (1979) 448–56.

Gurevitch, Zali, and Gideon Aran. "Never in Place: Eliade and Judaïc Sacred Space." *Archives de sciences sociales des religions* 39/87 (1994) 135–52.

Hadjiioannou, Emmanuel A. "A Study of the Helladic Autocephaly (1821–1852), Its Ideology and Consequences." ThM diss., St. Vladimir's Orthodox Theological Seminary, 1992.

Haight, Roger. *Christian Community in History*. Vol. 1. New York: Continuum, 2004.

———. "Systematic Ecclesiology." *Science et esprit* 45/3 (1993) 253–81.

Haldon, John F. "The Byzantine Successor State." *Oxford Handbooks Online*. Oxford, 2013.
Haney, Jack V. *Moscow-Second Constantinople, Third Rome or Second Kiev: The Tale of the Princes of Vladimir*. Offprint, 1968.
Harrison, William. "The Church." In *Brill's Companions to the Christian Tradition: A Companion to Richard Hooker*, edited by Torrance Kirby and Rowan Williams, 305–36. Leiden: Brill, 2008.
Hathaway, Ronald. *Hierarchy and the Definition of Order in the Letters of Pseudo-Dionysius*, Dordrecht: Springer, 1977.
———. "The Anatomy of a Neoplatonist Metaphysical Proof." In *The Structure of Being: a Neoplatonic Approach*. Edited by R. Baine Harris, 122–36, Norfolk, VA: International Society for Neoplatonic Studies, 1982.
Hauser, Robert M., David L. Featherman, and H. H. Winsborough. *The Process of Stratification: Trends and Analyses*. Burlington, VT: Elsevier, 2013.
Hebblethwaite, Peter. "The Status of 'Anonymous Christians.'" *Heythrop Journal* 18/1 (1977) 47–55.
Heller, Celia Stopnicka. *Structured Social Inequality: A Reader in Comparative Social Stratification*. New York: Macmillan, 1968.
Hess, Hamilton. *The Early Development of Canon Law and the Council of Serdica*. Oxford: Oxford University Press, 2002.
Himmelfarb, Martha. "The Temple and the Garden of Eden in Ezekiel, the Book of the Watchers, and the Wisdom of Ben Sira." In *Sacred Places and Profane Spaces: Essays in the Geographies of Judaism, Christianity, and Islam*, edited by Jamie Scott and Paul Simpson-Housley, 63–80. New York: Greenwood, 1991.
Hjälm, Michael. *Liberation of the Ecclesia: The Unfinished Project of Liturgical Theology*. Södertälje: Anastasis, 2011.
Hobsbawm, Eric J. *Nations and Nationalism Since 1780: Programme, Myth, Reality*. Cambridge: Cambridge University Press, 1990.
Honneth, Axel. *Pathologies of Reason: on the Legacy of Critical Theory*. New York: Columbia University Press, 2009.
Hooker, Richard. *Of the Lawes of Ecclesiasticall Politie. Books I–V 1594–1597*. Menston, UK: Scolar, 1969.
Hopkins, Clark, and Bernard Goldman. *The Discovery of Dura-Europos*. New Haven: Yale University Press, 1979.
Hopkins, Clark, and Paul Victor Christopher Baur. *Christian Church at Dura-Europos*. New Haven: Yale University Press, 1934.
Hopkins, James Lindsay. *The Bulgarian Orthodox Church: A Socio-Historical Analysis of the Evolving Relationship between Church, Nation and State in Bulgaria*. New York: Columbia University Press, 2009.
Hovorun, Cyril. "Apostolicity and Right to Appeal." In *Heiligkeit und Apostolizität der Kirche*, edited by Theresia Hainthaler, Franz Mali, and Gregor Emmenegger, 241–45. Innsbruck: Tyrolia, 2010.
———. "As Pan-Orthodox Council Approaches, Conflicts and Uncertainty Intensify." *The Catholic World Report*, June 8, 2016. http://www.catholicworldreport.com/Item/4835/as_panorthodox_council_approaches_conflicts_and_uncertainty_intensify.aspx.
———. "Autocephaly as a Diachronic Phenomenon and Its Ukrainian Case." In *A Jubilee Collection: Essays in Honor of Professor Paul Robert Magocsi*, edited by Valerii Padiak and Patricia Krafcik, 273–80. Prešov: Padiak, 2015.

———. "A Blessedly Unpredictable Council." *First Things*, July 7, 2016. http://www.firstthings.com/web-exclusives/2016/07/a-blessedly-unpredictable-council.

———. "Borders of Salvation: Reading Fathers with Russian Theologians." In *Für uns und für unser Heil. Soteriologie in Ost und West; Forscher aus dem Osten und Westen Europas an den Quellen des gemeinsamen Glaubens*, edited by Theresia Hainthaler, Franz Mali, Gregor Emmenegger, and Mante Lenkaityte Ostermann, 313–22. Innsbruck: Tyrolia, 2014.

———. "The Church in the Bloodlands." *First Things*, October 20, 2014, 41–44.

———. "Churches in the Ukrainian Public Square." *Toronto Journal of Theology* 31/1 (2015) 3–14.

———. "De regionale en universele kerk in de huidige orthodox-katholieke dialoog." *Digitaal Oecumenisch Theologisch Tijdschrift*, 20 (2013) 28–33.

———. "Does Primacy Belong to the Nature of the Church?" In *Primacy in the Church: The Office of Primate and the Authority of Councils*, edited by John Chryssavgis, 511–30. Yonkers, NY: St. Vladimir's Seminary Press, 2016.

———. "Evolution of Church Governance: From the Diaspora-Model to Pentarchy." *Iura Orientalia*, XI (2013) 91–99.

———. *From Antioch to Xi'an: An Evolution of "Nestorianism."* Hong Kong: Chinese Orthodox Press, 2014.

———. *Meta-Ecclesiology: Chronicles on Church Awareness*, New York: Palgrave Macmillan, 2015.

———. "On Formation of Jurisdictional Limits of Eastern Churches in 4–5th Centuries." In *Proceedings of the Orientale Lumen IX Conference*, 87–103. Vienna, VA: Society of St. John Chrysostom Eastern Christian Publications, 2005.

———. "Universal and Particular in the Church." Філософська думка, IV (2013) 194–201.

———. *Will, Action and Freedom: Christological Controversies in the Seventh Century.* Leiden: Brill, 2008.

Ivanovic, Filip. "The Ecclesiology of Dionysius the Areopagite." *International Journal for the Study of the Christian Church* 11/1 (2011) 27–44.

Jay, Eric George. *The Church: Its Changing Image through Twenty Centuries.* Louisville, KY: John Knox, 1980.

Jeffreys, Elizabeth, John Haldon, and Robin Cormack, eds. *The Oxford Handbook of Byzantine Studies.* Oxford: Oxford University Press, 2008.

Johnson, Lawrence J. *Worship in the Early Church: An Anthology of Historical Sources.* Collegeville, MN: Liturgical, 2009.

Johnston, Hank. "Religio-Nationalist Subcultures under the Communists: Comparisons from the Baltics, Transcaucasia and Ukraine." *Sociology of Religion* 54/3 (1993) 237–55.

Johnston, Sarah Iles. *Religions of the Ancient World: A Guide.* Cambridge: Harvard University Press, 2004.

Jones, Lindsay. *Encyclopedia of Religion.* Detroit: Macmillan Reference USA, 2005.

Kaegi, Walter. "Reconsidering Byzantium's Eastern Frontiers in the Seventh Century." In *Shifting Frontiers in Late Antiquity*, edited by Ralph Mathisen and Hagith Sivan, 83–92. Aldersho, UK: Ashgate, 1996.

Kanyike, Lawrence. "The Anonymous Christian and the Mission of the Church." PhD diss., University of Notre Dame, 1978.

Karamanolis, George E. *Plato and Aristotle in Agreement? Platonists on Aristotle from Antiochus to Porphyry*. Oxford: Oxford University Press, 2006.

Karpat, Kemal. "The Balkan National States and Nationalism: Image and Reality." *Islamic Studies* 36/2-3 (1997) 329-59.

Kingdon, Robert M. "The Church: Ideology or Institution." *Church History* 50/1 (1981) 81-97.

Kinnamon, Michael. "Ecumenical Ecclesiology: One Church of Christ for the Sake of the World." *Journal of Ecumenical Studies* 44/3 (2009) 341-51.

Kirby, W. J. Torrance. *Richard Hooker's Doctrine of the Royal Supremacy*. Leiden: Brill, 1990.

Kloppenborg, John S., and Richard S. Ascough. *Greco-Roman Associations Texts, Translations, and Commentary: Attica, Central Greece, Macedonia, Thrace*. Berlin: De Gruyter, 2011.

Koskela, Douglas. "Yves Congar's Vision of Ecclesiality: Pneumatological Development and Ecumenical Promise." PhD diss., Southern Methodist University, 2003.

Kraeling, C. H. *The Christian Building. The Excavations at Dura-Europos: Final Report VIII*, part II. Edited by C. B. Welles. New Haven: Dura-Europos, 1967.

Küng, Hans. *The Church*. New York: Sheed & Ward, 1967.

———. *Structures of the Church*. New York: Crossroad, 1982.

L'Huillier, Peter. *The Church of the Ancient Councils: The Disciplinary Work of the First Four Ecumenical Councils*. Crestwood, NY: St. Vladimir's Seminary Press, 1996.

Laidlaw, William Allison. *A History of Delos*. Oxford: Blackwell, 1933.

Lamoreaux, John C. "Episcopal Courts in Late Antiquity." *Journal of Early Christian Studies* 3/2 (1995) 143-67.

Lee, A. D. *Information and Frontiers: Roman Foreign Relations in Late Antiquity*. Cambridge: Cambridge University Press, 1993.

Leemans, Johan, Peter van Nuffelen, Shawn W. J. Keough, and Carla Nicolaye, eds. *Episcopal Elections in Late Antiquity*. Berlin: De Gruyter, 2011.

Lenski, Gerhard. *Power and Privilege: A Theory of Social Stratification*. New York: McGraw-Hill, 1996.

Liddell, Henry George, Robert Scott, Henry Stuart Jones, and Roderick McKenzie. *Greek-English Lexicon*. 9th ed. Oxford: Clarendon, 2006.

Lindbeck, George A. *The Church in a Postliberal Age*. Grand Rapids: Eerdmans, 2003.

Lora, Erminio, and Rita Simionati, eds. *Enchiridion delle encicliche*. Vol. 6. Bologna: EDB, 1995.

Lora, Erminio, ed. *Enchiridion Vaticanum. 19: Documenti ufficiali della Santa Sede 2000*. Bologna: EDB, 2004.

Louth, Andrew. *Greek East and Latin West: The Church, AD 681-1071*. Crestwood, NY: St. Vladimir's Seminary Press, 2007.

Lunn-Rockliffe, Sophie. *Ambrosiaster's Political Theology*. Oxford: Oxford University Press, 2007.

Luther, Martin. *Works*. Edited by Jaroslav Pelikan, Hilton C. Oswald, Helmut T. Lehmann, and Christopher Boyd Brown. Saint Louis, MO: Concordia, 1955.

Mannion, Gerard. *Comparative Ecclesiology: Critical Investigations*. London: T. & T. Clark, 2008.

Mannion, Gerard, and Lewis Seymour Mudge, eds. *The Routledge Companion to the Christian Church*. London: Routledge, 2008.

Mansi, Johannes Dominicus. *Sacrorum conciliorum nova et amplissima collectio*. Graz: Akademische Druck- u. Verlagsanstalt, 1961.

Marek, Pavel, and Volodymyr Bureha. *Pravoslavní v Ceskoslovensku v letech 1918–1953: príspevek k dejinám Pravoslavné církve v ceských zemích, na Slovensku a na Podkarpatské Rusi*. Brno: Centrum pro studium demokracie a kultury, 2008.

Marjanen, Antti. "Montanism: Egalitarian Ecstatic 'New Prophecy.'" In *A Companion to Second-Century Christian "Heretics,"* edited by Antti Marjanen and Petri Luomanen, 185–212. Leiden: Brill, 2005.

Markus, R. A. "How on Earth Could Places Become Holy? Origins of the Christian Idea of Holy Places." *Journal of Early Christian Studies* 2/3 (1994) 257–71.

Martini, Luciano. "Anonymous Christians, Anonymous Faith in Karl Rahner's Theological Thought." *Religioni e Società* 1/1 (1986) 68–81.

McDonnell, Kilian. "The Ratzinger/Kasper Debate: The Universal Church and Local Churches." *Theological Studies* 63/2 (2002) 227–50.

Meeks, Wayne A. *The First Urban Christians: The Social World of the Apostle Paul*. New Haven: Yale University Press, 1983.

Mettepenningen, Jürgen. *Nouvelle Théologie—New Theology: Inheritor of Modernism, Precursor of Vatican II*. London: T. & T. Clark, 2010.

Meyendorff, John. *Byzantium and the Rise of Russia: A Study of Byzantino-Russian Relations in the Fourteenth Century*. Cambridge: Cambridge University Press, 1981.

———. *Rome, Constantinople, Moscow: Historical and Theological Studies*. Crestwood, NY: St. Vladimir's Seminary Press, 1996.

Meyendorff, Paul. "Ethnophyletism, Autocephaly, and National Churches—A Theological Approach and Ecclesiological Implications." *St. Vladimir's Seminary Quarterly* 57/3–4 (2013) 381–94.

Michel Foucault. *The Archaeology of Knowledge and the Discourse on Language*. Translated by A. M. Sheridan Smith. New York: Pantheon, 1972.

Miller, J. Michael. *The Divine Right of the Papacy in Recent Ecumenical Theology*. Roma: Università Gregoriana editrice, 1980.

Miltchyna, Vera. "Joseph De Maistre's Works in Russia: A Look at Their Reception." In *Joseph De Maistre's Life, Thought and Influence: Selected Studies*, edited by Richard A. Lebrun, 241–70. Montreal: McGill-Queen's University Press, 2001.

Mironowicz, Antoni, Urszula Pawluczuk, and Piotr Chomik. *Autokefalie Kościoła prawosławnego w Polsce*. Białstok: Wydawn. Uniwersytetu w Białymstoku, 2006.

Mojanoski, Cane T. *Avtokefalnosta na makedonskata pravoslavna crkva: dokumenti*. Skopje: Makedonska iskra, 2004.

Mommsen, Theodor, and Paul M. Meyer. *Theodosiani libri XVI cum constitutionibus sirmondianis et leges novellae ad Theodosianum pertinentes: consilio et auctoritate Academiae litterarum regiae Borussicae*. Berlin: Weidmann, 1905.

Moore, Sheila E. "Karl Rahner's Notion of the Anonymous Christian." PhD diss., University of St. Michael's College, 1971.

Morris, Colin. *The Papal Monarchy: The Western Church From 1050 to 1250*. Oxford: Oxford University Press, 1989.

Mousnier, Roland. *Social Hierarchies, 1450 to the Present*. New York: Schocken, 1973.

Muehlberger, Ellen. *Angels in Late Ancient Christianity*. Oxford: Oxford University Press, 2013.

Nelson, John Robert. "Toward an Ecumenical Ecclesiology." *Theological Studies* 31 (1970) 644–73.
Niditch, Susan, ed. *The Wiley Blackwell Companion to Ancient Israel*. Chichester, UK: Wiley Blackwell, 2016.
North, Douglass C. *Structure and Change in Economic History*. New York: Norton, 1981.
———. *Institutions, Institutional Change, and Economic Performance*. Cambridge: Cambridge University Press, 1990.
Norton, Peter. *Episcopal Elections 250–600: Hierarchy and Popular Will in Late Antiquity*. Oxford: Oxford University Press, 2007.
O'Donnell, Christopher. *Ecclesia: A Theological Encyclopedia of the Church*. Collegeville, MN: Liturgical, 1996.
O'Keefe, John J., and Russell R. Reno. *Sanctified Vision: An Introduction to Early Christian Interpretation of the Bible*. Baltimore, MD: Johns Hopkins University Press, 2005.
Obolensky, Dimitri. "Byzantium, Kiev and Moscow: A Study in Ecclesiastical Relations." *Dumbarton Oaks Papers* 11 (1957) 21–78.
Olyan, Saul M. *Rites and Rank: Hierarchy in Biblical Representations of Cult*. Princeton: Princeton University Press, 2000.
Ormerod, Neil. "Recent Ecclesiology: A Survey." *Pacifica* 21/1 (2008) 57–67.
Ott, Daniel J. "The Church in Process: A Process Ecclesiology." PhD diss., The Claremont Graduate University, 2006.
Otto, Rudolf. *Das Heilige: uber das Irrationale in der Idee des göttlichen und sein Verhältnis zum Rationalen*. Breslau: Trewendt & Granier, 1917.
———. *The Idea of the Holy: An Inquiry into the Non-Rational Factor in the Idea of the Divine and Its Relation to the Rational*. Translated by John W. Harvey. Oxford: Oxford University Press, 1923.
Owen, Carol. *Social Stratification*. London: Routledge, 1968.
Öörni, Soili. "Autocephaly and Its Meaning for the Finnish Orthodox Church." MDiv diss., St. Vladimir's Seminary, 1986.
Papademetriou, Tom. *Render unto the Sultan: Power, Authority, and the Greek Orthodox Church in the Early Ottoman Centuries*. Oxford: Oxford University Press, 2015.
Papagiannes, Thymios, and Josep Maria Mallarach i Carrera. *The Sacred Dimension of Protected Areas: Proceedings of the Second Workshop of the Delos Initiative: Ouranoupolis, Greece, 24–27 October 2007*. Athens: Med-INA, 2009.
Papandrea, James Leonard. *The Trinitarian Theology of Novatian of Rome: A Study in Third-Century Orthodoxy*. Lewiston, NY: Mellen, 2008.
———. *Novatian of Rome and the Culmination of Pre-Nicene Orthodoxy*. Eugene, OR: Pickwick, 2011.
Parker, John. *Structuration*. Buckingham, UK: Open University Press, 2000.
Parsons, Talcott. *Social Structure and Personality*. London: Free, 1970.
Partykevich, Andre. *Between Kyiv and Constantinople: Oleksander Lototsky and the Quest for Ukrainian Autocephaly*. Edmonton, AB: Canadian Institute of Ukrainian Studies, 1998.
Pascuzzi, Maria. *Ethics, Ecclesiology and Church Discipline: A Rhetorical Analysis of 1 Corinthians 5*. Roma: Pontificia università gregoriana, 1997.
Peachin, Michael. *The Oxford Handbook of Social Relations in the Roman World*. Oxford: Oxford University Press, 2011.
Perkins, Ann Louise. *The Art of Dura-Europos*. Oxford: Clarendon, 1973.

Perl, Eric D. *Theophany: The Neoplatonic Philosophy of Dionysius the Areopagite*. Albany, NY: State University of New York Press, 2007.

Phidas, Vlassios. "The Limits of the Church in an Orthodox Perspective." *The Greek Orthodox Theological Review* 43/1–4 (1998) 1–13.

Photios. *Photii patriarchae Constantinopolitani epistulae et amphilochia*. Vol. 3, *Epistularum pars tertia*. Edited by B. Laourdas and L. G. Westerink. Leipzig: Teubner, 1985.

Plokhy, Serhii, and Frank E. Sysyn. *Religion and Nation in Modern Ukraine*. Edmonton, AB: Canadian Institute of Ukrainian Studies Press, 2003.

Poe, Marshall. *"Moscow, the Third Rome": The Origins and Transformations of a Pivotal Movement*. Washington, DC: National Council for Soviet and East European Research, 1997.

Poster, Mark. "Foucault and History." *Social Research* 49/1 (1982) 116–42.

Potter, David. *A Companion to the Roman Empire*. Malden, MA: Blackwell, 2006.

Prandy, Kenneth. "The Social Interaction Approach to the Measurement and Analysis of Social Stratification." *International Journal of Sociology and Social Policy* 19 (1999) 204–36.

Prusak, Bernard P. *The Church Unfinished: Ecclesiology through the Centuries*. New York: Paulist, 2004.

Rahner, Karl. *Theological Investigations*. Vol. 5. London: Darton, Longman & Todd, 1966.

Ramet, Sabrina P. "Autocephaly and National Identity in Church-State Relations in Eastern Christianity." In *Eastern Christianity and Politics in the Twentieth Century*, edited by Sabrina P. Ramet, 3–19. Durham, NC: Duke University Press, 1988.

Rapp, Claudia. *Holy Bishops in Late Antiquity: The Nature of Christian Leadership in an Age of Transition*. Berkeley: University of California Press, 2013.

Ratzinger, Joseph. *The Open Circle: The Meaning of Christian Brotherhood*. New York: Sheed and Ward, 1966.

Rauh, Nicholas K. *The Sacred Bonds of Commerce: Religion, Economy, and Trade Society at Hellenistic Roman Delos, 166–87 B.C.* Amsterdam: Gieben, 1993.

Rennie, Kriston R. *The Foundations of Medieval Papal Legation*. New York: Palgrave Macmillan, 2013.

Rhodes, P. J. *The Athenian Boule*. Oxford: Clarendon, 1972.

Richardson, Cyril. *Early Christian Fathers*. Louisville, KY: John Knox, 2006.

Roberts, Alexander, and James Donaldson, eds. *The Ante-Nicene Fathers*. Vol. 4. Grand Rapids: Eerdmans, 1956.

Rolt, C. E. *Dionysius, the Areopagite, on the Divine Names and Mystical Theology*. London: SPCK, 1920.

Ross, W. D. *Aristotelis politica*. Oxford: Clarendon, 1957.

Rostovtzeff, Michael Ivanovitch. *Dura-Europos and Its Art*. Oxford: Clarendon, 1938.

Roudometof, Victor. "From Rum Millet to Greek Nation: Enlightenment, Secularization, and National Identity in Ottoman Balkan Society, 1453–1821." *Journal of Modern Greek Studies* 16/1 (1998) 11–48.

Rousseau, Jean-Jacques. *The Essential Rousseau: The Social Contract, Discourse on the Origin of Inequality, Discourse on the Arts and Sciences, the Creed of a Savoyard Priest*. Translated by Lowell Bair, New York: Penguin, 1975.

Rubin, Paul H. "Hierarchy." *Human Nature* 11/3 (2000) 259–79.

Russell, Jesse. *Autocephaly*. Miami: Book on Demand, 2015.

Sanderson, Charles Wegener. "Autocephaly as a Function of Institutional Stability and Organizational Change in the Eastern Orthodox Church." PhD diss., University of Maryland, 2005.

Saunders, Peter. *Social Class and Stratification*. London: Routledge, 2001.

Scheid, John. "Graeco-Roman Cultic Societies." *Oxford Handbooks* Online. https://goo.gl/i5MZWD.

Schillebeeckx, Edward. *Church: The Human Story of God*. New York: Crossroad, 1990.

———. *The Church with a Human Face: A New and Expanded Theology of Ministry*. New York: Crossroad, 1985.

Schmemann, Alexander. *Church, World, Mission: Reflections on Orthodoxy in the West*. Crestwood, NY: St. Vladimir's Seminary Press, 1979.

Schwartz, Seth. "Ancient Jewish Social Relations." *Oxford Handbooks Online*. https://goo.gl/eZEUOA.

Sidanius, Jim, and Felicia Pratto. *Social Dominance: An Intergroup Theory of Social Hierarchy and Oppression*. Cambridge: Cambridge University Press, 1999.

Somers-Hall, Henry. *Deleuze's Difference and Repetition: An Edinburgh Philosophical Guide*. Edinburgh: Edinburgh University Press, 2013.

Sorabji, Richard, ed. *Aristotle Transformed: The Ancient Commentators and Their Influence*. Ithaca, NY: Cornell University Press, 1990.

Steinberger, Helmut. "Sovereignty." In *The Max Planck Encyclopedia of Public International Law*. Edited by Rüdiger Wolfrum. Vol. 10, Oxford: Oxford University Press, 2012.

Stephens, Christopher W. B. *Canon Law and Episcopal Authority: The Canons of Antioch and Serdica*. Oxford: Oxford University Press, 2015.

Stewart-Sykes, Alistair. *The Original Bishops: Office and Order in the First Christian Communities*. Grand Rapids: Baker Academic, 2014.

Strémooukhoff, Dimitri. "Moscow the Third Rome: Sources of the Doctrine." *Speculum* 28/1 (1953) 84–101.

Stuckrad, Kocku von, and Robert R. Barr. *The Brill Dictionary of Religion Vol. II, E-L*. Leiden: Brill, 2006.

Studstill, Randall. "Eliade, Phenomenology, and the Sacred." *Religious Studies* 36/2 (2000) 177–94.

Sullivan, F. A. *From Apostles to Bishops: The Development of the Episcopacy in the Early Church*. New York: Newman, 2001.

Tabbernee, William. *Fake Prophecy and Polluted Sacraments: Ecclesiastical and Imperial Reactions to Montanism*. Leiden: Brill, 2007.

———. *Montanist Inscriptions and Testimonia: Epigraphic Sources Illustrating the History of Montanism*. Macon, GA: Mercer University Press, 1997.

Tabbernee, William, and Peter Lampe. *Pepouza and Tymion: The Discovery and Archeological Exploration of a Lost Ancient City and an Imperial Estate*. Berlin: De Gruyter, 2008.

Theissen, Gerd. *The Religion of the Earliest Churches: Creating a Symbolic World*. Minneapolis, MN: Fortress, 2000.

Themelis, Petros G. *Mykonos-Delos: Archaeological Guide*. Athens: Apollo, 1977.

Thier, Andreas. *Hierarchie und Autonomie*. Frankfurt am Main: Klostermann, 2010.

Tillard, J. M. R. *Flesh of the Church, Flesh of Christ: At the Source of the Ecclesiology of Communion*. Collegeville, MN: Liturgical, 2001.

Tollefsen, Torstein. *Activity and Participation in Late Antique and Early Christian Thought*. Oxford: Oxford University Press, 2012.
Toumanoff, Cyril. "Moscow the Third Rome: Genesis and Significance of a Politico-Religious Idea." *The Catholic Historical Review* 40/4 (1955) 411–47.
Toynbee, Arnold J. *A Study of History*. Oxford: Oxford University Press, 1940.
Trevett, Christine. *Montanism: Gender, Authority, and the New Prophecy*. Cambridge: Cambridge University Press, 1996.
Tuominen, Miira. *The Ancient Commentators on Plato and Aristotle*. Berkeley, CA: University of California Press, 2009.
Volf, Miroslav. *After Our Likeness: The Church as the Image of the Trinity*. Grand Rapids: Eerdmans, 1998.
Wach, Joachim. *Sociology of Religion*. Chicago: University of Chicago Press, 1944.
Wallace-Hadrill, J. M. *The Frankish Church*. Oxford: Oxford University Press, 1983.
Walters, Philip. "Notes on Autocephaly and Phyletism." *Religion, State and Society* 30/4 (2002) 357–64.
Walzer, Michael. *Interpretation and Social Criticism*. Cambridge: Harvard University Press, 1987.
Ware, Kallistos. *Eustratios Argenti: A Study of the Greek Church under Turkish Rule*. Oxford: Clarendon, 1964.
Weber, Max. *The Sociology of Religion*. Boston: Beacon, 1963.
Weed, Ronald, and John von Heyking, eds. *Civil Religion in Political Thought: Its Perennial Questions and Enduring Relevance in North America*. Washington, DC: Catholic University of America Press, 2010.
Weisgerber, James. "Primacy and Collegiality." *The Furrow* 52/12 (2001) 696–99.
Weitzmann, Kurt, and Herbert L. Kessler. *The Frescoes of the Dura Synagogue and Christian Art*. Washington, DC: Dumbarton Oaks, 1990.
Wilberding, James. *Porphyry*. London: Bloomsbury, 2014.
Wiley, Charles Aden. "Responding to God: The Church as Visible and Invisible in Calvin, Schleiermacher, and Barth." PhD diss., Princeton Theological Seminary, 2002.
Williams, James. *Understanding Poststructuralism*. Chesham, UK: Acumen, 2005.
Williamson, Oliver E. *The Mechanisms of Governance*. Oxford: Oxford University Press, 1996.
Wittke, Anne-Maria, Eckart Olshausen, Richard Szydlak, and Christine F. Salazar. *Historical Atlas of the Ancient World*. Leiden: Brill, 2010.
Wolff, Robert Lee. "The 'Second Bulgarian Empire.' Its Origin and History to 1204." *Speculum* 24/2 (1949) 167–206.
———. "The Three Romes: The Migration of an Ideology and the Making of an Autocrat." *Daedalus* 88/2 (1959) 291–311.
Wong, Joseph H. "Anonymous Christians: Karl Rahner's Pneuma-Christocentrism and an East-West Dialogue." *Theological Studies* 55/4 (1994) 609–37.
Wood, Susan. "Continuity and Development in Roman Catholic Ecclesiology." *Ecclesiology* 7/2 (2011) 147–72.
Wright, J. Robert. *A Companion to Bede: A Reader's Commentary on the Ecclesiastical History of the English People*. Grand Rapids: Eerdmans, 2008.
Yale University, Académie des inscriptions belles-lettres France. *Excavations at Dura-Europos Conducted by Yale University and the French Academy of Inscriptions and Letters*. New Haven: Yale University Press, 1929.

Zernov, Nicolas. *Moscow, the Third Rome*. London: SPCK, 1937.
Zizioulas, John. *Being as Communion: Studies in Personhood and the Church*. Crestwood, NY: St. Vladimir's Seminary Press, 1985.
———. *The One and the Many: Studies on God, Man, the Church, and the World Today*, Alhambra, CA: Sebastian Press, 2010.
———. *Communion and Otherness*, London; New York: T & T Clark, 2006.

Ἀγαπίου καὶ Νικοδήμου. *Πηδάλιον τῆς νοητῆς νηὸς τῆς Μιᾶς Ἁγίας Καθολικῆς καὶ Ἀποστολικῆς τῶν Ὀρθοδόξων Ἐκκλησίας*. Ἀθῆναι: Ἀστήρ, 1993.

Γλαβίνα, Αποστόλου. *Το αυτοκέφαλο της Ορθόδοξης Εκκλησίας της Αλβανίας*. Αθήνα: Ίδρυμα Γουλανδρή—Χορν, 1986.
Γόνη, Δημητρίου. *Ιστορία των Ορθοδόξων Εκκλησιών Βουλγαρίας και Σερβίας*. Αθήνα: Συμμετρία, 1996.
Δημαρά, Κωνσταντίνου. *Νεοελληνικός Διαφωτισμός*. Αθήνα: Ερμής, 1989.
Καρμήρη, Ἰωάννη. *Τὰ δογματικὰ καὶ συμβολικὰ μνημεία τῆς Ὀρθοδόξου Καθολικῆς Ἐκκλησίας*. Vol. 1. Ἀθῆναι, 1960.
———. "Ἡ παγκοσμιότης τῆς ἐν Χριστῷ σωτηρίας." *Θεολογία* 51 (1980) 645–91.
Κεκαυμένου, Γιώργου. *Το κρυφό σχολειό: το χρονικό μιας ιστορίας*. Αθήνα: Εναλλακτηκές, 2012.
Κοραῆ, Ἀδαμαντίου. *Ἀριστοτέλους Πολιτικῶν τὰ σωζόμενα: ἐκδίδοντος καὶ διορθοῦντος Ἀ.Κ., φιλοτίμῳ δαπάνῃ τῶν ὁμογενῶν, ἐπ' ἀγαθῷ τῆς Ἑλλάδος*. Paris: Ἰ. Μ. Ἐβεράρτου, 1821.
Κωνσταντινίδου, Ἐμμανουῆλ. *Ἡ ἀνακήρυξις τοῦ αὐτοκεφάλου τῆς ἐν Ἑλλάδι Ἐκκλησίας (1850) καὶ ἡ θέσις τῶν Μητροπόλεων τῶν "Νέων Χωρῶν*." Ἀθῆναι, 1996.
Παπανδρέου, Δαμασκηνού. *Τὸ θέλημα τοῦ Θεοῦ*. Ἀθῆναι, 1981.
Ράλλη, Γεωργίου, καὶ Μιχαὴλ Ποτλῆ. *Σύνταγμα τῶν θείων καὶ ἱερῶν κανόνων*. Ἀθῆναι: Γ. Χαρτοφύλακος, 1854.
Φειδᾶ, Βλασίου. *Ὁ θεσμὸς τῆς πενταρχίας τῶν πατριαρχῶν*. Vol. 1. Ἀθῆναι, 1969.
———. *Ἐνδημοῦσα σύνοδος: γένεσις καὶ διαμόρφωσις τοῦ θεσμοῦ ἄχρι τῆς Δ' οἰκουμενικῆς συνόδου*. Ἀθῆναι, 1971.
———. *Ἐκκλησιαστικὴ Ἱστορία*. 2nd ed. Vol. 1. Ἀθῆναι, 1995.

Афанасьев, Николай. *Вступление в Церковь*. Москва: Паломник, 1993.
Бердяев, Николай. "Вселенскость и конфессионализм." In *Христианское воссоединение: экуменическая проблема в православном сознании*. Edited by Сергий Булгаков, 63–81, Paris: YMCA, 1933.
Булгаков, Сергий. "Очерки учения о Церкви." *Путь* 4 (1926) 3–26.
———. *Христіанское возсоединеніе: экуменическая проблема въ православномъ сознаніи*. Paris: YMCA, 1933.
Власовський, Іван. *Нарис історії Української Православної Церкви*. Vol. 4. New York, 1961.
Говорун, Сергей. "Исторический контекст 28-го правила." *Церковь и время* 2/27 (2004) 178–94.
Голубинский, Евгений. *История Русской Церкви*. Vol. 2. Москва: Университетская типография, 1900.
Дроздов, Филарет. *Собрание мнений и отзывов Филарета. по делам Православной Церкви на Востоке*. Санкт-Петербург: Синодальная типография, 1886.
Зернов, Николай. "Православие и англиканство." *Путь* 43 (1934) 49–61.

Карташев, Антон. "Соединение Церквей в свете истории." In *Христианское воссоединение: экуменическая проблема в православном сознании*. Edited by Сергий Булгаков, 82–120, Paris: YMCA, 1933.

Кириллов, И. А. *Третій Римъ: очеркъ историческаго развитія идеи русскаго мессіанизма*. Москва: И.М. Машистова, 1914.

Словарь книжников и книжности Древней Руси. Edited by Д.С. Лихачев. т. 2, Ленинград: Институт русской литературы, Пушкинский дом, 1989.

Оглоблин, Олександр. *Московська теорія ІІІ Риму в XVI–XVII стол*. Munich: Церковно-археографічна Комісія Апостольського Візитатора для українців у Західній Європі, 1951.

Светлов, Павел. *Христианское вероучение в апологетическом изложении*. Vol. 1. Киев, 1914.

Синицына, Н. В. *Третий Рим: истоки и эволюция русской средневековой концепции: XV–XVI вв*. Москва: Индрик, 1998.

Страгородский, Сергий. *Православное учение о спасении*. Сергиев Посад, 1895.

———. "К вопросу о том, что нас разделяет со старокатоликами." *Церковные ведомости* 40 (1903) 1249–52.

———. 1994. "Об отношении Церкви Христовой к отделившимся от нее обществам." *Журнал Московской Патриархии* 5 (1994) 80–98.

Троицкий, Иларион. *Очерки из истории догмата о Церкви*. Сергиев Посад, 1912.

Успенский, Борис Андреевич. *Царь и Патриарх*. Москва: Школа "Языки русской культуры", 1998.

Флоровский, Георгий. "О границах Церкви." *Путь* 44 (1934) 15–26.

Хомяков, Алексей. *Письмо к редактору «L'union Chrétienne» о значении слов «кафолический» и «соборный». Письма к В. Пальмеру*. Москва: DirectMEDIA, 2008.

Хомяков, Алексей. *Учение о Церкви*. Москва: Русская симфония, 2010.

Храповицкий, Антоний. "Ответ на третье письмо секретаря Всемирной Конференции Епископальной Церкви в Америке." *Вера и Разум* 8–9 (1916) 877–97.

Index

abaton, 30, 32
Abdülaziz, 119
Abdülmecid, 117–18
absolutism, 195
Ackrill, John, 134–35
acribeia, 176
acropolis, 29
admonisher, 8, 149
Adonis, 54
adyton, 29
aedes, 30
Aegean, 31, 91
Afanasiev, Nikolay, 178, 195
Africa, 29, 60, 65, 74, 85, 164, 180
ager, 30
agnosticism, 174, 177
agros, 29
Ahl, Valerie, 187–88
akribeia, 175–76
Alaska, 125
Albania, 82
Alberigo, Guiseppe, 23, 62, 141
Alexandria, 11, 39, 60–61, 65, 67, 80, 82, 85, 118–19, 140–41
Alexios III Angelos, 100
Alexiy of Moscow, 126
Allen, T.F.H., 187–188
almighty, 153
altar, 18, 29–30, 32–34, 54
altruistic, 147
ambiguum, 140
Ambrosiaster, 132, 140–41, 145–46, 158
Amphilochia, 91
anachronism, 70, 150
analogy, 12, 20, 22, 58, 158, 160

analytic, 24, 132
Anastasius of Sinai, 41
anathema, 21, 96, 102, 109, 112–13, 119, 124
Ando, Clifford, 75–76
angelic, 161
angelology, 140
Anglican, 168
Anglo-Saxon, 78
animal, 41, 134–35
annexation, 102
Annunciation, 115
anointment, 92, 108, 165–66
anomaly, 16, 86
anonymous, 172–73
antestes, 132, 141
Anthim of Bulgaria, 119
Anthimos of Jerusalem, 114
antichrist, 105, 119
antimensia, 34
Antioch, 8, 57, 60–61, 63, 65, 67, 79–80, 82, 90–91, 118–19, 152
Antiochus, 41
Aphrodisias, 61
apocrypha, 140
Apollinarianism, 109
Apollo, 31–32, 35
apologist, 32
apostasy, 17
apostolicity, 64
appeal, 63, 67, 77–78
Aquinas, 164
Arabic, 65, 68, 74, 78–79, 125
Aramaic, 58
archaeology, 31, 35, 53–54, 56, 182

250   Index

archangel, 161
archbishopric, 96–97, 100–101
archdeacon, 161
archdiocese, 45
archetype, 50, 94, 111
archimandrite, 112, 117
archipelago, 31
architecture, 39, 54, 113
Areopagite, ps-Dionysios, 37, 132, 139, 160–61
Argos, 111
Arianism, 5, 62–63, 79, 163
aristocracy, 156
Aristotle, 12, 41–43, 66, 129, 133–37, 140–41, 182
army, 29, 123, 158
Artemis, 31–32
Arthur, Rosemary, 140
ascetic, 68
Asclepius, 30
Ascough, Richard, 52
Asen Alexander, 99
Asia, 43, 60, 76, 83–84, 86
Asiana, 65
Athanasios of Paros, 175
Athens, 31, 51–52, 86, 113, 125, 151, 169
atomization, 196
Attikos of Constantinople, 77
Augustine, 17, 164, 174
Austro-Hungary, 83, 121
autarkic, 88, 163
authoritarianism, 188
autism, 46
autocephalism, 122
autocephaly, 2, 6, 44, 48, 62, 65, 80–83, 88–95, 97–107, 109–17, 119–29, 183, 185, 189, 197
autochthonous, 85
autocrat, 98, 101
autonomy, 44, 48, 59, 69–70, 82, 89, 95–97, 121–24, 154, 192, 195
awakening, 111, 122

Bailey, Leon, 10
Bair, Lowell, 115

Balkans, 69–72, 77, 84, 100, 103, 106, 108, 110–11, 116, 120–21
Balsamon, Theodore, 62, 165
Balthasar, Hans Urs von, 130, 173
Baltic, 121
baptism, 18, 39, 41–42, 47, 54–56, 95, 98, 103, 145–46, 164–166, 169, 171, 174–75, 183
baptistery, 53–55
barbarian, 73–74, 83–84, 113, 179
Barnes, Jonathan, 41
Barr, Robert, 26
Barth, Karl, 21–22
Barthes, Roland, 188, 198
Basil I emperor, 96, 99
Basil III of Moscow, 104–5, 107–8
Basil of Caesarea, 158
basileus, 98, 101
basilica, 39
Baum, Gregory, 170–71, 173
Baur, Christopher, 54
Bavaria, 112
Bede, 78
Belgrade, 84, 120
Bellah, Robert, 114
Bellarmine, Robert, 20
Benedict XIV of Rome, 173–74
Berdiaev, Nicholas, 168
bipolarity, 2, 196
Biriukov, Dimitry, 140
Birkelund, Gunn Elisabeth, 146
bishopric, 158
blasphemy, 181
Bodel, John, 53
Bogardus, Emory, 147
Bogatyrev, Sergei, 108
Bohr, David, 151
Bolshevik, 122, 125, 176
Boniface I of Rome, 77–78
Boniface VIII of Rome, 129
Bonnet, Jules, 19
borderland, 29
borderline, 2, 5, 9–11, 20, 40, 93, 126, 163, 179
Borgatta, Edgar, 148
Boris of Bulgaria, 94–96, 101
Bottero, Wendy, 186

boulē, 151
bouleutērion, 31
Bourdieu, Pierre, 186
Bowen, Harold, 70
Bowersock, G.W., 79
Bozveli, Neophyte, 117
Braaten, Carl, 24
Braude, Benjamin, 70
Breen, Richard, 146
Brent, Allen, 59, 153
bride, 24
Britain, 73–74, 78, 80, 187
Brown, Peter, 154
Brown, Raymond, 149, 151, 193
Brown, Stewart, 168
Brubaker, Leslie, 78
Bulgakov, Sergey, 169
Bulgaria, 6, 48, 72, 82, 91, 94–102, 108–9, 111, 113, 116–20, 126
bull, 32, 129, 165
bureaucracy, 156, 158
Burns, J.H., 129
Burtchaell, James, 51
Butler, Rex, 35

Cabasilas, Nilus, 143
Caesar, 98, 108
Caesarea, 60–61, 158
Cajetan, Thomas, 129
Calabria, 78
caliphate, 78–79
Calixtus of Rome, 154
Calvin, John, 18–19
Cameron, Averil, 74
Cameron, Ron, 59
Canaan, 28
Canada, 77, 123
Cappadocia, 40–41, 60, 63, 158
Caria, 61, 76, 91
Carolingian, 67
Carthage, 60, 164, 179–80
Caseau, Béatrice, 28–29, 33
catacombs, 33
catechist, 149
catechization, 39
catechumen, 160

causality, 2, 139, 192–93
Celtic, 78
censure, 93
centrifugal, 57, 74
centripetal, 38, 57, 74, 163
centrism, 190
Chadwick, Henry, 147
Chalcedonian, 5, 41, 67, 70
Chaldean, 137
Chandler, Alfred, 69
changeability, 185
charisma, 8, 35, 60, 108, 147–50, 154, 185
chauvinism, 122
Chenu, Marie-Dominique, 139
chiliastic, 35, 108
China, 106
Chlup, Radek, 137–38
chora, 29
chrismation, 108
Christendom, 4, 96, 170
Christocentrism, 13, 15, 172
Christology, 11, 20, 58, 79, 129, 141, 152
Christophe, Paul, 154
Chrysostom, John, 189
churchliness, 22
cizye, 70
Clapsis, Emmanuel, 169
Clement of Kyiv, 103
Clement of Rome, 140
Clements, R.E., 139
clerical, 158–160, 185, 197
clericalization, 159
Cohn, Ronald, 89
collegium, 51–53, 58–59, 75
Collins, Randall, 146
colonial, 6, 81, 83–85, 124
commonwealth, 68
communality, 71, 75
communist, 85, 123–24
conciliarity, 7, 16, 47, 62, 81, 122, 129
Congar, Yves, 22, 170, 173, 194
consent, 67, 76, 82, 88–89, 100–101, 103, 105, 127, 130, 155
conservative, 5, 48, 57, 113, 122, 154, 173, 175

conspiracy, 164
Constantine I the emperor, 5, 33–34, 39, 98, 106–7, 158
Constantine Manasses, 98–99, 108
Constantine Oikonomos, 113
contemplative, 160
Cooley, Alexander, 69
Cooper, Kate, 156
Cornelius of Rome, 154
coronation, 102
Corrigan, Kevin, 192
corruption, 5, 26, 38, 71, 104–6, 182, 188, 191
Cosmas Indicopleustes, 39–40
cosmology, 28
Costa, Gavin, 172
countryside, 29, 159
creed, 21, 141
Crete, 16, 48–49, 120
Crimea, 124
Crompton, Rosemary, 146
Crossley, Nick, 196–97
crusade, 100
curia, 53, 158, 189
Cyclades, 31, 35, 112
Cyprian of Carthage, 164, 177, 179–180
Cyprus, 61, 65, 82, 89–91, 97, 119
Cyril equal-to-apostles, 119
Cyril of Alexandria, 11, 141
Cyril V of Constantinople, 166
Cyrus of Alexandria, 67
Czech Lands and Slovakia, Church, 82, 121, 126
Czechoslovakia, 83, 121

Dacia, 74
Dadeshkeliani, Ilamez, 89
Damascus, 41
Danube, 73
Darrouzès, Jean, 97
deacon, 33, 43, 146, 149–50, 152, 157, 160–61, 196–97
decolonization, 6
deconstruction, 6, 181, 188, 195
deimperialization, 89
deity, 28, 142

Deleuze, Gilles, 185, 191
Delos, 31–32, 35, 39, 52, 192
Demacopoulos, George, 6
Demetrios of Ochrid, 100
democracy, 113, 120, 124–25, 156, 194–95
demon, 29
denomination, 165–67
Denton, Jeffrey, 139
Denysenko, Nicholas, 159
Denzinger, Heinrich, 165
Derrida, Jacques, 181
desacration, 26
despotism, 188
DeVille, Adam, 6
devolution, 93
dhimmah, 70
diakonia, 185, 192
dialectics, 39, 41–42, 129, 136, 182, 196
dialogue, 7, 35, 128, 168, 172, 194
diaspora, 6, 16, 51–52, 58, 81, 83, 85–87, 123, 125, 168
Diatessaron, 56
dichostasia, 120
dichotomy, 18, 24, 187, 197
dictator, 188
Didachè, 43
Didascalia apostolorum, 153
Didymus, 140
Diocletian, 64
Dionysus, 52
diptycha, 16, 131
Directoria, 122
discipleship, 51
discipline, 14, 21, 50, 152, 154, 184
dissent, 123–24
ditch, 2, 5–6, 73–75, 77, 79, 81, 83, 85, 87, 192
Dods, Marcus, 17
domestication, 46
domination, 4, 7, 29, 32, 38, 44, 59, 61, 68, 73, 110, 152, 170, 191
Dominus Iesus, 173
Donaldson, James, 33
Donatism, 164
Drake, H.A., 158

dualism, 20, 24–25, 34, 36–39, 179, 187
Dulles, Avery, 1, 20, 191
Dunn, Geoffrey, 77–78, 129
Dura Europos, 53–56
Durkheim, Émile, 25
dysfunction, 38, 190, 192

Easter, 101–2, 118
Easton, Burton Scott, 151
ecclesia, 19, 21–23, 42, 44, 97, 164–66, 169, 173, 196
ecclesiocentrism, 10, 192
Eckstein, Arthur, 8
eclectism, 178
Edessa, 61
edict, 75, 117
education, 106, 111, 116–17
egalitarianism, 3, 7–9, 35, 149, 194
Egypt, 26, 65, 68, 79
eidos, 41, 134
Elder-Vass, Dave, 2
elders, 149, 151, 159
Eliade, Mircea, 25
Elias legate, 66
Elias philosopher, 41
emanation, 137
emancipation, 4, 80, 103, 121, 194–96
empress, 108
encosmic, 138
enculturation, 46
encyclical, 22–23
England, 19, 78
Enlightenment, 4, 110–11, 115–17
Enneads, 133
enthronement, 97, 101, 104, 108–109
eparchia, 60
Ephesus, 6, 8, 60, 65, 79, 89–91, 149
Epidauros, 111
Epirus, 100
eschatology, 34, 43, 108, 168
Estonia, 49, 82–83, 121
ethnic, 4, 6, 16, 72, 84, 120, 125–26
ethnicism, 47
ethnophyletism, 89

ethnos, 72, 115
Evagrius Ponticus, 192
Evangeliou, Christos, 41
Evans, J.A.S., 78
Evtimiy of Tirnovo, 99
exarch, 63, 119–20
exarchate, 119, 124
excommunication, 44, 156, 190

fanaticism, 120
Feodosiy of Moscow, 107
fermânı, 117, 119
feudal, 162
Filaret of Kyiv, 124
Filaret of Moscow, 167
Filo, Julius, 85
Filofey from Pskov, 107–9
Finland, 82–83, 121
Fisher, Greg, 78
Florovsky, Georges, 176–78
Foucault, Michael, 182
foundational, 3, 52, 136
fragmentation, 86, 127
France, 21
Franks, 67, 78, 95
Frazee, Charles, 111
frontier, 5, 9–10, 54, 73–74, 79, 163, 165, 167, 169, 171, 173, 175, 177, 179–80, 187
Fulgentius of Ruspe, 164
fullness, 36, 47, 171, 174–75
Fulton, John, 63, 156–57
FYROM, 84–85

Gaetuli, 179
Galicia, 103–4
Gallia, 65
Galych, 103
Gangra, 61
Garamantes, 179
Gavrilyuk, Paul, 177
Gennadios Scholarios, 69
genos, 41, 115, 134
gentile, 7, 27, 34, 57–58, 147–48, 158
genus, 41, 72, 134–36
geopolitics, 79, 94

254 Index

Georgia, 82, 89, 126
Gerasim of Smolensk, 104
Gerd, Lora, 58
Germanos of Old Patres, 115
Germany, 20, 25, 73–74, 78, 80, 95, 123
gerousia, 151
Gholaia, 28–29
Gibb, H.A.R., 70
globalization, 15, 85
gnosticism, 35–37, 152
goddess, 29
Godfrey, John, 78
godless, 26, 109
gods, 29–32, 54, 137
Godunov, Boris, 109
Goldman, Bernard, 53–54, 56
Golubinsky, Yevgeny, 105–6
Gooder, Paula, 58
Gorodetsky, Platon, 167
Granfeld, Patrick, 21
Greece, 6, 82, 86, 106, 110–13, 116–17, 120, 169
Gregory of Nazianzus, 189
Gregory V of Constantinople, 71, 112
Grigorieff, Dmitry, 125
Gritsch, Eric, 191
grotto, 31
gymnasium, 31
Gyzis, Nikolaos, 115

Habermas, Jürgen, 196
habitat, 29, 79
Habsburg, 121
Hadjiioannou, Emmanuel, 89
Hadrian's wall, 74
Hadrill, Wallace, 67
Haight, Roger, 13–14, 53, 57–59, 148, 152, 194
Haldon, John, 8, 78
Hammon, 29
Hammond, Phillip, 114
Haney, Jack, 107
Harrison, William, 19
Hathaway, Ronald, 136–37
Hauser, Robert, 146

healer, 8, 149
Hebblethwaite, Peter, 172–73
Hebrew, 26, 58
Heidegger, Martin, 181
Heidelberg, 35
Hellas, 89, 113, 115–16
Hellenist, 28, 31, 57
Hellenization, 57
Hellespont, 91
henad, 137–38, 142
Heraclius emperor, 67, 79, 99
Herod, 27
Hertford, 78
Hess, Hamilton, 63
heterodoxy, 119, 169, 175, 178
Heyking, John Von, 114–15
hierarchism, 3, 10, 141–42, 188, 190
hierourgy, 159
High Porte, 71, 112, 117
Hilarion of Kyiv, 103
Hilarion of Makarioupolis, 117–18
Hillner, Julia, 156
Himmelfarb, Martha, 26
Hippolytus of Rome, 140, 151, 154
Hjälm, Michael, 196
Hobsbawm, Eric, 110
Honneth, Axel, 184
Honorius emperor, 78
Honorius I of Rome, 67
Honorius III of Rome, 101
Hooker, Richard, 19–20
Hopkins, Clark, 53–54, 56, 94
horia, 73
horos, 29, 120, 166
Hosios of Cordoba, 63
household, 53–54, 56, 148–49, 190
Hovorun, Cyril, 40, 42, 49, 58, 60, 63, 67, 79, 88, 124, 128, 167, 188, 196
Hümayun, 118
Humbert, 165
Hünermann, Peter, 165
Hus, Jan, 18
Hütter, Reinhard, 24
hypercosmic, 138
hypocritical, 176
hypostasis, 41–42, 45, 131, 183
hypostatic, 42, 45, 189

Index   255

hypotyposis, 165
hyppodrome, 31

iconoclasm, 66, 78
idealism, 12–14, 20
ideology, 4, 10, 21, 74–75, 99, 107–10, 113, 127, 152–53, 188
Ignatius of Antioch, 8, 43–44, 96, 152–153
Illyria, 65, 77–78, 95, 129
immanent, 25, 140
imperialism, 122, 125
imperialization, 121
Imvros, 69
inauguratio, 30
Incarnation, 7, 22–23, 25, 27, 37, 41, 44, 176, 181, 183
inclusivism, 167, 171, 173
indigenization, 89
infallibility, 15, 181
institutionalism, 10, 191
intercommunion, 153
investiture, 67
Irenaeus of Lyon, 36–38, 44
Isidore of Kyiv, 104–5
Islam, 70, 78
isolationism, 37–38
isonomia, 52
isopoliteia, 52
Israel, 24, 26–28, 108, 139
Istanbul, 80, 116–18
Italia, 65
Ivanovic, Filip, 139, 160
Izbicki, Thomas, 129
Izyaslav of Kyiv, 103

Jay, Eric, 155, 164
Jeremiah II of Constantinople, 109
Jeremiah III of Constantinople, 166
Joanikije of Serbia, 101–2
Job of Moscow, 109
John Tzimiskes, 98
John VI Kantakouzenos, 102
Johnson, Lawrence, 153
Jonas of Moscow, 104–5, 109
Judea, 28
Julius of Rome, 63

Jupiter, 29
jurisdictionism, 190
jus, 128, 146
Justinian emperor, 78–79, 91, 107, 188

Kaegi, Walter, 79
kakodoxia, 119
Kanyike, Lawrence, 172
Kapodistrias, Ioannis, 112
Karamanolis, George, 41
Karmires, Ioannis, 169
Karpat, Kemal, 70–71
Kartashev, Anton, 168
Kasper, Walter, 48
katholou, 136
Keefe, John, 140
kenotic, 3, 192
Kessler, Herbert, 53
khan, 94
Khomiakov, Alexey, 174–75
Khrapovitsky, Anthony, 175–76
Kingdon, Robert, 21
Kinnamon, Michael, 24
Kirby, Torrance, 19–20
Kloppenborg, John, 52
knyaz', 103–108
koinonia, 152
Konstantia, 61
Koraïs, Adamantios, 111, 117
Korostyshev, 168
Koskela, Douglas, 22, 170
kosmos, 39
kral, 101
Kremlin, 105, 108
Krewo, 103
Kritovoulos, 69–70
Küng, Hans, 1, 7, 11–12, 18, 62, 173, 194–95
Kyiv, 102–7, 122, 124, 165, 167–68

L'Huillier, Peter, 64, 77
laicization, 159
Laidlaw, William, 31
laity, 9, 71, 81, 92, 121, 154, 159, 161, 185–86, 195–96
Lakeland, Paul, 194

Index

Lamoreaux, John, 158
Lampe, Peter, 35–36
Lampsakion, 100
Laodicea, 155
Laourdas, B., 91
lapsi, 16
Lavers, Anette, 188, 198
lector, 146
Lee, Robert, 74
Leemans, Johan, 155, 158
legate, 66, 96, 132, 141
Lenski, Gerhard, 146
Leo I of Rome, 155
liberalism, 48, 113, 117
liberation, 10, 52, 111, 113, 115–16, 120, 125, 194, 196
liberator, 90
liberty, 81, 115, 118
Libya, 28, 65, 179
Liddell, Henry, 51
limes, 74
Lindbeck, George, 24
Lithuania, 103–4
liturgiolatry, 159
locality, 37, 45–46
Logos, 37, 41–42
lordship, 99, 161
Lorenzo da Brindisi, 165
Louth, Andrew, 68, 140, 161
Lubac, Henri de, 130, 173
luci, 31
Lumen Gentium, 22, 171
Lund, 23
Lunn-Rockliffe, Sophie, 132, 141, 145–46
Luther, Martin, 18–19, 165
Lycia, 61
Lydia, 76
Lypkivsky, Vasyl, 123

Macedonia, 84–85, 96, 101
Macedonius of Antioch, 67
magisterium, 21
magistrate, 52
Mahmud II sultan, 117
Maidan, 124
Maistre, Joseph de, 5–6

Makary of Moscow, 108
Mallarach i Carrera, Josep Maria¶, 31
Mannion, Gerard, 13, 15, 58, 194
Mansi, Johannes, 21, 66, 166
Manuel I of Constantinople¶, 100
Marcion, 35
Marjanen, Antti, 35
marks of the church, 18–19, 141
Markus, R., 34
Mary Magdalene, 182
Maurer, Georg, 112
Maximilla, 35
Maximus the Confessor, 41–42, 140, 153, 183, 186
McDonnell, Kilian, 48
McPartlan, Paul, 130
Meeks, Wayne, 53
Mehmet II sultan, 69
Meletios of Constantinople¶, 48, 125
Mesopotamia, 26, 53–54, 61, 74
metaphor, 5, 9–10, 198
metaphysics, 24, 132, 135–36, 188
Metropolia (OCA), 126
metropolis, 2–4, 45–46, 58, 62–65, 76, 86, 97, 103, 190
Mettepenningen, Jürgen, 130, 169
Meyendorff, John, 89, 104, 107
Meyer, Paul, 77
Mihajlovski, Stojan, 117
militia, 71
Miller, Merrill, 59
Miller, Michael, 129
millet, 3–5, 70–72, 80, 117–18, 120
    Ermeniyan, 70
    Rum, 4, 70, 118, 120
    Yahud, 70
Miltchyna, Vera, 6
Minucius Felix, 32–33, 38
Mironowicz, Antoni, 121
Misyur'-Munekhin, Mikhail, 107
Mithraïc, 54
modernism, 154
modernity, 139, 173, 194
Moesia, 65, 91
Mojanoski, Cane, 89
molestation, 90

Mommsen, Theodor, 77
monad, 66
monarchy, 3–5, 13, 67–69, 108, 112, 131, 161
monastery
    St Catherine, 40
    Stoudion, 161
    Valaam, 125
    Vatopedi, 48
monenergism, 67
Mongols, 103, 106
mono-episcopacy, 8–9, 152–54
monophysitism, 163
monothelitism, 67
Montanism, 17, 35–36, 153–54
Montanus, 35
Montenegro, 84
Montgomery, Rhonda, 148
Moore, Sheila, 172
Morris, Colin, 68
Moscow, 6, 49, 82, 84–85, 102–10, 121–22, 124–26, 165, 167, 176–78
mosque, 106
mount
    Athos, 99, 101, 118
    Cynthus, 32
    Sinai, 40
Mousnier, Roland, 139
Mudge, Lewis, 58, 194
Muehlberger, Ellen, 140
mültezim, 71
Muscovy, 94, 103–10, 165
Mutimir of Serbia, 99
myrrh, 92, 97–98, 100, 119, 165–66
Myrrha, 61
Mysia, 76
mystery, 22–23, 30, 47, 160, 171, 173–77
Mystici Corporis, 21, 23, 46, 164

Nasamones, 179
nationalism, 2, 4–5, 70–71, 110, 121, 124–25
NATO, 85
Naxos, 32
Nazi, 123

Nea Ionia, 86
Neapolis, 86
Nelson, John, 23
Neoclassicism, 113
Neoplatonism, 37, 41, 133, 135–37, 139–41, 143, 160–61, 185
Neoscholasticism, 129
Nestorianism, 79, 163
New Delhi, 23
Nicea, kingdom, 100
Nicodeme the Hagiorite, 175
Niditch, Susan, 139
Nikephoros of Constantinople, 67
Niketas Stethatos, 161
Nilus Cabasilas, 143
Nisibis, 61
Nobel Prize, 92
nobility, 162
Nockles, Peter, 168
nomadic, 78
noncanonical, 127
normative, 111, 175
Norton, Peter, 154, 156–58, 189
notitiae, 97
nouvelle théologie, 130, 169
Nova Justiniana, 91
Novatian, 154
Novatianism, 154, 164
novelty, 154
Novgorodok, 103

O'Donnell, Christopher, 42–44
Obolensky, Dimitri, 102–3
ochlos, 155
Ochrid, 100–101
Odessos, 91
oikonomia, 37, 175–77
Oikonomos, Constantine, 113
oikos, 149
Olbia, 52
Olyan, Saul, 53, 139
oneness, 11
onta, 160, 181
ontological, 38, 48, 137, 142, 181, 185, 196
ontology, 136–37, 139
Öörni, Soili, 89

openness, 52
Optatus of Milevis, 164
oracle, 30
orator, 158
ordination, 76, 83, 89–90, 154–56
ordo, 9, 141, 158, 195
Oriens, 65, 90
oriental, 32
Origen, 17, 155, 188
Ormerod, Neil, 12–13
Orphic, 137
Ott, Daniel, 12
Otto, Rudolf, 25, 112
ousia, 41
overseeing, 151
overseer, 29, 132
Owen, Carol, 146

pagan, 39, 158, 175
Palestine, 57, 59, 61, 65, 68
Palmyrene, 54
Panaretos of Tirnovo, 116
Pannonia, 65
pantheon, 137
papacy, 44, 67, 129–30, 156, 164, 189
Papademetriou, Tom, 70–71
Papandrea, James, 154
Papandreou, Damaskinos, 169
Papanikolaou, Aristotle, 6
Paphlagonia, 61
Paphos, 61
papyrus, 56
parchment, 56
parish, 44, 47–48, 125
Parker, John, 197
paroikia, 44
Parsons, Talcott, 197
Parthenios II of Constantinople, 166
Parthia, 54
particularism, 2, 46–47
Partykevich, Andre, 122
Pascuzzi, Maria, 50
Patara, 61
paterfamilias, 53
patristic, 13, 43–44, 77–78, 140
Pax Romana, 5, 73, 75, 78, 179

Peace of Westphalia, 5–6, 80–84
Pelikan, Jaroslav, 19
Peloponnese, 112
pentarchy, 3–4, 58, 66–67
Pentecost, 49, 57
Pepouza, 34–36, 39
Perge, 61
Perigenes of Corinth, 77–78, 129
perilampsis, 133
Perkins, Ann, 53
Perl, Eric, 137, 139
Persia, 68, 79
Petrine keys, 190
Phanar, 48, 112
Pharisees, 106, 182
Pharmakides, Theokletos, 112–13
Phazania, 179
Pheidas, Vlasios, 60, 63, 176
phenomenology, 25
Philippi, 60
Photios of Constantinople, 91, 96
Phrygia, 34–35, 76, 155
phyletism, 89, 119–20, 125
phyrama, 50
physis, 182–83
Picts, 74
Piedmont-Sardinia, 5
Pisidia, 61
Pius XII of Rome, 21–22, 46
Plato, 41, 133, 137
Platonism, 12–13, 41, 133, 135–37, 140
plebs, 52
Pliska, 95
Plokhy, Serhii, 122
Plotinus, 133
pluralism, 14–15, 54, 167
pluriformity, 106
pneuma, 172
pneumatocentrism, 15
Pnyx, 52
Poland, 82–83, 103, 121
polis, 29, 31, 51, 58, 94, 151
Polish, 104, 123, 126
polytheism, 26, 28, 32, 75, 137, 187
pomerium, 30
Pompiioupolis, 61
pontifex, 75, 153

Index   259

Pontus, 65, 74, 83–84, 192
populism, 189
populus Romanus, 159
Poros, 32
Porphyry, 41–42, 136–37, 140–41, 182
portico, 31
postapostolic, 152
Poster, Mark, 182
postliberalism, 24
postmodernism, 14
poststructuralism, 1, 10, 132, 181, 183–85, 187–89, 191–93, 195, 197–98
praetorian, 64
pragmateia, 37
Pratto, Felicia, 7
pre-Constantinian, 53
predestination, 20
prefecture, 64, 79
presbyterium, 8, 151, 155
priesthood, 155–56, 172, 186–87
primate, 5, 49, 59, 68, 82, 89, 91, 97–98, 100, 109, 118, 120, 131, 146, 186, 190
principality, 103–4, 136, 161
Priscilla, 35
privilege, 4, 6, 9, 44, 69, 82–83, 143, 146–47, 156, 158, 185
Proclus, 133, 137–38, 140, 142
profanity, 36
propaganda, 124–25
property, 3, 5, 70, 141, 182
prophetism, 35
prostitution, 188
protectorate, 112
Protestantism, 20, 166, 170, 173
protos, 101
providence, 37, 146
Prusak, Bernard, 53, 60, 62, 149, 152, 155, 158–59, 161–62
Prussia, 181
prytaneion, 31
Ps-Dionysius Areopagite, 37–38, 132–33, 137, 139–41, 143, 145, 160–61, 188
pseudonym, 37
psychè, 197

psychikoi, 35
psychology, 25, 36, 175
purity, 18, 34, 106
pyramid, 2, 7, 9, 128–31, 133, 135–37, 139, 141–43, 160, 192
Pyrrhos of Constantinople, 42

qadosh, 26

Rahner, Karl, 172–73
Ramet, Sabrina, 111
Rapp, Claudia, 146
Ratzinger, Josef, 48, 173
Rauh, Nicholas, 31
rebaptism, 165, 175–76
recapitulatio, 37
reduction, 66, 89, 94, 154
Reformation, 17, 19–20, 80, 165, 171, 194
Reformed theology, 21
regency, 112
Renaissance, 139, 177
Rennie, Kriston, 77
Reno, Russell, 140
republic, 21, 122
resurrection, 21, 37, 50, 57, 171
Revelation, 35–36, 43, 139, 160, 184
revolution, 71, 111–12, 115, 124–25, 168, 176
Rheginus of Cyprus, 90
Rheneia, 31
Rhodes, 49, 151
Richardson, Cyril, 8, 152
ritual, 30, 51–52, 106, 114, 196
ROCOR, 176
Rolt, C.E., 38
Romania, 25, 72, 82, 119
Romanides, John, 195
Romanos I Lekapenos, 98
Romans, 28–30, 76, 98, 101
Romanticism, 113
Ross, W.D., 66
Rostovtzev, Michael, 53
Rottenburg, 48
Rottman, David, 146
Roudometof, Victor, 120
Rousseau, Jean-Jacques, 115

routinization, 147–48, 154
Rubin, Paul, 7
Runciman, Steven, 70
Rus', 103, 105
Russia, 5–6, 104, 106–8, 111–12, 119, 125, 166, 168, 176

sacer, 30
sacerdos, 132, 141, 159
sacerdotalization, 159
sacramentalization, 160
Sagala, 61
Sanderson, Charles, 89, 92–93
Sardica, 63
sarkic, 35
Saunders, Peter, 146
Sava of Serbia, 99–102
Scheid, John, 52, 59
Schillebeeckx, Edward, 12, 53, 147, 149–50, 152–55, 158, 190, 194
Schleiermacher, Friedrich, 20
Schmemann, Alexander, 110–11, 126, 195
scholasticism, 43, 129
Schwartz, Seth, 58
Scythia, 91
sectarian, 35–36, 38, 42, 195
secular, 25, 31, 90, 156, 158, 161, 187–89, 194
secularist, 115
secularization, 9
senate, 30, 53, 83, 98, 143
Serbia, 6, 72, 82, 85, 94, 99–103, 108–9, 119–20
Serdica, 63
serf, 161
Sergius of Constantinople, 67
servant, 9, 53, 147, 159
Shishkov, Andrey, 131
Sicily, 78
Sidanius, Jim, 7
Simeon of Bulgaria, 97–98, 101
Simionati, Rita, 21
simulacrum, 10, 33, 191
Skopje, 101
Skoropads'ky, Pavlo, 122

Skrypnyk, Mstyslav, 123
slavery, 53, 115–16
Slovakia, 82, 121
Smyrna, 86
socialism, 122
solidarity, 71
Somers-Hall, Henry, 191
sovereignty, 5–6, 72–75, 77, 79–85, 87, 107, 110, 112, 121, 128
Soviet, 84, 121, 123–24
species, 41, 134–36
Stalin, Joseph, 123, 178
statehood, 4, 98, 108, 110
Stefan Nemanja, 99
Steinberger, Helmut, 80–82
Stephens, Christopher, 63, 158
Stethatos, Niketas, 161
stoa, 31
Strabo, 76
Stragorodsky, Sergiy, 177–78
strata, 2, 9, 145–47, 149, 151, 153, 155, 157–61, 163, 185–86, 192, 195
Strémooukhoff, Dimitri, 107
structuralism, 1, 10, 181, 183–85, 187, 189, 191, 193, 195, 197
Stuckrad, Kocku von, 26
Studstill, Randall, 25
subculture, 124
subordination, 75, 93
substructure, 152
Sullivan, F.A., 146, 150
sultan, 4, 70–71, 112, 114, 117–19
superstructure, 185
supremacy, 20, 81, 99
Svetlov, Pavel, 168
Sykes, Stewart, 75, 151, 188
Symeon the New Theologian, 68
Synaxis, 49
synedrion, 48
synodality, 62, 68
synoptic, 58, 147
Syria, 53–54, 56, 60, 68, 79, 140, 199
Sysyn, Frank, 122

Tabbernee, William, 35–36
taktika, 97

Tanner, Norman, 76, 83, 90, 141, 143, 157, 166, 171
Tanzimât, 72, 117
Tatian, 56
teleology, 37
temenos, 29
Temple, 26–29, 31–32, 51, 187
templum, 30, 33
territoriality, 45, 61, 73, 75–76, 85–86
Tertullian, 17, 35
thanksgiving, 18, 50–51
thema, 79
Theodore I Laskaris, 100
Theodore of Raithu, 41
Theodore Studite, 66
theogony, 137
Thrace, 65, 83–84
Tillard, Jean-Marie, 23
Tirnovo, 97–99, 116
Titov, Vladimir, 118
togetherness, 41
Tollefsen, Torstein, 133, 140
tongues, 8, 149
tonsure, 100, 159
Torah, 51, 139–40
Toth, Alexis, 125
Toumanoff, Cyril, 107
Toynbee, Arnold, 68
Trajan Decius, 153
Tralleis, 61
Trevett, Christine, 35
Trinity, 41, 131, 142, 165, 181
Tripolitania, 28
Troitsky, Hilarion, 175
Troizena, 111
tsar, 97–99, 101–2, 106–10, 166, 168
tsardom, 108–10
Tuominen, Miira, 41
Turkey, 34, 68, 71–72, 106, 109, 113–15, 117
Turkocracy, 113
Tymion, 34–36
tyranny, 111
tyrant, 70
Tyre, 136

U-hierarchy, 69
UAOC, 123–24
Ukraine, 6, 85, 88, 120, 122–25, 168
Ukrainization, 123
unchangeability, 141
UOC, 124
Uspensky, Boris, 108, 110

Vamvas, Neophytos, 113
Varna, 91
Vatican, 21–22, 46, 48, 159, 171–74, 194
Veniaminov, Innocent, 125
Venice, 21
vicarius, 77, 132
Vienna, 65
Vilno, 103
Vladimir upon Klyazma, 103
Vladimir-Suzdal, 103
Volf, Miroslav, 195–96
Volhynia, 103
Volodymyr of Kyiv, 103
Vukan of Serbia, 100

Wach, Joachim, 148
Wallace-Hadrill, J.M., 67
Walters, Philip, 89
Walzer, Michael, 184
Ware, Kallistos, 130, 165
Warsaw Pact, 85
WCC, 23–24, 47
Weber, Max, 147–48
Weed, Ronald, 114–15
Weisgerber, James, 7
Weitzmann, Kurt, 53
Westerink, L.G., 91
Whitehead, Alfred, 12
Wilberding, James, 41
Williams, James, 132, 185, 188
Williamson, Oliver, 92
Wittelsbach, 112
Wittke, Anne-Maria, 65, 74, 79, 180, 199
Wolff, Robert, 98, 103, 107, 109
Wong, Joseph, 172
Wood, Susan, 46–47
Wright, J. Robert, 78

Yahweh, 37, 43
Yugoslavia, 84

Zacchaeus, 182
Zephyrinus of Rome, 154
Zernov, Nicolas, 107, 168
Zeus, 30, 54
Zion, 28
Zizioulas, John, 45, 130–31, 195
Zoe Palaiologina, 108
Zwingli, Ulrich, 18

www.ingramcontent.com/pod-product-compliance
Lightning Source LLC
Chambersburg PA
CBHW030614230426
43661CB00053B/1977